Tarot as Storyteller

"Salicrow's *Tarot as Storyteller* is a luminous guide that goes beyond instructions on how to read the cards—this is about learning to listen to the whispers of the unseen, then translating those whispers into empowering guidance. This book is imbued with Salicrow's warmth and approachable wisdom. A work that bridges the mystical and the accessible, *Tarot as Storyteller* is a truly inspired resource."

BENEBELL WEN, AUTHOR OF *HOLISTIC TAROT* AND *I CHING, THE ORACLE*

"If you are ready for a new and exciting book on tarot, make sure you add *Tarot as Storyteller* to your collection. This book is an absolute must-read that approaches tarot as a living, breathing oracle. This book is like having a personal mentor to guide you through the seasons, lunar cycles, and life-changing moments. What truly sets this book apart is its emphasis on personal empowerment. Salicrow encourages and inspires readers to trust themselves and to think 'outside the spread,' guiding people in the use of original tarot card spreads and creative layouts that go beyond mundane questions. Salicrow's *Tarot as Storyteller* is your portal to a world brimming with wisdom and wonder—a condensed book for beginners and a breath of fresh air for seasoned tarot readers that helps uncover the layers of each reader's own history and future."

LEANNE MARRAMA, COAUTHOR OF *READING THE LEAVES* AND *LIGHTING THE WICK*

"Salicrow's practical and accessible guide is full of techniques, spreads, rituals, and meditations for psychic and intuitive development. I especially appreciate her attention to the connections between cartomancy and the wheel of the year, such as lunar and solar cycles and celebrations, as well as other spiritual practices. This fresh new approach to tarot practice deserves a place in every cartomancer's library."

RUTH ANN AMBERSTONE, DIRECTOR OF *THE TAROT SCHOOL* AND COAUTHOR OF *UNLOCKING THE SECRET LANGUAGE OF TAROT*

"Salicrow's *Tarot as Storyteller* is an essential and insightful guide for anyone looking to integrate and expand their psychic development, cartomancy, and magickal practices. She skillfully takes the seeker on a journey through psychic unfoldment and builds on this to use cartomancy as a way to weave the story. Salicrow does this through original spreads, exercises, meditations, and spells that are powerful tools to support your work in an easy-to-follow and accessible fashion. She shares how to use your psychic insight to gain clarity on details in situations often brought up during readings. Salicrow offers an in-depth look at the meanings and symbolism of tarot and oracle cards and how to best work with your deck in divination and magick. Take your readings and storytelling to the next level with this invaluable resource—for those new to the path and experts alike."

DANIELLE DIONNE, AUTHOR OF *MAGICKAL MEDIUMSHIP*
AND *CHRONICALLY MAGICKAL*

"Salicrow effortlessly weaves in the history and intricacies of tarot reading while putting the power in the hands of the reader and supporting them through the journey. She supports the reader through the entire book in a way that instills confidence and removes doubt no matter what their goals are for reading tarot. It's so beautiful to see that she has left no stone unturned in her quest to help people understand, trust, and use this powerful and enlightening method of divination."

ANDREA LOVETT, FOUNDER OF SWEET RELEASE HEALING SCHOOL

"In writing *Tarot as Storyteller*, Salicrow has successfully married two age-old and beloved traditions: tarot and storytelling. She bridges the gap between the two, allowing the reader the ability to analyze the cards through psychic storytelling, impelling one to use their innate abilities to tap into the mysteries of the universe. Salicrow instructs us to create our own allegorical techniques to master the cards. *Tarot as Storyteller* teaches us to merge our intuition and imagination, culminating in clarity and insight. Through Salicrow's many years of prolific experience and teaching, she has provided us with the ultimate guide, suitable for experienced practitioners and novices alike!"

DIANE CHAMPIGNY, ALEXANDRIAN HIGH PRIESTESS AND WITCH

Tarot as Storyteller

Psychic Development, Cartomancy, and Reading the Web of Fate

A Sacred Planet Book

SALICROW

Destiny Books
Rochester, Vermont

Destiny Books
One Park Street
Rochester, Vermont 05767
www.DestinyBooks.com

Destiny Books is a division of Inner Traditions International

Sacred Planet Books are curated by Richard Grossinger, Inner Traditions editorial board member and cofounder and former publisher of North Atlantic Books. The Sacred Planet collection, published under the umbrella of the Inner Traditions family of imprints, includes works on the themes of consciousness, cosmology, alternative medicine, dreams, climate, permaculture, alchemy, shamanic studies, oracles, astrology, crystals, hyperobjects, locutions, and subtle bodies.

Copyright © 2025 by Salicrow

All rights reserved. No part of this book may be reproduced or utilized in any form or by any means, electronic or mechanical, including photocopying, recording, or any information storage and retrieval system, without permission in writing from the publisher. No part of this book may be used or reproduced to train artificial intelligence technologies or systems.

Cataloging-in-Publication Data for this title is available from the Library of Congress

ISBN 979-8-88850-206-8 (print)
ISBN 979-8-88850-323-2 (ebook)

Printed and bound in the United States by Lake Book Manufacturing, LLC

10 9 8 7 6 5 4 3 2 1

Text design and layout by Priscilla Harris Baker
This book was typeset in Garamond, with Benguiat, Fleur, Gill Sans, Legacy Sans, and Majesty used as display typefaces
Tarot card artwork by Pamela Coleman Smith

To send correspondence to the author of this book, mail a first-class letter to the author c/o Inner Traditions • Bear & Company, One Park Street, Rochester, VT 05767, and we will forward the communication, or contact the author directly at **salicrow.com**.

 Scan the QR code and save 25% at InnerTraditions.com. Browse over 2,000 titles on spirituality, the occult, ancient mysteries, new science, holistic health, and natural medicine.

I dedicate this book to magical women of my family who follow the line of Isola: My grandmother Florence Isola; my sisters Sandy, Stahr, and Corey; my cousin Morgan; my daughter Levi Nirvana and my granddaughters Persephone and Rosemary; my nieces Eden, Thyme, Odaiya, and Piper; and my great nieces Aphelia, Hallie, Brynlee, Maeve, and Elenor; and to the generation of powerful women who will follow!

Contents

Welcome, Seeker 1

Psychic Storytelling

Becoming the Seer 4

Divination, 5 ✦ Cartomancy, 8 ✦ Psychic Evolution, 11 ✦ Empathic Ability, 13 ✦ Sacred Space, 14 ✦ Divine Timing, 18 ✦ Training the Brain, 24 ✦ Body Dowsing, 32 ✦ Building Your Symbolic Language, 35 ✦ Guided Meditation and Intuition, 38 ✦ Self-Care and Personal Healing, 43

Telling the Story 47

Ethics, Morals, and Reputation, 47 ✦ A Book of Shadows, 51 ✦ Choosing a Deck, 53 ✦ Blessing and Programming Cards, 54 ✦ Oracular Storytelling, 57 ✦ The Web of Fate, 61 ✦ Karma in the Cards, 65 ✦ Asking the Right Questions, 66 ✦ The People in the Neighborhood, 68 ✦ How Are We Connected, 71 ✦ Telling Time, 72

Spreads and Layouts

Seasonal Card Spreads 78

Winter Solstice: The Wheel of the Year, 78 ✦ Imbolc: Hearth and Home, 81 ✦ Spring Equinox: Balancing Personal Energy, 83 ✦

Beltane: Relationship Readings, 85 ✦ Summer Solstice: Blessings and Bounty, 90 ✦ Lughnasa: Career/Life Path, 91 ✦ Autumn Equinox—A Year in Review, 93 ✦ Halloween: Lessons from Guides, 94

Rare Moon Spreads 96
Blue Moon: Self Viewing, 96 ✦ Black Moon: Soul Healing, 98 ✦ Lunar Eclipse: Hidden Potential, 99

Soul-Level Card Spreads 100
Soul Purpose, 102 ✦ White Raven, 105 ✦ Past-Life Readings, 108

Thinking Outside the Spread 119
Long-Term Draw, 121 ✦ Cartomancy in Activated Prayer, 122 ✦ Cartomancy Spells, 126 ✦ Playing Card Charms, 127 ✦ Intuitive Healing Boards, 134 ✦ House of Cards Travel Altar, 140 ✦ Journey of the Oracle, 146

The Tarot

The Major Arcana 154
The Fool, 156 ✦ The Magician, 159 ✦ The High Priestess, 163 ✦ The Empress, 167 ✦ The Emperor, 171 ✦ The Hierophant, 175 ✦ The Lovers, 180 ✦ The Chariot, 184 ✦ Strength, 188 ✦ The Hermit, 192 ✦ Wheel of Fortune, 197 ✦ Justice, 201 ✦

The Hanged Man, 205 ✦ Death, 209 ✦ Temperance, 213 ✦
The Devil, 217 ✦ The Tower, 221 ✦ The Star, 224 ✦ The Moon, 228 ✦
The Sun, 232 ✦ Judgement, 235 ✦ The World, 239

The Suits—The Minor Arcana 242
Wands, Staves, and Clubs, 243 ✦ Pentacles, Coins, Discs,
and Shields, 244 ✦ Cups, Chalices, and Goblets, 246 ✦
Swords, Spades, and Blades, 247

The Court Cards 250
The Pages, 250 ✦ The Knights, 255 ✦
The Queens, 260 ✦ The Kings, 265

Numerology and The Tarot 272
Ace, 273 ✦ Two, 276 ✦ Three, 278 ✦ Four, 281 ✦ Five, 283 ✦
Six, 285 ✦ Seven, 287 ✦ Eight, 290 ✦ Nine, 292 ✦ Ten, 295

A Final Wish for the Seeker 299

Index 300

Welcome, Seeker

The psychic arts are my passion, my life path, and my craft. I have worked on developing my skills since childhood, and I have a great love of helping others do the same. Cartomancy, the tarot in particular, has been a love of mine for the past thirty-five years. As a professional psychic I have used its imagery to tell thousands upon thousands of psychic stories, weaving bits of fate with intricacy. Many like me have made professions out of their skill as readers and teachers of arcane lore, and many more have developed the skill for the love of it! It is my hope that the information in these pages offers you, the reader, a different way of seeing by using the cards, infusing traditional symbolism with personal experience, alternate perspectives, and an open intuition.

The journeys, techniques, and spreads of this book have been tested in workshops in-person and online, and they were designed to help you develop your psychic abilities and create a personal relationship with your cards. In addition, the final part of this book goes into detail about the Major and Minor Arcana of the tarot, including questions to ask when looking at each card to help the reader seek alternate perspectives. I wish you luck and an open mind as you begin your journey!

SPREADING LOVE,

SALICROW

PSYCHIC STORYTELLING

THE CHARIOT.   DEATH.   THE EMPEROR.   THE EMPRESS.   THE FOOL.   THE HERMIT.   THE HIEROPHANT.   JUDGEMENT.

Becoming the Seer

Intuition is not limited to a few, but something we are all naturally endowed with. The problem is that society has crushed it out of us for many generations! Many of us have experienced moments of precognition, such as knowing our friend was going to call moments before they did or having a feeling that something had happened to someone we care about before being told. Often these experiences are referred to as "gut feelings" or "hunches," and often they are written off as coincidence. Personally, I do not believe in coincidence!

Becoming a Seer requires us to put aside our doubts, choosing instead to look at all our coincidences, hunches, and gut feelings as something more: they are clues that help us connect the dots and see the bigger picture, as opening our awareness requires us to engage with the belief that everything is connected. In many ways, the mind of the Seer is like that of a detective, as both understand that clues can be found anywhere and that observation is key!

Seer

A person with supernatural insight capable of perceiving the future and unknown.

There are many names for psychic seers, such as psychic reader, oracle, prophet, diviner, mystic, soothsayer, and fortune-teller. A reader who specializes in the tarot, oracle, or playing cards is also known as a cartomancer.

The term *Seer* is somewhat misleading, as not all who develop their precognitive skills will receive information through seeing. The means by which we perceive the unknown are unique to the individual and come in various forms, which we will discuss in more detail later in the book. To be a Seer, simply put, means that we perceive information about people and situations through supernatural means before being informed by mundane sources.

Supernatural

An event or manifestation beyond the laws of nature.

When we hear the word *supernatural* we often think of it as beyond reality, when in fact it simply means "a force beyond the understanding of science," much like that other word, *magic*, that can be described as "science that has not yet been explained." Neither of these words deny the possibility of the thing being true; they simply state that we don't know how they work! Without understanding how something functions we must first rely on faith, and that is challenging if we grew up being told that psychic abilities and magic were fake.

The first step to becoming a Seer is belief in oneself and making the decision to reconsider the coincidences and *wyrd* experiences of our lives. (*Wyrd* means "being connected to Fate.") Becoming a Seer requires that we first put aside the societal programming that has told us that precognitive perception is something outside the normal range of being, and then we must recognize that, like most things we want in life, we will have to dedicate time to it if we wish to see true results.

DIVINATION

Divination is the psychic art of seeking and receiving information from the unknown—future and unseen—through magical means.

6 ✦ Psychic Storytelling

Magic is simply science that has not yet been discovered!

I refer to divination as a psychic art because, like drawing and painting, it is something everyone can develop to some degree of skill; but, like art, not everyone will be capable of developing it to a professional level. While we may not all have the psychic capacity necessary to perform on a professional level, we are all capable of developing our skill to a point in which we can utilize our intuition to make better choices in our own lives and develop a deeper understanding of who we are on a soul level. I encourage you to approach learning divination, cartomancy in this case, with a focus on exploration and a desire for expanding your consciousness, for such study is not meant to be rigidly academic; instead, it is meant to be experienced like art with our consciousness open and fluid.

We are living in an amazing age in which the veil between our physical world and that of spirit, and the line between science and magic, are simultaneously thinning. As science and magic merge, divination is becoming an acceptable tool for personal guidance. This is due in part to the changes in science—particularly through studies on the quantum level that show time is not linear but instead happening all at once, making it easier to understand how people can perceive future events.

It is important to recognize that just as two people remembering the past will remember it differently, the future is also malleable; this makes it possible to change our path, as all things are happening at once, providing numerous ways in which our choices can play out. When reading cards or practicing divination of any form, we are looking for the most likely path the querent will take.

Querent

The person the psychic reading is for.

The way in which a psychic reader receives information can vary between the psychic senses, also called *clair* or "clear" senses: clairvoyance, clairaudience, clairsentience, claircognizance, and clairsalience. Most people have a combination of these ways of receiving. In divination, the word *Seer* can refer to the use of any of the psychic senses; we do not need to be *clairvoyant* ("clear seeing") to be a Seer!

Clairvoyance (psychic seeing). Receiving psychic information through the mind's eye/third eye, which is located in the center of one's forehead between the brow and back into the middle of the brain, connected to the pineal gland. Images may appear like snapshots or moving videos. Tarot and oracle cards are helpful for those with clairvoyance, as the pictures on the cards often trigger other images in the Seer's mind.

Clairaudience (psychic hearing). Receiving psychic information through voices and sounds heard when no external sound is present. While received telepathically, these clairaudient experiences can be physically audible to the receiver, as if they are hearing it outside of their head. Mediums and channelers utilize this clair often.

Clairsentience (psychic feeling). Receiving psychic information through feeling the emotional and physical pain of others. Many healers have developed clairsentience through their regular contact with clients, particularly those that do hands-on forms of healing such as Reiki, massage, physical therapy, and nursing. Clairsentience also includes the ability to feel wounds in buildings and on the land.

Claircognizance (psychic knowing). Receiving information about the unseen/unknown as thoughts in one's mind. Information may pop into the receiver's consciousness out of nowhere with a feeling of knowing it to be true. Claircognizance is the first voice to speak in our mind, before logic and reason step in. When developing our psychic knowing, it is important to remove doubt words from our speech, which changes our words from questioning to affirming: "I think I see a move in your future" to "I see a move in your future."

Clairsalience (psychic smelling). Receiving information about the

8 ✦ Psychic Storytelling

unseen/unknown through our sense of smell. Our olfactory senses are incredible, allowing us to be transported back in time simply by smelling something from our past. Clairsalience is often used in channeling and mediumship, as one of the easiest ways for spirits to communicate with us is by using scents we associate with them to prove that they are around. In divination, those who experience clairsalience may find that they smell things that direct them to certain people, places, and times.

In this book we are focusing on divination skill—specifically on the art of cartomancy. When practicing cartomancy, developing psychic readers will likely find that they utilize clairvoyance, clairsentience, and claircognizance most often.

Cartomancy
Fortune-telling and future seeing using a deck of cards.

CARTOMANCY

Cartomancy is the practice of divination in which the Seer makes predictions based on images displayed on cards. Tarot cards are the most popular tool for performing cartomancy; however, oracle cards and traditional playing cards are also commonly used. In truth, cartomancy can be performed with any deck of cards that utilizes imagery, color, and/or symbolism: from Uno to Go Fish to a stack of grandma's old greeting cards! The key to utilizing cartomancy is in the visual perception and intuitive imagination of the reader.

As a psychic skill cartomancy is often easier for visual thinkers to pick up, as they perceive the world through symbolism, noting what something they see makes them feel and the connection that feeling has to people and events they have known. Artists, healers, and philosophical thinkers often experience the world through a heightened symbolic perception; their brains intuitively connect emotions and situations to visual images. Psychic sensitivity of this nature is a combination of clairvoyance (psychic seeing) and claircognizance (psychic knowing).

When practicing cartomancy, it is best to be led visually, noting whatever catches the attention of our eyes—regardless of how small a detail we are drawn to—as attention to detail is an integral part of psychic development, whether we are reading cards or walking down the street. When we are led by our intuition, we begin to unfold the depth of information available in every card, noting that the same card can have ten different meanings for ten different readings.

As an oracular art, cartomancy is a form of scrying, a type of divination relying on the reader's mind being triggered by imagery. However, unlike other clairvoyant forms of divination, readers are not solely reliant on their ability to formulate facsimiles in their mind. Instead, they are utilizing the images on the cards to trigger thoughts, allowing them to use not only their free-flowing intuition but also their analytical detective brain. *In my opinion the best readers are those who have both a deep intuition and an inquisitive, analytical mind.*

The use of cards in divination became popular in the fourteenth century, shortly after playing cards came into use. Most likely the oracular use came about naturally, as the images stimulated intuitive thinking and the numbers featured on the cards invited the user to incorporate numerological symbolism—something mystics of multiple cultures had practiced for thousands of years.

Cards have been a constant in my life! As a child my grandmother used playing cards in her readings, often through the innocent looking game of solitaire, and helped develop my psychic knowing through card games like memory and rummy. As a teenager I began carrying playing cards in my purse and often would just sit and shuffle them as I chatted with my friends. At the time I didn't really know why I carried them, as I was not a big game player; in fact, I don't think I ever pulled them out for that use. I simply liked to sit and shuffle them while I talked

10 ✦ Psychic Storytelling

about deep subjects. Now, I look back at it as a memory of the future, understanding that something inside of me knew how important a role cards would play in my life! At eighteen my future husband brought home a deck of tarot cards to study; I recognized instantly that the cards were mine and began my personal relationship with cartomancy.

While we can use any type of cards in our readings, finding our favorite flavor goes a long way in the development of skill, for the relationship between the Seer and their cards is a personal one. Some people like to use many decks, and some use only one specific deck that they treasure. Some readers only work with one type of card—oracle, tarot, or playing—while others incorporate multiple types simultaneously.

To begin it is helpful to understand the use and flavor of each type of card, as understanding the strengths and weakness of each will help us get clearer answers in our divination.

Playing cards, while offering the least symbolism, have the benefit of being ordinary and, for the most part, above suspicion. They are also cheap and easily accessed, available for purchase at most drug stores and mini-marts. This accessibility and acceptability make them popular for many "home psychics" who tell fortunes to their family and friends around the kitchen table. Playing cards were a popular divination tool before the days of the internet, when purchasing tarot cards meant first finding them, and oracle cards were not yet a thing. While some folks still prefer to use playing cards, oracle and tarot cards far outsell them in oracular use!

Oracle cards come in hundreds of varieties as their simplicity and ease of use make them approachable to all. Whatever your interest or spiritual beliefs, you are sure to find a deck geared toward your needs. Oracle cards are great for daily divination, checking in, and getting a broad overview of a situation. Most often oracle cards are used for personal inspiration and guidance. Oracle decks are compatible in readings with either playing cards or tarot by giving the general view of the situation, often representing the energy that the querent is experiencing, where the playing cards and tarot provide the finer details.

Tarot cards are, in my opinion, the real deal of divination through cartomancy, offering intricate images laden with symbolism. The tarot can be a bit intimidating for this reason, and often people explore oracle cards before making the leap to the tarot. If we approach the tarot as a storytelling tool, we will find that the images on the cards are eagerly awaiting an opportunity to share their knowledge. Books upon books, websites upon websites, share details and angles of approaching this wonderful tool, with many of the images designed to trigger our consciousness, whispering in our mind a deeper knowing!

While cartomancy is primarily devoted to divination, the cards can be used for manifestation as well, offering the serious student a powerful tool on their path to co-creating their life. For this reason, I have included material on spell work and prayer through the use of cards as well. Exploring cartomancy in alternative ways helps us develop a deeper understanding of each card, making our readings more concise.

PSYCHIC EVOLUTION

We are living in a time of psychic evolution, in which we as a species are experiencing an expansion of our consciousness. People are finding themselves more aware of their surroundings, feeling and sensing emotions and physical sensations of other humans, animals, as well as the general vibe of the world. This awakening is something that affects all of us, regardless of whether we are looking for it or not. Many are finding this enhanced experience of reality to be difficult to navigate, often finding themselves struggling to balance their emotions. Exhaustion, anxiety, and overwhelm are common maladies of the time we are living in, with most people experiencing some form of the above. While adjusting to this new level of input can be overwhelming, it truly is a gift that once adjusted to can enhance our lives in many ways.

Having worked as a professional psychic for the past three decades, I have had a ringside seat for observing this mass change in consciousness. When I began my work in the early 1990s very few people I read for were personally experiencing psychic phenomenon, with approximately one out of ten clients showing up with unexplained psychic experiences. In 2011 I began noticing a change in the number of my clients having extrasensory experiences, and by 2012 the change was so noticeable that I started offering a class for empaths with tips and tools for opening and protection. In 2024 the number of clients I see experiencing supernatural phenomena is more like eight out of ten, with the most common manifestation being empathic awareness!

While I saw the beginning of this uptick in 2011, it is my belief that the catalyst for intuitive opening was the winter solstice of 2012. On this significant astrological date the solstice sun aligned with the center of our galaxy, something that happens every 26,000 years. This alignment was much speculated on during the day, as it was interpreted as being significant to the Mayan calendar, described as "the end of the world." Like most things this was misinterpreted, but it was potent all the same as there was an ending and beginning of sorts in which the rigidity of our collective mind cracked, allowing us to perceive in ways we had not been allowed for many centuries.

In sync with this astrological alignment were major changes in our social structure and technology. The internet became mainstream, allowing us to perceive the idea of gathering information from all over the world at the touch of a button, and the interweb showed us we were all connected. Our media began to change rapidly, and concepts and ways of living different than the ones we were raised in were available for us to explore from the comfort of our own homes. Spirit communication and divination became mainstream, with spirit mediums and paranormal investigation being featured regularly on television and internet channels like YouTube. This acceptance and the knowledge it carried helped everyday people recognize the unexplained phenomena of their own lives, and the belief that we are capable of perceiving with more than our five senses became common, spreading out like water seeping into the very fabric of our consciousness.

EMPATHIC ABILITY

The most common form of psychic phenomenon experienced is that of empathy, which is the ability to share and understand the feelings of others. People who experience this regularly are often referred to as empaths or empathic.

Empathy is not a new concept, as humans have always had the ability to sense the feelings of others. What is new is the level in which we are perceiving. Like turning up the radio, our awareness has been turned up a notch or two. Now many people find themselves struggling to separate their own emotions from those of others, making simple things like going to work and attending family gatherings an ordeal that often leaves us drained, anxious, and questioning our mental health. It doesn't have to be this way! We can learn how to protect and rebalance ourselves.

In truth, if someone is having psychic phenomenon spontaneously—such as feeling the emotions of others—they will have a hard time stopping those experiences. But we do have a choice between suffering with it or learning how to navigate it. I often describe it this way, "If you and I were in the woods and I was hurt badly, you would drive me to a hospital even if you did not know how to drive. However, the chances of us getting there safely would greatly increase if you knew how to drive the vehicle!"

Just as learning to drive opens our lives to new possibilities—as we can navigate to locations once outside of our reach—so too does learning how to work with our intuitive gifts. After all, there is a reason they are referred to as gifts. Developed intuitive abilities, such as empathy, make communication easier as we are capable of truly understanding a situation. We must learn to trust our gut instinct when it comes to first impressions, because sudden feelings of fear or hyperalertness often help us to avoid dangerous situations and bad relationships.

This heightened sensitivity to the emotions and physical feelings of others is not limited to our relations with humans but reaches out into the natural world, including animals, plants, and landscapes. And for those of you who are here as seekers, it's just the beginning of a grand adventure of self-discovery, and cartomancy offers the perfect tools for developing those abilities.

SACRED SPACE

Accuracy in divination requires the reader to be in a balanced state of mind. This is something our surroundings play a big part in, particularly in the beginning of our psychic development, as our hopes and fears can sway the way we interpret the cards. With this in mind, we can see how cartomancy benefits from being performed in sacred space, where we feel grounded and open. Skilled readers learn how to control and check their emotions at the door; they often use personal techniques to create sacred space whenever and wherever they need it, making it possible for them to give clear readings regardless of what is happening or where they are.

Personal rituals that help us to create sacred space allow us to recognize that what we are doing is outside of our everyday routine. In the beginning of our journey, we benefit from choosing a location where we can be undisturbed and in taking the time to sanctify our space. With time and dedication most readers personalize their sacred space, some with lots of bits and bobs, and others with little to no accoutrements.

It is possible to create sacred space with our intention alone, but this is often challenging for beginners to perceive as viable; therefore, I recommend lighting incense and burning herbs to clean and clear the surroundings of residual energy and emotions that may interfere with getting a clear reading. Setting up an altar adds another layer of intent to the working, showing that we recognize the relevance of what we do.

If this is something you are unfamiliar with, I recommend experimenting a bit until you find a method that feels natural to you. First perform a reading in a space in your home that gets regular traffic without any preparation, and make sure to write down your results where you can review them. Later that day or week do a second reading, only this time go through the effort of creating sacred space. Write down your results, making sure to compare your findings to those of the previous reading.

◇◇◇◇◇◇◇◇

RECIPE

SACRED SPACE SPRAY

With essential oils readily available at metaphysical and health food stores, making our own sprays is easy! All we need is a spray bottle (ideally glass), a few essential oils, water, and witch hazel. When doing so, we want to be thoughtful in the amount of oil we use, as it takes a ridiculous amount of plant matter to make that little bottle. The recipe below is using some of my favorite oils, but there is a plethora of recipes online, making it easy to find one you love.

You Will Need

A four-ounce bottle (preferably glass), witch hazel, water (from a spring if possible), a small funnel, essential oils of sage, rosemary, and cedar. Optional: small crystal chips.

1. Make sure your bottle is clean, and then add one-quarter cup witch hazel to the bottle using the small funnel.
2. Add thirteen drops each of rosemary for purification and cleansing, sage for sacred intentions, and cedar for protection and purification.
3. Add crystal chips if you like. I recommend rose quartz for love, black

16 ✦ **Psychic Storytelling**

tourmaline for protection, labradorite for psychic opening, and clear quartz to raise the vibration.

4. Top the bottle off with water.
5. Shake, label, and use.

◇◇◇◇◇◇◇◇◇◇◇◇

TECHNIQUE

CREATING SACRED SPACE

When it comes to creating sacred space, I like to keep it simple, particularly as my clients are for the most part pretty normal, non-mystical folks. When I have control of my space I tend to rely on permanent space holders, like altars. When I do not have this option, I generally rely on sacred sprays, crystals, or, in a pinch, my voice! I recommend doing a quick cleaning and clearing on any space that is used for mundane purposes before doing psychic work.

For the technique below we will be creating sacred space with crystals and a sacred spray. Use the recipe above or one of your favorites. If you do not have any crystals, river or ocean rocks will do.

―――――――――――― **You Will Need** ――――――――――――

Eight small crystals, fist-size or smaller—I prefer rose quartz for love, black tourmaline for protection, labradorite for psychic opening, and clear quartz to raise the vibration. You will also need your sacred spray and your Book of Shadows (a sacred journal used to record your psychic and magical workings; we will discuss these later in the book, see page 51).

1. Start by clearing the space you plan on working in of clutter and debris.
2. Place the eight crystals or stones around you in the cardinal directions (north, northeast, east, southeast, south, southwest, west, northwest). *You can find where they are in your space by using the compass on your phone.*
3. Spray the room liberally with your sacred spray.
4. Record your experience in your Book of Shadows.

TECHNIQUE
CREATING DIVINATION ALTARS

Altars are external representatives of our spiritual work. They can be created for a plethora of reasons, including holidays, magical working, ancestor honoring, and healing to name a few. Here we will be talking about altars dedicated to revealing the unseen/unknown and developing our skill as a Seer. An altar is a place of prayer as we ask for deeper guidance and more access to our gifts, and it's also a place of focus that helps us to dial into the mystery we seek unraveling. There are two types of altars: temporary and permanent.

Temporary altars are set up purposefully for a magical event and taken down shortly after completion of the working. There are many benefits to creating temporary altars, including offering privacy to those who are not yet ready to share their explorations with others, and, most importantly, the intention-setting power that focusing on creating your altar brings to the divination. Temporary divination altars should include incense or herbs to honor the element of Air and the spirit of inspiration, a candle to honor the element of Fire and the spirit of dedication, a bowl of water to honor the element of Water and the spirit of intuition, and a crystal of your choosing to honor the element of Earth and the spirit of manifestation. Along with these items I suggest adding religious or spiritual talismans, photos of your ancestors, and other items that represent your sacred journey.

Permanent altars, like their temporary counterpart, are designed to help us focus our intent, whether it be on receiving clear messages during our reading or manifesting the things we see on the horizon. The benefit of a permanent altar dedicated to developing our ability as a Seer is that it shows we have committed ourselves to the work. As we care for and maintain our altar, we acknowledge that the path we are taking is sacred to us, and we are prepared to work with it over the long haul.

Caring for our permanent altar means cleaning away debris, lighting the candle at every reading, bringing fresh water and incense as offerings, and

18 ✦ Psychic Storytelling

holding our crystal for a few moments in connection before we begin our work. One of the added bonuses of a permanent divination altar is you can place a card or three on it for days and weeks at a time; something that allows you to explore the situation more deeply.

DIVINE TIMING

Just as setting up space helps us to focus our intention, so too does timing! While we can do cartomancy at any time in any location, beginners and ritualists find it helpful to utilize the phases of the moon and sun in their readings. Full moons are luminous, shedding light on all inquiries, making them a great time for doing monthly forecasts, whereas dark moons (the waning moon before the rising moon) are more specific, offering us the perfect energy for looking at our shadows! For those who are looking to develop their skill at reading each month, I suggest doing personal divinations under the full moon.

Lunar Cycles
The full moon names and correspondences that I introduce below are according to the *Old Farmer's Almanac* and based on a northern climate with significant seasonal change. Please note that there are many names for each of the full moons and that these are simply the most used. You may find that these correspondences do not work for your location. If that is the case, tune in to your environment; notice what is happening in the natural world that surrounds you. Is something blooming or dying off? Is there a particular feel to the full moon of each month where you live? Feel free to explore and create monthly focuses based on the moon where you are! I have included descriptions of each of the full moons and suggestions for the kinds of readings that are best suited for them here.

January—Wolf Moon. January is often the coldest month of the year. It is a time of clear skies and plummeting temperatures. We call this the Wolf Moon because it is a time when the wolves' cry carried far on the cold empty night, filled with the hunger that the heart of winter carries. This is a great time to do readings based on connecting to that which we long for.

February—Snow Moon. February is the month in which we notice the return of sunlight in the northern hemisphere. It is often a time of heavy snow and warm temperatures. This is a time of great inspiration; it's when the returning light wakes our creative minds and activates our inner desire to create. This is the perfect time for readings based on that which we wish to birth in the new year.

March—Worm Moon. The name Worm Moon is believed to be associated with the thawing of the Earth and the movement of earthworms associated with such. In practical terms this is a time when things are beginning to awaken, with the Earth showing the early signs of spring. Remembering that early spring is a time of fast movement, the focus of this reading is on the practical ways we should be focusing our energy.

April—Pink Moon. The Pink Moon gets its name from the wild phlox that comes forth this time of year covering the ground. It is a time of early blossoms, pussy willows, and budding trees, rich with the potency of new beginnings. This is the perfect moon for focusing on what "gifts" we would like to bring forth this year, particularly those of the extrasensory type.

May—Flower Moon. Oh, the flowers! May is the month of spring fully loaded; filled with flowers and blossoms, it is month of ripening, celebration, and fertility! The Flower Moon is perfect for readings focused on that which you want to fertilize, be it your womb or a project important to your heart.

June—Strawberry Moon. The Strawberry Moon is one of sweetness and bountiful celebration of the Earth. Here our focus is best directed at the richness of life, family, friends, community, and that which makes our hearts sing! Readings done during June's Full Moon are best focused on community, friendship, and family.

20 ✦ Psychic Storytelling

July—Buck Moon. This moon is named after the buck as male deer's antlers are fully developed by July. As deer antlers are both seen as a sign of masculinity and prowess, this moon best serves for readings focused on our external drive, that which we are projecting into the world, be it our careers or projects we are pushing forward in our lives.

August—Sturgeon Moon. Sturgeon is a type of fish, and the August moon is named after them, as it is a time when the Great Lakes find their waters fully stocked. It is a time of harvest, and readings done at this time are often done so we can fully appreciate what we have accomplished.

September—Corn Moon. Sometimes called the Harvest Moon (the Harvest Moon is traditionally the full moon closest to the autumn equinox and can take place in either September or October), this is a time of surveying the land, examining the scale of the crop we have grown, and examining how best to harvest it. Whether you are a farmer or not, this is a good time for looking at that which we have created during the year and focusing on how best to utilize it throughout the dark months of winter.

October—Hunter's Moon. This is the last of the Harvest Moons, and the one associated with livestock and game: recognizing the importance of life given so that others may be sustained. This is a deeply introspective time, and readings done during the month of October are often associated with what needs to be sacrificed to sustain growth. It is also a time of deep reverence for those who have gone before us, making it a perfect time to utilize your cards as a way of receiving messages from our ancestors.

November—Beaver Moon. In November beavers prepare their lodges, securing them for the long winter. The full moon in November is perfect for going deep within, exploring our shadowy bits that we often hide from the light of day. Knowing that a healthy relationship with our own shadow is greatly important for developing our psychic vision, this is, in my opinion, one of the most important forms of divination we can do for ourselves.

December—Cold Moon. The Cold Moon of December is one of darkness and light, as the sun disappears below the horizon, only returning for a few short hours a day. In this time of darkness, we humans celebrate with lights of our own, bedecking our storefronts and homes with glittering lights and hearth fires; this makes the full moon of December the perfect time for exploring the contrasts between our own darkness and light.

In addition to these full moons of the year, there are other lunar events of significance: the blue moon, the black moon, and lunar eclipse. I include cartomancy spreads for these events in the "Rare Moon Spreads" chapter of this book (page 96).

Solar Cycles

The sun, like the moon, transforms itself through seasonal phases as the year turns, marked by the solstices, equinoxes, and the places in between. Modern Pagans refer to this passage as the Wheel of the Year and loosely base its attributes on the ancient Celtic and Germanic practices celebrated by our ancestors to the North. It's important to note that one does not need to be descended from either culture to take part in the Wheel of the Year, for these solar holidays are connected to the changing of our living planet not our ancestral bloodlines. Likewise, such holidays are devoid of manmade religious constructs, making them approachable regardless of your personal spiritual beliefs. You can find suggested card layouts for each of the solar holidays as well as the solar equinoxes in the "Seasonal Card Spreads" chapter starting on page 78.

Halloween (Samhain)—October 31. This time of dying, in which the leaves have fallen from the trees and the life-giving Earth has settled into slumber, is recognized and celebrated by many names and cultures. Recognized as one of the times of the year in which the veil that separates the worlds of the living and that of the dead is at its thinnest, Halloween is a potent time for magic of all kinds, including divination! Currently recognized as the turning point of the year—equivalent to New Year's Day in the Gregorian calendar we currently live by—Halloween is often referred to as the Witch's New Year. Agriculturally it marks the last harvest, in which livestock are culled before the winter.

In our modern world, Halloween is a time to celebrate the dark, with many of our cultural practices turning to the unseen world of spirit, and the hauntingly fictitious fears the dark brings with it. Halloween is one of the cross-quarter holidays of the Wheel of the Year, falling directly between the autumn equinox and the winter solstice. In divination, Halloween is the best time to perform a Wheel of the Year forecast for the year ahead.

Winter Solstice (Yule)—December 21–23. The winter solstice is an astronomical event; therefore, it varies in date from year to year, generally falling between December 21 and 23. Marking the shortest day of the year, and the longest night, the winter solstice has been celebrated throughout history by a plethora of names, including Yule and Christmas. It is a time of great darkness, in which many of our ancestors—particularly those who lived in the far north—questioned whether the light would return. In this time when the shadow holds heavy, we humans seek out light in other forms, from candlelit menorahs to twinkling lights on trees; we revere the light when it is away. This is a great time to focus on the light you bring to the world, and what light fills your soul the most fully.

Imbolc—February 2. Like Halloween, Imbolc is a cross-quarter holiday, falling directly between the winter solstice and the spring equinox. It is a time associated with the first signs of spring, when the light begins to grow stronger and stay stronger in the sky. It is a time of celebration for the hearth and home, the perfect time to do readings focused on our home and family life.

Spring Equinox (Ostara)—March 21–23. The spring equinox (also called the vernal equinox) is an astronomical event; its date varies year to year, generally taking place between March 21 and 23. It is a time of balance, in which there are equal hours of daylight and the dark of night, with the hours of light growing longer each day. Like the autumn equinox that shadows it in September it is a time of seeking internal balance, with an awareness that the most productive time of the year lies in front of us. This is a time of planning the best use of our time, and divination done at this time should be focused on finding that balance.

Beltane—May 1. Oh, Beltane . . . the holiday of lovers and lovemaking! Falling directly between the spring equinox and the summer solstice, Beltane is one of the cross-quarter holidays. Like Halloween, which shadows it from the other side of the wheel, Beltane is a time in which the veil between the worlds is thin. However, due to the life-bearing greenness of the landscape, it is connected most deeply with the unseen world of the fae folk, fairies, nature beings, and elementals. This is the perfect time to do a reading for deeper connection to our elemental and fairy guides.

Summer Solstice (Litha)—June 21–23. The summer solstice is an astronomical event marking the longest day and shortest night of the year. Located directly across from the winter solstice in the Wheel of the Year, it is a time of celebrating the living green world, family, and community. This is a time of giving thanks to our community and the promised bounty of the growing season. Readings done at this time are best focused on recognizing the blessings being presented to us and how we can, in turn, return those blessings to the world around us.

First Harvest (Lughnasa)—August 2. The beginning of August marks the first of three harvest holidays. Located directly between the summer solstice and the autumn equinox, Lughnasa is a busy time—regardless of whether we farm the land or not. Our world is at the height of abundance at this point, with fresh vegetables and fruit being plentiful, and long days of warmth and satiating sunlight lasting well into the evening. This is a time of basking in the

24 + Psychic Storytelling

goodness of life! Readings done at this time are best focused on our career and life path.

Autumn Equinox—September 21–23. The autumn equinox is an astronomical event marking the balance of night and day, as the Wheel of the Year moves into its season of darkness. It is the second of three harvest holidays and marks the time of balance between day and night, in which we celebrate our hard work and do the final planning for the winter months. It is a time of assessment, marking the last holiday of the modern Wheel of the Year. Readings done at this time are best focused on our accomplishments, recognizing all that we have gained and given over the past year.

Solar Eclipse—Solar eclipses are energetically powerful, rare opportunities to look at the BIG STUFF in our life. They occur when the moon passes between the Earth and the sun, blocking the view of the sun for a short period of time. Readings done at this time are best focused on the big picture, what we are trying to achieve on a soul level, not only in this lifetime, but in the multitude of lifetimes that make up our being. This is a time for calling in our spiritual allies—including ancestors, guides, and deities—and creating a bigger ceremony around such readings, placing focus on my altar and offerings.

Utilizing the passage of the moon and sun in your readings will guide you to look at life differently, as you learn to approach blessings and burdens through an alternative viewpoint. While I have suggested particular readings for each of the lunar and solar events, these are just suggestions. I encourage you to follow your intuition and utilize the cartomancy spreads featured in this book in whatever way best suits you, and to create your own spreads that are tailored to your individual needs.

TRAINING THE BRAIN

The difference between being a psychic reader who works with cards and being a card reader comes down to the methods we employ in our reading, whether we lean toward memorization or intuitive flow. While the psychic reader benefits from having a strong symbolic vocabulary and an educated understanding of whatever form of cartomancy they are practicing (oracle, playing cards, tarot), the true key to detailed, accurate readings lies in the mental state of the reader.

Developing psychic abilities requires us to find stillness in our minds, even when the world around us is loud! In the beginning this can be difficult, as we are living high-frequency lives, filled with electrical currents, Wi-Fi signals, and 5G cell service. Background noise hums in our ears so frequently that we don't notice it most of the time, yet it affects us, keeping us buzzing like bees with little time for stillness. Meditation, sacred solitude, intentional sound, and movement help us to develop this stillness, and through practice we can learn to call upon that internal quiet without any outward preparation. Like art, the subtleties and details become clearer with proper technique and practice.

When beginning anything new, there are often more steps necessary to get the results that we seek than are necessary once we have developed skill. Cartomancy is no exception!

Just as it is important to create a peaceful environment for our psychic work, it is equally—if not more—important for us to create such space in our minds. With time and practice such a mindset is easy to achieve and can be accomplished in just a few moments. The key is to create little rituals that help us slip into a light trance state.

What is a light trance state?

Light trance feels like that sweet, drowsy state of consciousness we experience when listening to relaxing music or rocking in a rocking chair. In this state our mind drifts easily but is still aware enough to be pulled back into ordinary consciousness by any signs of alarm. People often find themselves naturally in this state while daydreaming.*

---

*From Salicrow, *Spirit Speaker: A Medium's Guide to Death and Dying* (Rochester, VT: Destiny Books, 2023).

Most of us are comfortable in light trance state and spend short intervals in this state multiple times a day. Psychics utilize this state of mind to connect more deeply with the world, allowing insights and answers to come to them more fluidly. In this state, we are more deeply connected to our higher self, the part of our soul that is conscious throughout all incarnations and capable of perceiving both the past and the future with more accuracy. When working in this state of consciousness information flows into and through our minds easily, and our serious inquiries are generally answered with the first thoughts that come to mind.

It's important to remember that doubt words like *maybe, kind of,* and *I think so* get in our way and often stop us from utilizing our intuitive minds. *If you are prone to throwing those words around, I suggest repeating your statements without them, as they often hinder our intuitive development!*

When beginning our path as a Seer, it is important to develop a personal meditation practice. Meditation comes in many varieties: from the recognizable sitting on a cushion in silence to ecstatic dance to vocal toning meditation, there is a form of meditation that fits everyone. My personal favorite is soaking in my cast-iron bathtub while listening to hypnotic music, like binaural beats, recorded river sounds, or Norse trance music.

I enter my tub like others enter church, with my heart and mind focused on going deep into my own consciousness. I close my eyes and take deep breaths, occasionally reminding myself to release any unnecessary burdens on the exhalation, and to pull deeply of the calm on the inhalation; this simple breathing reminder is something I can use as an access point when I am doing readings. By remembering to release burden on the exhale and to inhale calm, I connect my consciousness to that moment in the tub, just like an experienced yoga practitioner can find peace the moment they step onto the mat and take their first deep breath.

If you already have regular meditation practice you are ahead of the game. If you do not, I recommend experimenting with some of the forms below.

Traditional Meditation. Sitting on the floor cross-legged, eyes closed, working with either deep breathing or a mantra. (A mantra is words or sounds repeated during meditation to maintain focus.)

Rocking Meditation. This form of meditation can be performed while sitting in a rocking chair or by rocking the body gently back and forth or in small circles.

Vocal Toning. Sitting in a comfortable position or standing, with a straight back, close your eyes and begin to sing/vocalize simple vowel sounds, such as "Oh," and "Ah," allowing yourself to pull out the sound as if you were singing opera. Simple words can be added to the process, like my favorite: "open." *When toning "open" I am imaging that I am opening my consciousness.*

Ecstatic Dance. Movement, particularly dancing, is a part of many trance-inducing spiritual practices. I like to describe ecstatic dance as "dancing ugly," as the practitioner cares little for how their dance looks, and instead focuses on how it feels.

Finding a form of meditation that we connect with, and practicing it regularly, helps us to create shortcuts to deep relaxation and light trance. While we will not be able to break out into ecstatic dance or vocal toning before every reading, we can use pieces of the practice as keys that allow us access to a grounded, open state of mind with ease. Long, deep breathing reminds us of our sitting meditation; making micro-rocking movements reminds our brain of our ecstatic dance practice; and quietly toning "Ooohh" on our exhalation reminds us of our practice of vocal toning. The more regular our practice, the better the keys work!

28 ✦ Psychic Storytelling

◇◇◇◇◇◇◇◇◇◇◇◇

TECHNIQUE
ROCKING

Rocking is a simple technique that can be used anywhere; in fact, children often practice this as a form of self-soothing. While no tools are required, you can use a rocking chair if you have one.

1. Take note of your surroundings, as this will determine how elaborate your rocking can get; note that small movements can be quite effective for lulling the mind into a light trance state.
2. Taking deep, even breaths through the nose, bring your consciousness to your root chakra (at the base of your spine), noting the sensation of sitting upon the ground or chair. Take a few breaths here feeling yourself relax.
3. Begin to slowly make small counterclockwise spirals with your upper body, or your head only. The size of the spiral's dependent on your surroundings. If you are in a public place, they can made so small they are hardly noticeable. *The counterclockwise spiral helps unwind overthinking minds.* Do this for a few moments, continuing to breathe deeply and steadily.
4. Reverse the direction of your spiral, now moving in a clockwise direction. Continuing to keep your breath even, imagine you are opening your consciousness as you invite your mind to slip into deep relaxation. *Clockwise spirals help us recharge.* Do this for a few moments, making note of how it feels.
5. Now move into a simple back and forth rocking, making small movements with your body. Note how the sensation makes you feel.
6. Make sure to write about your experience in your Book of Shadows.

I use rocking often in my daily work, making simple movements when I am sitting with clients in person or on Zoom. My movements are often so small that they don't even notice I am making them, however these micromovements help me stay in a light trance state, making it easier for me to use my psychic perception.

As we advance in our meditation practice—whether it be in the tub, nature, the dance floor, or a yoga mat—we will want to start directing our focus, particularly if we are serious about developing our psychic intuition. One of the easiest ways to do so is to clearly form your intention before entering mediation, whether that intention be focused on a particular problem or simply on opening our consciousness. For those who are seriously interested in opening their psychic gifts, I recommend focusing your mediations on opening the third eye.

The third eye is the chakra (energy center) located in the middle of our forehead between and above the brow. It is often associated with psychic seeing (clairvoyance) and psychic knowing (claircognizance); however, all forms of psychic input can be experienced through this energy center.

When meditating on our third eye it is helpful to move our focus from the chakra point in the middle of our forehead, back to the pituitary gland in the center of our brain. You can simply focus on this space inside your mind as you take deep full breaths, or you can try the guided meditation I have created for you below. *I recommend recording yourself reading the meditation on your phone. For best results, speak in a slow, calm voice with very little fluctuation in volume or speed.* Begin in a comfortable position sitting or lying down. If you are prone to falling asleep during deep relaxation, I suggest sitting.

◇◇◇◇◇◇◇◇◇◇◇◇

TECHNIQUE

THIRD EYE OPENING

Close your eyes and begin taking deep, even breaths in through and out through your nose. On the inhale imagine you are filling your energetic body with light, and on the exhale releasing all the everyday worries you do not need with you in this moment. Inhaling . . . filling your body with light, exhaling . . . stress and everyday worries.

30 + Psychic Storytelling

Continuing to breathe in deeply, bring your attention to your feet . . . notice that they feel heavy, and warm. On the inhalation allow your consciousness to rest in the warm heavy feeling of your feet, reassuring yourself that you are deeply grounded and present in this moment. On the inhale, imagine that feeling to be spreading, moving up your body into your ankles. Exhale and inhale deeply, as the heaviness and warmth move up your legs, encompassing your knees, and thighs. On the inhale, move that energy up into your pelvis, allowing it to spread around your hips and buttocks.

You feel warm and comfortable as you focus on your breath moving in and out of your lungs, filling your body from the hips down with warmth and a feeling of deep relaxation. Continuing to breathe allow this energy to move up your torso, feeling it on both the front and back sides of your body . . .

Moving the energy with your breath, imagine it moving up into your chest, arms, and shoulders. Notice how your body from the neck down feels heavy and warm, as you move the energy once again with your deep, steady breathing. Notice the warmth moving up into your neck and jaw, allowing you to release any tension you are carrying . . . pushing it out on the exhalation.

As you continue to breathe, allow that warm, heavy energy to move once again until it is entirely encompassing your body. Sit with this energy for a few moments as you breathe deeply, once again focusing on the even, steady pace of your breathing. Inhaling, and exhaling . . . and inhaling, and exhaling.

As you focus on your breathing, you become aware of a small white light emanating from between your eyes in the middle of your forehead, where your third eye is located. Take a few breaths here.

Continuing to breathe, you notice that the small circle of light in the center of your forehead begins to slowly expand as if opening. You might notice a sensation of pressure in the center of your forehead as you do this. Continue to breathe and stay relaxed. Resist the temptation to clench your brow . . .

Imagine that with every inhalation you are expanding your third eye, opening it, allowing light to shine through. On the exhale, relax your brow, consciously letting go of any tension you are holding there. Continue breathing for a few moments: Inhaling . . . expanding the light in the middle of your forehead, exhaling . . . relaxing your forehead. Inhaling, expanding the light . . . exhaling, relaxing your forehead. Again, inhaling, expanding the light . . . exhaling, relaxing your forehead.

Taking a deep breath in, allow yourself to expand your third eye, holding your breath on the inhale and keeping that light expanded, counting . . . one, two, three, four, five. Exhaling, and releasing all tension. Repeat: Taking a deep inhalation, expanding your third eye, and hold . . . one, two, three, four, five . . . and exhale releasing all tension. One more time: Deep inhalation, expanding the third eye, hold . . . one, two, three, four, five, and a nice deep exhale as you release.

Return your breathing to a deep, steady, rhythmic pace, and spend a moment here. When you are ready you can start wiggling your fingers and toes, as you bring yourself back into regular consciousness.

Make sure to take a few moments to write about your experience in your Book of Shadows, remembering that tracking our progress helps greatly in psychic development.

Like any new exercise we may experience fatigue or slight discomfort or pressure; this is normal. For many people the pressure felt in the center of our forehead feels like having our eyebrows pulled up, and the natural reaction to this feeling is to want scrunch up our brow. I do not recommend doing this, as scrunching up our brow when our third eye is expanding often creates a pulsation that leads to headaches. Instead, try to relax into the feeling of expansion in the center of your forehead. With practice this sensation will lessen or go away completely. Patience and repetition go a long way. In the beginning I do not recommend doing this meditation more than three times per week.

BODY DOWSING

Trusting our psychic abilities requires us to believe in our own wisdom, something society has tried very hard to keep us from doing. Many of us find we are constantly seeking validation, wanting to check and double check to see if the answers we are receiving are valid. This is particularly true if we are looking at emotionally difficult situations. Remembering to ground and center is helpful, but there will still be times when we feel the need for confirmation. That's where body dowsing comes in!

Body dowsing is like using a pendulum in that it works primarily through yes or no answers, but where pendulum dowsing requires us to add another tool to the belt, body dowsing is something we can do at any time, in any place, as our body is the tool! *If you find it easier to work with a pendulum for confirmation, feel free to do so.*

When learning body dowsing, we must first determine whether we respond to the lie or the truth, or both, and how we respond. To do this we begin by making both a truthful statement and a lie about something we know the answer to. Once we are clear on our statement, we repeat both sentences a few times slowly, noticing any sensations we feel in our body.

When teaching body dowsing, I use the example "I am going to Texas on vacation," and "I am not going to Texas on vacation," knowing that I am not going to Texas on vacation. When doing so, I notice that my solar plexus tightens in response to the lie, and I feel no noticeable sensation to the truth.

Not everyone responds the same way. Some people respond to the truth, others to the lie, and still others have responses for each. Responses can come in a variety of forms, such as cold chills, pressure behind the eyes or at one of the chakra points, and a feeling of knowing. Through practicing with things that we know the answer to, we become adept at understanding how our body responds, and capable of utilizing this response as a form of confirmation to our divination.

I recommend practicing this skill throughout your readings, checking in from time to time to gain clarity. Write down your responses, knowing that the more we study our own ability the more skill we will develop. After a while body dowsing will become something you do without thinking about it, your subconscious picking up the cue and giving alerts in your everyday life when people are lying to you. This skill is a major boon in psychic development, as most of our precognitive needs happen in an instant.

One of the reasons I included alternate forms of psychic development in this book is because the more we develop our skills of observation, and learn to trust our intuition, the better we will be at psychic divination. Our body is sensitive! Many people experience a feeling of heightened energy in their body; often described as a feeling of anxiousness or excitement, their body is agitated in the anticipation of "Something is coming!" We must learn to listen to this feeling, to explore it, instead of trying to outrun it. When such feelings come up, take the time to check in with your intuition through body dowsing or cartomancy.

Understanding how our bodies react to psychic stimuli offers structure to our intuition, allowing us to incorporate our bodies' responses into the core of how we process our experiences. Along with developing our yes or no psychic lie detector, it is beneficial to make note of how our body responds to sudden psychic input, such as prophetic dreams or big revelations during a reading. Most people will have an area they are noticeably blocked in, usually located on or near one of the seven primary chakras.

When I was a girl developing my psychic abilities, I blocked incoming psychic information through my sacral chakra, which generally manifested in me getting sick to my stomach, cramped up, before something significant happened. Once I realized this, I was able to utilize the block, seeing its appearance as notice that something of relevance was about to happen. My daughter blocked with her throat chakra, often having to clear her throat or coughing when trying to talk about a prophetic dream she had. Again, recognizing the block can

34 ✦ Psychic Storytelling

turn it into an early warning sign, giving us a heads-up. Over time we become more sensitive to the sign, and soon we are getting our heads up without the pain and discomfort, and knowing where we personally block our intuition helps us direct our efforts more effectively when working to break through the block!

Over the years I have expanded my body dowsing check-in to include questions that help me narrow in on that which is causing me precognitive anxiousness. Below is the method I developed for getting clarity when it is elusive. Like all things, practice makes skill, so the more you practice the more reliable the skill will be when you need it.

◇◇◇◇◇◇◇◇◇◇◇◇

TECHNIQUE
NEAR OR FAR:
ADVANCED BODY DOWSING

Even the best readers will have times in which they are unable to get a clear answer to their inquiry, often because the situation is personal and/or emotionally charged. In these moments I have taken to asking questions that approach the inquiry from a roundabout trajectory, asking questions about the people surrounding the situation and secondary situations that would be affected by how the situation turns out. When experiencing a sudden psychic response of anxiousness triggered by intuitive input during a reading, in a dream, or through a premonition, it is helpful to determine how close the situation is to us personally.

Taking a few moments to create sacred space and quiet our thoughts by taking deep rhythmic breaths and rocking slightly, we feel more balanced as we slow our heart rate and release some of the anxiousness associated with big feelings of knowing. Utilizing our internal pendulum, begin slowly and steadily repeating out loud: "It's near!" "It's far!" "It's near!" "It's far!" The first time we ask this question if our response determines the situation is near, it means it will affect us personally. If it is far, repeat the process again.

On the second round of stating "It's near!" "It's far!" if we feel the answer is near it means it will affect someone in our close family circle: husband/wife/romantic partner, or child. If it is far, we will repeat the process again! If the response shows it is near on the third round it means it will affect our extended family and/or close friends. If it is far, our process is repeated. The fourth round is for personal community, the fifth round our state or province, every circle out moving farther and farther from affecting us personally.

Generally, when we are hit with a sudden and profound psychic knowing that leaves us unable to get a clear message it is likely to affect us personally or those who are within our extended family or close friends, unless the situation we are being affected by is on a global scale. Having had such experiences myself, I have had my circle of effect extended many rings out. Understanding how far it is and how it still will affect me shows me how intertwined we really are.

BUILDING YOUR SYMBOLIC LANGUAGE

Symbolism is the unspoken language of humanity that allows us to share information through shapes and colors, images, and association. In fact, reading this book requires the use of symbols—known as the alphabet. While interpretation of symbols can vary, there are some that are universally understood, such as arrows that point in the direction we must go, red hexagons that represent the need to stop, and heart shapes representing love.

Symbols work as a shortcut for the brain, allowing a simple image to transmit a broader understanding. In psychic development symbolism is recognized as a key way in which intuitive information is transmitted—something that is particularly true in cartomancy, with even the humble playing card being laden with symbolic meaning.

Symbolism is the language of intuition, and like all languages the better we understand it the easier it is to communicate. It can be both

36 ✦ Psychic Storytelling

universal and uniquely personal in its meaning, as it relies primarily on the effect it has on the mind of the receiver; therefore, our personal reaction to the symbol holds more sway than anything we will read in a book, including this one!

Cartomancy relies heavily on symbolism as it is a visual form of divination based on how we interpret images seen on cards. The number of symbols present is based on the type of cards we are working with and the design of each deck. Generally playing cards hold the least symbolism, oracle cards are bedecked with magical symbols, and tarot—particularly the Rider-Waite Tarot and decks influenced by it—are loaded with esoteric symbolism intentionally placed like clues around each card to activate the reader's psychic mind.

Many people experience the effects of symbols without understanding their common meaning, something that is particularly true if the symbol is esoteric in nature. In my opinion, being of an animistic nature, this is due to the fact that symbols, like all things, gain a sense of purpose when used accordingly by a large group of people. I find analytical understanding of a symbol's meaning is highly beneficial, as it allows us to both intuitively respond to its meaning and question its appearance for deeper introspection.

When I was developing my own understanding of symbolism, I studied symbols regularly by both picking one or two symbols at a time to analytically study, and by looking up symbols when they popped into my everyday world. As this was in the early days of the internet, my study revolved primarily around one book, *The Woman's Dictionary of Symbols and Sacred Objects* by Barbara G. Walker. I still recommend this book today, noting that the title is a bit outdated, as the information is not restricted to women's eyes only. Now there are a plethora of options when it comes to developing a symbolic language, with many books and websites dedicated to such.

With so many options available it can seem overwhelming to figure out which sites are the best. My advice is to read the booklet that comes with your cards, visit a bunch of websites, and peruse books on symbolism at the local bookstore. Look for similarities in the definitions given, as this shows an accurate view of the collective meaning. When you find sources you like and trust, bookmark the pages and add the books to your personal bookshelf for easy access.

Along with books and websites on dream interpretation and the tarot, we can find rich sources of symbolism exist in the magical schools we study: be it Reiki healing, astrology, Witchcraft, or ceremonial magic, as well as religious symbols associated with churches and sects. Personal symbols with emotional or spiritual significance to us, like family crests, and references from pop culture also activate our minds symbolically, as do color, numbers, and animals, as symbolism is a natural way of communication. Moreover, we have the everyday symbolism that is crafted from our mundane life, influenced by our jobs, hobbies, the environment we live in, as well as our ethnic and community traditions. For example, a person who lives in Tennessee may respond to the image of heavy snow differently than a person from Vermont; heavy snow in Tennessee represents a minor disaster as they are unequipped to deal with it, but a Vermonter could easily interpret it as a sign to go skiing!

While developing our symbolic language it is helpful to record our personal reactions and interpretations of symbols in our Book of Shadows, noting that our insights are highly important and likely to become the ones we rely on. When I come across a new symbol, I like to meditate on it for a few minutes, noting both my intuitive knowing and my analytical observations, then I write down my thoughts in my Book of Shadows, and finally I look it up on websites and in books. I find that most of the time my thoughts are like that of the written description given by others, although there have been exceptions in which my reaction was completely different. In such cases I always go with my interpretation, knowing that as the one receiving psychic input it's the one that matters most!

Developing one's symbolic language is a lifelong pursuit for most psychics, with new signs and symbols leading us further and further into the web of wyrd!

38 ✦ Psychic Storytelling

When building our symbolic language, it is helpful to make note of what symbols present themselves to us throughout the day. While there are many possible ways in which this can happen there are some common ones to keep an eye out for, such as animals that catch our attention, number sequences, colors that stand out to us, and symbols we notice in emails, store windows, nature, and our dreams.

Many people experience psychic communication in the form of symbolism within their dreams. These dreams do not leave us when we return to our wakeful consciousness, but instead generally keep us questioning throughout the day. Dreaming of this sort often takes us to the astral realm, where we can access our higher consciousness and the world of spirit. Such dreams are often filled with symbolism that helps bring deeper understanding to situations that affect our life and soul. Through the lens of symbolism, we begin to dissect our dreams, recognizing that seeing a Bear sitting in our grandmother's kitchen most likely does not mean grandma will be entertaining bears!

Astral Realm

A nonphysical plane of existence accessed by our astral self or spirit.

Developing our understanding of symbolism in this abstract way helps us to make our mind flexible, teaching it to jump from an image to a thought with ease; all of which is beneficial when learning to trust our intuition. For those who want to go deeper into the dreamscape, I recommend journey work.

GUIDED MEDITATION AND INTUITION

Journey work is a form of meditation in which the participant travels deep into their consciousness in search of answers. The level of guidance is variable, with some people needing more direction than others. A variety of such meditations can be found on YouTube, Spotify, and

Apple. Guided meditations are similar to journey work but generally have someone guiding the listener where to look through telling an interactive story. When choosing which journey to take, I recommend looking for ones that focus on third eye opening and psychic development. It's important to note that not all guides are the same, so find one you like listening to! Make sure your Book of Shadows is close by for writing down your experiences after you are done.

Actively developing our symbolic vocabulary though guided meditation is another way to help our mind become more fluid, easily moving between images and thoughts, and like most things it gets easier with practice! While dedication is necessary for the serious practitioner it doesn't have to feel like work. We need to remember that we are developing this skill with a desire to know ourselves better and to see what we are capable of as intuitive human beings. We need to step away from the capitalist mindset that focuses on the fastest route to the top, for there is much to learn by taking the side roads.

Guided meditation is often referred to as journey work because the participant is traveling to the astral realm via their mind. By calling our experience a journey we are enforcing the belief that what we went through was real; albeit, not necessarily real on the material plane.

◇◇◇◇◇◇◇◇◇◇◇◇

TECHNIQUE
PREPARING TO JOURNEY

1. Practice is necessary if we want to get anywhere. Some people will naturally have vivid experiences with journey work, while others will struggle in the beginning, getting little to no input; know you are developing a skill, and development takes time.

2. Not everyone's journeys are the same. This means some people will have technicolor visual dream sequences, with full-on details including audible soundtrack, and others will have very little visualization, instead experiencing their information as more of a knowing.

40 ✦ Psychic Storytelling

3. Don't be afraid to ask questions and reexamine things. A good psychic should think like a detective, looking at clues, reviewing things that puzzle them, and asking lots of questions. This is true of the work we do while journeying as well as when we are reading cards.

4. Repeating the same journey is helpful. Repeating the same journey multiple times is helpful, as we can go a little deeper into our mind each time, accessing symbols and signs we may have previously missed.

5. Sit up if you fall asleep easily. Many people will fall asleep during journey work if they are too comfortable. If you are one of these people, making yourself a little uncomfortable is good. You can try sitting in a comfortable chair, and if that is still too comfy, sit on a cushion or the ground with your legs crossed.

6. Journey in sacred space. Make sure you will not be disturbed. Take the time to set up an altar, or simply light a candle. Burn incense or herbs or mist your favorite cleansing spray. Call in your spiritual allies, particularly the ones you are hoping to connect with. Treat your work as sacred and you will have better results.

7. Cover your head. Placing a scarf over your head to shade your eyes is helpful for people who have a hard time closing out the world. This not only blocks out light and our surroundings, but it also adds another layer of sacredness to the act of journeying.

8. Utilize herbs for deeper work. For those who are looking for a deeper exploration in journey work, herbal smokes and tinctures—such as cannabis and mugwort—are helpful aids for entering a deeper trance state. Proper knowledge of the herbs mentioned, and your personal response to them, should be considered before taking this step.

9. Use the rocking technique to go deeper. See the description on page 28.

10. Record your experiences. Journaling is key to the development of psychic abilities.

11. Audio is best. When using a written journey, such as the one below, use the voice recorder app on your phone to record yourself reading the journey. In leading a journey for yourself or others it is important to talk in a slow, even pace.

Now that you are prepared to journey, using as many of the tips listed above as possible, we shall begin.

◇◇◇◇◇◇◇◇◇◇◇◇

TECHNIQUE

GUIDED MEDITATION TO OPEN THE THIRD EYE

Close your eyes and begin taking deep, even breaths through your nose. On each inhalation imagine that you are pulling in bright white light, and on the exhalation imagine that you are releasing burden and fear in the form of a gray cloud. Continue to breathe like this for a few moments, until you feel you no longer see the gray cloud on your exhalation.

When you have done so, continue to breathe in an even, rhythmic pattern. If your mind drifts, remember you can bring yourself back to the center and your journey's purpose by coming back to your breath.

Bring your attention to your body, allowing yourself to first feel the physical sensations of your body. Take a few breaths here, allowing yourself to deeply connect with the physical world, noticing how warm and heavy it feels. Continuing to breathe, in and out . . . fully filling your lungs on each breath.

Now imagine that you are beginning to levitate just above your body. With every breath in you fill yourself with more light, and on every exhale, you rise out of your body. Take a few breaths here, noticing how light and free you feel.

As you continue to breathe, you notice you are now floating above your body, and that you can see seven orbs of light rising in the middle of your spine, in the colors of the rainbow. Recognizing them as chakras, you begin to examine each a bit closer.

Making your way from bottom to top, focus first on your root chakra, the luminescent red located in your pelvis. Red like a fire truck, red like an apple. Take a few breaths here visualizing the red orb growing brighter on every inhale.

On the exhale move your eyes up the body, now focusing on your sacral chakra, the glowing orange orb just below your body's navel. Orange

42 ✦ Psychic Storytelling

like fruit, orange like a summer sunset. Take a few breaths here visualizing the orange orb growing brighter on every inhale.

On the exhale move your eyes up the body to the orb spinning in your solar plexus, as it illuminates your upper torso with yellow light on every breath, spilling out golden light like the sun on every inhalation.

On the exhale move your eyes up the body to rest on your heart chakra, located in the center of your chest. Here you see a glowing green orb, green like summer grass, green like emeralds. As you inhale imagine the orb becoming more luminescent.

As you exhale, bring your attention to the throat chakra, noticing the brightly lit turquoise sphere spinning in the center of your throat, blue like the summer sky grows brighter with each inhalation.

On the exhalation you are drawn up once again to the center of your forehead, just above your eyes. Here you see a deep azure-blue orb spinning. Looking at it reminds you of the night sky, sparkling with the light of the stars. This is your third eye, the center of your intuition. As you focus on it you notice that twinkling light of the internal star seems to make patterns, like constellations, or dew sparkling on a spider web. You begin to see patterns emerging and seek light to illuminate the weave.

Taking a deep breath allows yourself to focus on the top of the head. Here you see a large glowing white orb, the crown chakra. As you breathe imagine that light getting brighter and brighter. Now imagine you can focus that light, shining a bright stream of light from the crown chakra into your third eye.

Continuing to breathe, the hidden patterns sparkling in your third eye come into view, illuminated by the light of your crown chakra. Take a few moments here, directing the light into the dark spots, focusing on the symbols that are presenting themselves to you. As you do so, ask that you be shown a symbol or symbols that will be helpful for you as you develop your skills as a psychic. Take a few moments here, carefully examining the web of sparkling light for all symbols.

Continue breathing, deep inhalations and exhalations, taking a few moments to focus on your third eye. When you feel like you have received all the symbols being shown to you, return your focus to the bright white light streaming in from your crown. Illuminate your third eye with this light, filling it with light. It should now be vibrantly glowing a deep purple, like an amethyst. As you continue to focus on it, imagine it expanding, growing larger until it appears to cover your face from below your nose to the top of your forehead. You may feel a sensation now, like raising your eyebrows, or a tugging in the middle of your forehead above the brow. Relax, and take a few additional breaths here.

Now relax your mind, and take a final look at your body, seeing it illuminated brightly by your chakras. On the exhalation, focus your mind on the silver thread attaching you to your body, and on the inhalation imagine you are being pulled back into your physical form.

Breathe evenly for a few more rounds as you begin to wiggle your toes and fingers, coming fully into your physical body. Remember to write down your experiences, particularly any symbols you may have seen, remembering that animals, colors, and numbers can also be symbolic.

SELF-CARE AND PERSONAL HEALING

Healing is an important part of developing psychic ability, as utilizing these skills requires the use of our personal energy. While this energy is a naturally renewing source it takes time to recharge, just as our muscles need time to repair after a workout. It is also a common belief that we have a finite amount of personal energy, and that most people waste much of their energy on unhealed wounds and self-sabotaging behavior. For the serious seeker, there will come a time in which personal traumas and damaging behaviors need to be healed if we are to truly step into our potential.

There are a couple of big reasons why it is so important to heal ourselves if we want to truly develop our psychic skills. The first has to do with freeing up energy that is stuck in our physical and emotional bodies, and the second is so we are not triggered into weaving our own wounded story into the readings of others. I have seen readers who could give a good reading if things were going well for them, but their readings all became laden with emotional drama when the readers were struggling with their own relationships.

As psychic readers we must be capable of looking into the lives of others with clear vision, so we can give advice that is centered and truthful. When we are overcome with our own pain, it has a way of trickling into everything we do and creating a mess that is often hard to see clearly through. This does not mean we can't develop our psychic ability before we heal, but it does mean that doing so will make us do the work to clean things up! This is where journey work and doing readings for us come in, helping us to see things from a different angle so that we may begin to have a better understanding of self. For those with deep trauma, it is helpful to work with a skilled healer and/or counselor as we move through our psychic development.

Cleaning up our personal garbage has another effect, in that we will no longer be wasting hours of our day on the things that hurt us and make us feel bad about ourselves. With this extra energy we have more available to fuel our psychic skills. Just as dropping extra weight makes it easier to perform physical activities.

I should add that along with these big ones there is another subtle but powerful gift that comes out of personal healing, experience, and perspective. Having walked through our wounding and out the other side we are often far more compassionate and understanding of other people's situations, and sometimes our personal experience is what holds the best path for others as well. This is particularly true of those who would approach divination as a storyteller as the perspective in which we deliver our information is as important as the information itself.

This information is shared with the serious practitioner! The more we expand our consciousness and peer into the unknown, the more we realize that life is far more complex than the mundane world would have us believe. This epiphany requires a lot of reconfiguring! It's important to remember that the growth of this nature takes place over time, as healing and growing are lifetime achievements that play out throughout our years incarnate, creating a path we will walk for the rest of our lives. Embracing such growth, as painful as the process can sometimes be, comes with many rewards outside of the psychic realm as well, particularly in the quality of our lives.

Just as healing ourselves is necessary, if we are to reach our full potential, it is also important that we learn early on to let go of other people's stories and the wounds woven into them. To help us disconnect it is helpful to go into the situation protected. We can do this through personal spell work and prayer, by wearing crystals for protection (I recommend a rose quartz or labradorite worn close to the heart chakra), through Reiki, or through imagery.

When I was starting out in my career, I used to pretend I was wearing a "psychic hat." I would put it on before sitting with a client and take it off when I was done with my work for the day. Through repetition this simple action became a powerful tool.

Self-care is vitally important as we develop our psychic skills, particularly in the form of prayer, meditation, or spell work, as these practices offer a time to center our thoughts and balance our energy, making the whole process of opening far more pleasant. These practices are even more beneficial if we incorporate our personal divination into these moments, as psychic opening opens doors in our mind, and it often comes with energetic downloads in which our consciousness receives information in a compacted form that will be incorporated over time. Much like downloading a file to our computer, we understand a small portion of it in the moment with the rest of it expanding into our mind over a period. This kind of growth often triggers emotional release and moments of awe. In truth it can be fabulous and wonderous if we are caring for ourselves properly, but when we are just pushing through without making accommodations for our changing selves, we are likely to burn out, finding our life a bit overwhelming.

It's OK to take a break! It's OK to slow things down! Listening to our bodies by eating right, getting enough sleep, and connecting with our spiritual allies on a regular basis will greatly benefit our well-being. This does not mean we have to live like saints; it is simply a reminder that *sensitive means sensitive*! We do not simply develop sensitivity in the areas we wish; often heightened psychic awareness means we have less tolerance for irritants. I like to believe that this sensitivity is akin to an early warning system, advising us to change our path before those irritants become a much bigger problem.

My final thoughts on self-care come in the form of understanding that a developed intuition sets us apart from others, in the sense we are picking up more information at any given time. This means we may find we volunteer to do more for others than they do for us, creating an imbalance in our relationships. When this happens it's important to think as if the other person were blind or deaf. In which case, we would need to provide more information for them to understand our needs. In short, there is a good chance we are picking up on things they are thinking, responding to random thoughts in their head, thoughts and requests they are not actually saying!

I do hope that this sparks a desire to become a psychic practitioner, for the journey is filled with magic and mystery!

Telling the Story

Now that you have started your personal path of psychic development, we'll focus on the art of storytelling through the use of tarot cards. While our focus will be on the tarot this concept can be utilized with oracle and playing decks as well.

ETHICS, MORALS, AND REPUTATION

One of the most important questions we should ask as a reader is, Should I reveal this information?

When people come to a psychic for a reading, they are asking the Seer to look deeply into their lives. But what about the people they ask about—their lovers, friends, family, and adversaries? Is it right for us to reveal information about someone who has not agreed to having their story revealed?

This kind of inquiry most often occurs when the querent is asking about someone they are in a relationship with. In such scenarios they are often seeking hidden knowledge about the person's actions and feelings. While it is helpful to understand where someone else is coming from—particularly when our lives are interwoven—we must ask ourselves at what point are we eavesdropping on someone else's private life. In determining this, it is helpful to ask ourselves whether

48 ✦ Psychic Storytelling

the person inquired about would want the querent to have this knowledge about them. It can be tricky, as often the question is asked with good intentions, but we all have things we just don't want to share with others.

When I encounter such situations, I work both with my common sense, asking, "Would I want someone receiving psychic knowledge of this sort about me?" and with a simple thought that I have programmed into my higher consciousness, asking that I be blocked of seeing things the person inquired about would not want revealed, unless such things involve danger.

As psychic readers we are held to a higher level of honesty and morals, as we are dealing with people's personal lives. We are also more likely to be scrutinized than a therapist or life coach, as our workings have a "magical" nature to them, which makes many people uncomfortable to begin with. In truth, our reputation is highly valuable, and we must do what we can to keep it on point. *We must be cautious in the advice we give, recognizing that we are neither doctor, lawyer, nor therapist, and while we may clearly see the issue, it is against the law for us to claim our advice as authority!*

This means, when we see medical conditions, we cannot diagnose; instead, we need to weave our words carefully, suggesting that there may be a problem in a particular area of the person's health, and advise them to seek medical attention. The same goes with mental health issues and legal battles. I regularly advise my clients that I cannot give them such information. Some psychics go so far as to post this information on their websites and social media feeds, making it clear that they are not suggesting psychic knowledge should override that of guidance from medical and legal professionals.

Another keynote when it comes to being a professional reader is that—unlike therapists, doctors, and lawyers—it is not advised that we keep documentation on our clients, other than email addresses and other logistical things. In truth, it's best if we put their information out of our minds shortly after the reading is done. This not only helps us keep our lives balanced, but it also means you do not have to worry about where we store and dispose of the files, and whether our client's life secrets are being kept that way.

While I do allow recordings of my sessions, those who see me in person are advised to record on their phones, and for online readings, in which I record for them, I advise them to download their recording within one week, as I will be deleting it after that point.

Reputation is everything when it comes to developing a career as a reader, particularly for those who wish to read cards as part of their occupation! It is important that we see ourselves as a professional, which means not only developing our psychic skills but also those of consistency and composure, as it's important to create a grounded atmosphere where the querent can feel at peace while receiving their reading, allotting them the comfort necessary to clearly hear and understand the messages being presented. It is helpful to establish regular locations and hours we are available for readings, and in this day and age to have such information available on our websites and social media feeds; this includes scheduled times we will be at psychic fairs and wellness events.

It also means taking time to set the stage, making our environment inviting and peaceful, regardless of whether we have our own reading room or a table set up at a psychic fair. If we are still in the mobile stage of our professional career, doing the psychic fair circuit, I recommend using the same props and tools for every fair, as we know that items retain a memory of their own over time. It also provides us with a small ritual to prepare ourselves every time we enter a new space, allowing us to slip more deeply into our role as psychic advisor as we lay out our table covering, and set out a few crystals.

Along with physically setting our space it is helpful to energetically set our space, something I like to refer to as "programming the empathic pool." To do this we must learn to reverse our empathic ability, so that instead of being bombarded by the emotions of each client

50 ✦ Psychic Storytelling

that arrives, we create an energetic space like a calm pool in which they can feel at ease.

◇◇◇◇◇◇◇◇◇◇◇◇

TECHNIQUE
PROGRAMMING YOUR EMPATHIC POOL

Psychic energy is a lot like water in that it can expand out to encompass whatever area it is placed in, filling the nooks and crannies, leaving no empty space untouched. An empathic pool is just that: filling the empty space around you with energy of your choosing—in this case, warm, calm, and grounded. But this same skill can be used to create a totally different energy if we need, such as an air of danger around us if we feel we need protection, showing that we are not easy prey!

This exercise works best if we have control of our space, such as a personal office or classroom. However, we can do this anywhere, at any time; in fact, I do it every time I get on an airplane! In such cases, it is helpful to work with a particular item, such as a ring or crystal, that we use as a trigger, remembering that repetitive use of an item creates ease and flow. In the technique below we will be creating an empathic pool filled with peaceful, grounded energy, so that our clients can relax and fully hear their reading. Note: This exercise can be done out loud or in your head, depending on your situation.

─────────── **You Will Need** ───────────

A talisman of some sort that can be used repeatedly, such as a crystal, pendant, ring, or lucky rabbit's foot, and your Book of Shadows.

1. Begin by holding your talisman in your hands and taking a few deep breaths, as you survey the area (card table, office, etc.). Engage Reiki or other healing modalities currently if you work with them.
2. Call in your spiritual allies, asking that they aid you in your work of creating sacred space.

Telling the Story + 51

3. Focus your mind on what you want your space to feel like, speaking to the space as you do (in your head or out loud).

4. Imagine there is a pinprick of white light in the center of your heart chakra. On every inhale it gets brighter, and on every exhale you expand it. Continue doing this until the room is filled with the energy of your choice.

5. Make note of your working in your Book of Shadows, as well as the reactions of your clients and self to the space.

A BOOK OF SHADOWS

When approaching psychic ability, it is helpful to think of it as an art form, for there are multiple ways of developing psychic intuition, just as there are a plethora of paths for creating art. We may learn techniques from others, but ultimately the formula in which we do so is our own, which is why it is so important for us to track our progress.

――――――――――― **Book of Shadows** ―――――――――――

A sacred journal used to track our psychic and spiritual development.

Unlike a journal that may contain entries regarding our personal, emotional experiences processed aloud through its pages, a Book of Shadows is more like a college notebook, containing processes and noteworthy facts. The term "Book of Shadows" has its roots in Witchcraft, referring to esoteric or hidden information—knowledge intended only for eyes that are capable of understanding. In many ways it is the most important book of knowledge we will ever possess, as it is personalized and dedicated to us!

While you can put all your magical workings into one Book of Shadows, I recommend separating your magical subjects. Having a book dedicated just to cartomancy and your developing psychic intuition will make it easy to track your progress; plus, you never know, you may

turn your Book of Shadows into a published book someday—I did!*
Noting that our Book of Shadows is in many ways the holiest of the
holy of personal journals, make sure to choose a notebook that feels the
part for you, and feel free to customize it in any way you like, knowing
that—like all things—the more time we spend with it, the deeper the
connection.

I do have a suggestion for choosing the right book. Remembering
that you will be recording readings you do for yourself here, as well
as your experience with techniques for psychic development, symbolism, and messages that come through while doing journey work, it
is helpful to have a notebook with margins. Margins give us a place
to write when we reflect on our past entries, something we will
do often.

Like all Books of Shadow, your cartomancy Book of Shadows
should be reviewed often. This is particularly true when working with
a form of divination, as tracking our progress is vital to believing in
ourselves, and believing in ourselves is vital to development of skill. I
recommend going back over old entries every two weeks, or cyclically
with the moon. The dark moon is a great time for reflection! When
reviewing your entries make sure to leave a comment in the margin
if what you foresaw came true. It is also helpful to record if you were
wrong, and how so; often we are not completely wrong, but instead it's
more of a misinterpretation of information.

For example: In the reading it appeared that the querent would
soon be pregnant. Instead, the querent's sister became pregnant. In that
situation the child coming into the querent's life was accurate, but how
it came in was not. Knowing this, we would want to ask more questions
when such a thing comes in again.

Have fun and write shit down! Review your entries often and learn
from your mistakes as much as your successes.

---

*The Path of Elemental Witchcraft: A Wyrd Woman's Book of Shadows (Rochester, VT:
Destiny Books, 2022) was crafted from my personal Book of Shadows.

CHOOSING A DECK

In this book I focus on the three main forms of cartomancy: tarot, oracle cards, and playing cards. While each is a viable tool, most people will find themselves drawn to one more than the other. Choosing the right deck starts with understanding what you want to look at and how much detail you are hoping to get.

Playing cards are the most inconspicuous of all the cards, their mundane use as a game making them highly acceptable. Playing cards are the most uniform of divination cards, with each deck having fifty-two cards, broken into four suits: Diamonds, Clubs, Hearts, and Spades. While art style may vary, the four suits generally carry uniform colors and symbolism.

On the downside, they are the least symbolic of card types, with their symbolism being focused primarily on the difference between the suits and numerological value (numerology). For this reason, playing cards are often seen as the most difficult to use; however, those with an understanding of numerology will likely appreciate them.

Oracle cards come in a large variety, designed to be tools of self-reflection and personal growth; each deck focuses on our spiritual development and magical growth from a different perspective. Oracle cards do not have a set style or number of cards, and they rarely have numerological value. In many ways oracle cards are specialized, allowing people to find a deck that fits their needs, such as animal guides, angels, and beloved dead. One of the other benefits of oracle cards is their ability to set the stage in a reading, something I will talk about in the "Oracular Storytelling" section of this chapter (page 57).

Tarot cards are my true love when it comes to divination tools! Loaded with symbolism and numerological value, tarot cards are the most advanced of all the cards, offering the reader a deep view of the unknown. Traditionally tarot cards have seventy-eight cards: fifty-six Minor Arcana cards and twenty-two Major Arcana cards, although some modern decks have additional cards added by the artist. The

54 ✦ Psychic Storytelling

Minor Arcana is like a deck of playing cards, with one additional card per suit: the Page. The suits of the Minor Arcana have similar meaning to that of playing cards, with slightly different names: Pentacles replace Diamonds, Wands replace Clubs, Cups replace Hearts, and Swords replace Spades. The twenty-two cards of the Major Arcana stand alone, with each of the cards having a unique meaning.

Tarot cards can be intimidating, but in truth they are the best storytellers of all the cards, and taking the time to learn their secrets will allow the reader to gain far more information. The Rider-Waite deck is the most well-known tarot deck, with its symbolism being repeated by many other artists; this is primarily because the deck was created by two members of the Hermetic Order of the Golden Dawn, and the cards reflect a deep mysticism. If you are new to working with the tarot, I highly recommend working with a deck based on the Rider-Waite Tarot!

Once you know what kind of deck you want, then it comes down to the artwork! As psychic development and magical studies have become more and more popular, so has the call for divination cards of all kinds, making it easy to find a deck or two that appeals to our personal aesthetic and spiritual needs. If you're like most readers, you will find yourself with a collection of cards before you are done!

BLESSING AND PROGRAMMING CARDS

Years ago, I took part in a sacred gifting ceremony in which we were asked to give away something sacred to us—meaning it had to hurt a little bit to do so. Each of us spoke in turn about our gift, and when all had told their tale we took turns choosing the gift we felt most drawn to. I chose to give away a deck of my cards that I had been working with for many years, their wax long worn away by repetitive usage. Months after the ceremony, the person who received my cards shared that they found the re-gifted deck the easiest they had ever worked with. I believe this to be due to the programming of the cards that came from the thousands of times they have been used in divination.

One of the ways of understanding this programming is to see it as a form of psychic residue left behind by the user, something that psychics who utilize psychometry read.

Psychometry

A form of extrasensory perception in which the psychic gleans knowledge of the object through physical contact.

Understanding that items, particularly those utilized for sacred and psychic work, retain memory of their purpose, we can see how important care of the item is. Cards used for divination are such an item, regardless of whether they are cheap playing cards from the drugstore or gilded tarot cards from an exclusive metaphysical store. Once we know their purpose, we need to treat them as the sacred tool they are. This begins with blessing and programming!

◇◇◇◇◇◇◇◇◇◇◇◇

TECHNIQUE
CARD BLESSING AND PROGRAMMING

This is a simple blessing you can do with any new deck, as well as old decks you have had for years. Adding intention to our developing relationship with our cards helps us to acknowledge them as magical tools. Recognizing that they build memory and understanding of purpose over time, making using them easier and easier as we go along, we begin to believe more strongly in our ability to receive accurate information from them. Like all magical ceremonies, choosing the right timing for your blessing will enhance your work. I recommend working with the full moon for this. Please note that this is a suggested blessing, and you are free to change it any way you feel fit.

56 + Psychic Storytelling

—————————————— **You Will Need** ——————————————

Your cards, a working altar, incense or herbs for cleansing (sage, cedar, mugwort, palo santo), a candle, your Book of Shadows, and a scarf or piece of fabric long enough to wrap the cards in.

1. Begin by sitting in front of your altar with your cards. Take time to call on your spiritual allies (ancestors, guides, and deities) asking them to support you in your work. Light your incense or herbs and move the smoke over your cards thoroughly, imagining that you are removing any heavy, unwanted energy from your cards.

2. Closing your eyes and opening yourself to the moment, utilizing one of the light trance–inducing techniques if you need to, speak from your heart, asking your deities and spirits to bless your cards, clearly stating your intent for their use: "These cards are meant to be my sacred tool in divination, helping me to connect more deeply with my intuition."

3. Wrap your cards in the scarf or piece of fabric and place them in the windowsill for three days of the full moon. (Full moon energy is potent three days before and three days after the full moon.)

4. When you have completed your ceremony, thank your spiritual allies and write down your experience in your Book of Shadows.

When you take the cards from the window in three days, unwrap them carefully, focusing again on your intention for them to be a powerful tool in divination. When continuing your care of your cards consider wrapping them in the scarf at the end of every use and unwrapping them with intention at the beginning of every reading. Over time this little ritual will add to the potency of your tool!

◇◇◇◇◇◇◇◇◇◇◇◇

TECHNIQUE

STORING YOUR CARDS AND MAKING A SIGIL

There are many ways to store your cards, including the box they came in. Whichever method you choose for storage, the importance again lies in intent. I have many decks and keep them stored together in an ornate glass bowl on the table in my office. I store them this way as I often change what deck I am using depending on what type of reading I am doing and who I am doing it for. Although my cards are left open and exposed, they are being stored sacredly, as my whole office is like a temple, and I have placed them there with purpose.

Another simple bit of magic we can use when programming our cards, and ourselves, is to write our intention on a small piece of paper and place it on our deck during storage. If you want to go deeper with this, you can create a magical sigil to represent your intention.

Magical sigils are a simple a form of magical alchemy, changing our intentions from everyday words into a symbol or sign.

1. Start by writing all your intentions on a piece of paper, using one word to describe each intention.
2. Break down the words into one letter each.
3. Take each of the final letters and combine them into a symbol; the design made by the final letters is completely up to you!
4. Finally, draw your newly created symbol on a separate piece of paper and store it with your cards. Make a point of looking at the sigil every time you take your deck out for a reading.

ORACULAR STORYTELLING

Divination is a form of psychic storytelling, in which the teller receives prompts from the universe; clues, like breadcrumbs, appear on the path leading the reader to the answers they seek. Oracular tools like playing cards, oracle decks, and tarot provide us with the characters and situations, their image portrayed on the cards triggering memories in our mind that help us understand the unfolding story. *If you are new to cartomancy, it is helpful to get as much symbolism as you can! In my experience it is easier for most people to see the story when using oracle*

58 ✦ Psychic Storytelling

cards and tarot, as playing cards usually only have elaborate imagery on the Court cards.

In my professional practice I work primarily with tarot and oracle cards, incorporating both in my readings. Having many decks, I choose which cards I work with at the beginning of each session. If you have more than one deck, I recommend beginning your readings by first determining which deck best suits the questions being asked. Choosing which deck to use helps us determine the environment in which our reading will be set, and the type of players involved in the story. Structured decks with plain, easy images are often easier to interpret and are useful for all readings but are particularly beneficial for readings based on everyday life and practical matters. Stylized images with lots of mystical symbolism are often best suited to readings that have to do with spiritual matters and personal growth. Once we have chosen a deck or decks to work with it is helpful to take a few moments to connect with it, shuffling and asking a few simple questions as we center ourselves and tune in to the cards. If you are like me and prefer to work with both oracle cards and tarot, make sure you handle both decks before starting your reading, knowing that each plays an intricate part in your divination.

Handling our cards is a great way to become acquainted with their symbolism, and I recommend doing so often! When learning, make a point of playing with your cards when you're sitting on the couch half-watching television. Ask random questions, knowing that each time we flip a card and sit with it we are developing our relationship with the cards, making it easier for us to fully understand their symbolism.

Setting the Stage

Oracle cards are perfect for creating ambiance; like the broad stroke of a paint brush, they lay down color and feeling, stirring the imagination and intuition. Imagination is an important part of intuition as it allows the mind to open, making way for the impossible to happen—like perceiving the unknown! Choosing the right oracle deck for the divination

Telling the Story ✦ 59

is important, as it lays down the understructure of the reading, just as stagecraft lays the foundation of a play. *If you have only one oracle deck, then that is the right one!*

The Players

Most readings have characters or players within their story—people who are contributing either beneficially or not in the querent's tale.

Court cards (King, Queen, Knight, Page) and some Major Arcana cards are more likely to represent people in a reading than the numbered cards of the Minor Arcana. When they show up in readings they are often speaking of particular people or organizations; however, this is not an absolute—so, as always, trust your intuition! Court cards often come with physical descriptors listed in the meaning of the card for this reason. Make sure to check out "The Court Cards" chapter later in the book (starting on page 250). But remember that while the descriptors can be helpful, they are not absolute! I recommend reading the physical descriptions for each but advise readers to trust their own intuitive input foremost, and rely more on the images, thoughts, and knowing that come into our mind when looking at the card.

<><><><><><><><>

TECHNIQUE

MEETING THE COURT

I love exploring things with my intuition before looking at the meanings someone else gives to things, interpreting my own symbolism before looking at the definitions given by others. I invite you to sit with the Court before looking at their definitions in the back of the book, or in the little booklet that comes with most card decks. If you are familiar with tarot, you will no doubt already understand each card's meaning. This exercise will likely give you new insight.

I recommend creating sacred space and setting up an altar if you are

60 ✦ Psychic Storytelling

doing this for yourself, particularly if you are new to divination and psychic development. Try it again when you're sitting wasting time.

──────────────── **You Will Need** ────────────────

The Court cards of a tarot deck or playing cards, your Book of Shadows, a pen, a candle, and incense.

1. Take a moment to create sacred space; setting up an altar if you wish, light your candle and incense and welcome in your spiritual allies (ancestors, guides, and deities).
2. Take deep even breaths, taking a moment to quiet your mind and slip into a light trance state. (Try the rocking technique on page 28.)
3. Begin by placing all the Pages in front of you. If you are working with playing cards, skip to step 4. Notice the similarities in the cards, and then the differences; note the colors used for each card, and the items they carry.
4. Picking up each of the Pages, one at a time, feel into their energy, imagining what kind of person they would be. First study the card with your eyes open, then close your eyes and see what images and thoughts come into your mind. You may find that they remind you of someone you know already, and with that imagery you can imagine further what their occupation or hobbies may be.
5. Take time to write your intuitive thoughts about each Page in your Book of Shadows, including similarities and differences they have.
6. Repeat the process with the Knights, first looking at them as a group, noting similarities and differences, then as individuals. First studying them with your eyes open, then closing your eyes and allowing your intuition to inform you. Make note of your findings in your Book of Shadows before moving on.
7. Now for the Queens, following the same procedure as used for the Pages and Knights. Make sure to record your thoughts.
8. And finally, the Kings! Following the same instructions used by the rest of the court.

In divination, like most things, skill requires practice. Repeat this exercise with each of your decks, as the artist's depiction of cards greatly plays into how our intuition responds. I recommend doing the same exercise with the Major Arcana cards that are people oriented, like the Fool, the Magician, the High Priestess, Hierophant, Emperor, and Empress.

Once you have a feel for the personalities of the Court cards and the players of the Major Arcana, find the card that you feel best represents you, noting that this may vary from deck to deck. Once you have identified yourself, identify the cards that best represent the players in your own life story.

Situations and Circumstances

Now that we have set the stage and are familiar with our possible players, it is time to explore the situations and circumstances of the reading. This is where the rest of the cards come in! Using the remainder of the deck—the Court cards set aside—begin to explore them one by one. Again, it helps if you do so from a light trance state, but sitting on your couch casually shuffling through them is good enough here. The key is to revisit them often, noting the similarities in cards of the same suit, and similar numbers; both of these topics are covered thoroughly later in the book (see "The Suits—The Minor Arcana," page 242, and "Numerology in the Tarot," page 272).

Take your time, handling each card individually. Sit with it for a while, allowing the card to tell you it's story. Don't worry about whether your meaning will match one given in a book; simply let yourself drift into the story being told by the images on the card. Make sure to write your thoughts in your Book of Shadows as recording our progress is key to developing skill!

THE WEB OF FATE

When it comes to divination and looking into the unseen realms of future scrying and possibilities, I love the image of the web! Throughout time, fate has been seen as a woven thing, with tales

62 ✦ Psychic Storytelling

told throughout mythological history of Wyrd Sisters who spin, cut, and weave the future of existence. They know through their craft that changing direction from one's set course often requires following threads back into the past so we may better understand how to navigate the future.

In our modern world the image of the web is ever-present in our information-hungry minds, as we all utilize the internet: the world-wide web! The image created for us imprints our mind with crossed lines connecting the globe in a technological grid or "web." Without understanding how it works we all, nonetheless, use it in our daily lives, with people surfing the web for an average of just under seven hours per day, according to most polls. Now imagine connecting to the Web of Fate for seven hours a day . . .

Our ability to divine is not limited to the time we spend in front of our cards, nor is the information we are gathering always meant for immediate understanding. Our minds are picking up clues throughout the day, as our subconscious mind is drawn toward noticing things it will need to know later. These clues can happen anywhere: in the grocery store line or driving to work.

One such experience that stands out in my memory happened years ago, when I was still having psychic home parties, traveling to people's homes to do readings.

> On my way to the party, I noticed a used car lot on the side of the road, one I had seen thousands of times before. I recognized that I was really noticing it, and how that meant I would need the information for something. That night, as I was finishing up one of the readings, I asked the querent if they had any questions, and they replied, "Yes, I need a good cheap used car, do you know where I should look?" I laughed and said, "Yes, I do. I picked up this information for you on my way to work!"

Like a police detective's map, with red string connecting clues in weblike fashion, our mind is often putting pieces of the puzzle together. Divination, such as cartomancy, helps us to organize the pieces, fleshing out the details of their connection, allowing the developed psychic mind to navigate the web of wyrd with agility, noting what intersection in the web we can change course on, and which turns are unavoidable.

Wyrd

Connected to Fate.

The Web of Fate is a mental construct, an image the Seer can place in their mind, allowing them to see multiple possibilities—and the likelihood of each—in a readable format. When utilizing the image of a web, it is helpful to first focus our mind on seeing the path the querent is most likely to take. When doing a reading this is the story we begin with, sharing the most likely outcome. As the story evolves through the cards there will inevitably come times when the path followed leads to hardship, and we seek a different route to change our path. Here we again focus our mind on the web, this time looking for alternative routes.

For me these alternative routes show up in my mind's eye like points of light, or water droplets glistening on a spider's web. I see look for these intersections, directing my mind to them as I draw cards for clarity.

When seeking clarity in reading don't be afraid to draw more cards, as each card is a player in the story unfolding. *If we are new to our journey with cartomancy, we may find we need to draw extra cards often.* This is a great way of getting more details, so go for it!

◇◇◇◇◇◇◇◇◇◇◇◇

TECHNIQUE
VISUALIZING THE WEB

While intuition is a much-needed ability in divination, a lot can be credited to the power of the analytical brain and its orderly desire to connect the dots. Much of what we receive during card reading depends on our ability

64 ✦ Psychic Storytelling

to create a map, with pathways of possibility. The web is a great example of such an image!

I recommend trying this technique regardless of whether you have experience with cartomancy or divination of any kind, as it is helpful to see what comes to us intuitively, before training.

You Will Need

A deck of cards, your Book of Shadows, a candle, incense, and a working altar if you choose.

1. Create sacred space, setting up a working altar, lighting a candle, incense, and calling in your spiritual allies (ancestors, guides, and deities).
2. Use a spread of your choice, laying the cards out in front of you. I recommend using the traditional Celtic Cross spread that comes with most tarot decks.
3. Soften your gaze, and begin to take deep, even breaths in through your nose and out through your nose. Do this for a few breaths, slowing your heart rate and racing mind, and allowing yourself to slip into a light trance state.
4. Now close your eyes and imagine you can see a web in your mind, with an illuminated pathway representing the path the querent is most likely to take. Hold onto this image for a few moments, then open your eyes.
5. Begin your reading knowing you have actively instructed your mind to find the path most likely to be taken.
6. If you see an obstacle in the pathway of the querent, or that their road leads to an outcome they would rather avoid, close your eyes again and go back to the image of the web. Remember not everyone will visually see, and that the word *see* in this instance means "sense." Now redirect your mind, enhancing the web in your mind to now show you the pathway around the obstacle. Note that this will most likely be difficult and could involve backtracking. Just as taking a wrong turn on the road can cause us many hours to get on the right route.
7. Share your thoughts with the querent.

When the querent in the reading is yourself, make sure to write down your findings and experiences in your Book of Shadows, noting that recording and reviewing our readings helps to develop skill.

KARMA IN THE CARDS

When giving readings it's important to remember that not everything is set in stone. Instead, a reading shows what is most likely to happen if the querent stays on their current path. In many ways reading helps us to navigate the future, showing us pitfalls and ways in which we can avoid unpleasant outcomes. We learned through focusing on the image of a web we could not only see what was likely, but also ways around and through difficulty.

While much of the future has multiple pathways, there are unavoidable aspects as well. Regardless of what route we take we will face these things, as they are part of the agenda we created before birth, representing our karma.

Karma

Cause and effect created by a person's mental and physical actions, created in this life or previous (parallel) lifetimes.

I describe karma, as seen in readings, as the lessons we have chosen to learn. While most things are mutable, allowing us to make changes along our path, karma represents the things that are inevitable. While these things can sometimes be postponed, they will keep showing up repeatedly until we deal with them, often becoming more persistent the longer they are ignored. In truth, I advise my clients to lean into the karmic lessons, knowing that we are the ones who placed such things on our agenda, and that resisting the lessons generally makes them harder.

Finding a way of recognizing these lessons in our readings helps us better navigate life's path, as well as giving better guidance when reading for others. I recommend designating a card or series of cards that

66 ✦ Psychic Storytelling

point to the inevitable. I personally use Aces, found both in playing cards and tarot cards, for this purpose, something I talk about in detail later in the book under "Numerology and the Tarot."

Having cards designated to determine the hand of fate that can't be avoided brings a new level of understanding to readings, as we are able to see what is inescapable. When karmic cards show up, we can expect the situation associated with them to be a major part of the reading, as the future wraps itself around the lessons that need to be learned. It is sometimes helpful to draw a few extra cards—looking at what obstacles hinder the path, and what tools aid it—when such cards are present.

When karma is present in a reading it's important to remember that karmic lessons are those that were chosen by the querent before incarnating, which means the things coming are planned experiences, showing up at programmed times. Working with these lessons often leads to soul-level growth and avoiding them is generally pointless as they will follow us around until we tend them. I advise my clients to lean into the change that such lessons usher in, knowing that they are part of life's plan!

ASKING THE RIGHT QUESTIONS

In my opinion, the magic combination for a psychic seer is someone who has a deep intuition, a clever, analytical mind, a nosy disposition, and a strong moral compass—particularly when it comes to keeping other people's secrets. Many people are surprised by the analytical bit, believing such thinking to be restrictive to our intuition. While it is true that overthinking can create initial obstacles in development, an inquisitive mind benefits the intuition, allowing it to explore side paths where further information can be found.

Difficult situations often require more cards. Sometimes this is because the card we are looking at doesn't fully provide us with a clear answer, and sometimes because the answers provided lead us to questions outside those provided by the spread. Do not be afraid to keep asking questions and drawing cards until you feel satisfied! Over time you will become comfortable with the idea that the card spread is simply an outline, and that there are times when these assigned questions do not provide us with the answers we seek.

Two of the most important questions to incorporate into a reading are "Is there another path that can be taken?" and "How can the querent move through the situation with the least difficulty?" as people often come to psychics when they are in dire straits, feeling as if they have exhausted all avenues they can see. In which case, providing hope and direction is often the most important thing we can offer! Here it is important to remember that the first thing we see is the path the querent is most likely to take; in cases where this path leads to unnecessary hardship, we can look for alternatives and suggest ways in which they can alter their path. This, after all, is the true reason people seek out the advice of psychics: they want to know what they can change and what is inevitable!

There will be times when the path in front of the querent is so challenging that we cannot get a clear read—including heavy emotions, and factors outside the querent's control. In such moments it is helpful to inquire about things that could be residually affected by the situation, such as asking how the querent's partner will handle the situation instead, recognizing that if it was really bad it would affect them as well, and questions about duration to see how long the challenging situation will persist. This kind of side investigation helps relieve the pressure created by hopes and fears, allowing for the querent and reader to relax enough that they may eventually be able to look at how it affects them personally.

As psychic storytellers we must lean into our readings, like a detective on a case, questioning the situation from all angles. When something stumps us, we must turn it upside down and sideways until its secrets are revealed. Seeing each reading like a mystery waiting to be revealed, letting our curiosity explore possibilities, we must ask questions, and pull cards until we are satisfied with the knowledge presented.

68 + Psychic Storytelling

This questioning becomes natural over time, flowing in and out of our structured card spreads with ease, until we may find we step away from structured readings completely. Experienced Seers often create a selection of personal questions that they rely on far more than a spread provided in this book or others. With that in mind do not be afraid to create your own spreads, or to use none and just let the cards lead you to the next inquiry!

THE PEOPLE IN THE NEIGHBORHOOD

We all need help from time to time, and identifying helpers in a reading is one of the best things we can do to support our clients! All too often it is who we know that makes a change in our lives, as we humans are communal creatures; we rely on our connections to others not only to help hold us upright when things are challenging, but also to help us find opportunities and connections that make life more rewarding. While education and experience play a big role in our accomplishments, most of us would not have had the chance to try without someone else opening the door for us. A good psychic reading will shine light on these connections, showing the querent not only what path to take, but who the support players and quest givers are.

Many card spreads will allocate a space for outside influence, showing those that help and hinder the path of the querent, but this often comes through as a vague emotional influence, when in truth what the client could use is a more direct "talk to this person" approach. I like to make space for such things in my reading, looking for helpers that make the path easier. This is important whether they are looking for a new job, new relationships, or direction on their spiritual path.

One of the most common places of inquiry in which helpers are important is in employment. When clients are looking to change their occupation or simply find a job, pointing them in the right direction helps streamline the search and often gives them a contact of entry. In most cases we are not going to get a photo of the person, name tag included, in our mind; instead, we should focus on things like how the querent knows them, what they look like, what position do they hold, and the best way to contact them. This latter is important to remember in all readings, as we often do not know the people we are reading for, let alone who they know.

For those that experience clairvoyance, the images seen are often created through images we already hold in our mind. Much in the way that AI creates images, our psychic mind moves through our memories and creates an image or images that show us the person or thing we are searching for, giving us a visual image that we can describe in a way that the recipient of the information will know whom or what we speak of. However, if we were to be shown a photograph of that which we imagined in our mind, it would be slightly different. The more we know about a subject the clearer the images are going to be.

Psychics often work as a form of counselor, giving advice to their clients on how to best interact with situations and people in their lives. This means that people often come up with interpersonal problems involving their relational interactions. While we must remember that it is illegal for us to diagnose someone's mental health, in most places it is legal to give relationship advice. The truth is many people have never been taught communication skills, and emotional intelligence is like all forms of intelligence—in that some of us have more of it than others. While we are not required to get a degree, it really does help to educate ourselves about communication. I highly recommend *Nonviolent Communication* by Marshall B. Rosenberg, as it teaches the basics on how to communicate without triggering the other person's defense, and how to identify our needs as opposed to our wants.

While I like to focus on the helpers, we can use the same techniques when looking for adversaries, remembering that once they have been identified, the key is to ask additional questions regarding how to best interact with these individuals.

70 ✦ Psychic Storytelling

In relationship readings, which are one of the major reasons people come to a psychic, people are often looking for love . . . or trying to figure out why the relationship they are currently in is not working. In the latter looking for helpers can point us in the direction of who may help us get greater understanding. This may show up in the form of a counselor, a friend, or family member who can intervene or help us see the situation more clearly. In the case of looking for love, helpers are crucial, as modern dating through apps is failing—often leaving people feeling lonely, lost, and unsafe in the dating world. In the case of adversaries, we may be looking for who is getting in the way of the querent having a healthy relationship. Is there someone they are holding onto, is there someone in their life giving them bad advice or leading them in the wrong direction?

> When doing love readings for those looking for love, I advise my clients to ask five friends, who are not friends with each other, to invite them and a single friend of theirs over for dinner. This is not a set-up, simply friends having dinner, with the understanding that two of the folks are single and interested in a relationship. If it goes well, contact info can be exchanged at the end of the date. Unlike a blind date, the worst that can happen is dinner with friends. In such cases, I will often investigate the cards for the helpers I think will be the most helpful in this connection. Sometimes the "person" who is the helper is a thing, such as seeing that the client would benefit from joining a particular club or organization.

The other most common relationship factor discussed is that of the family dynamic. When dealing with such issues the reader should look at all the key players: the parents, siblings, cousins, and so on that are part of the situation. Knowing how each player affects things makes it easier to create a harmonious situation, which may mean cutting some folks out of their life and/or creating stronger bonds with a family member.

Humans are emotional beings; we communicate not only with our words and body language, but through the energetic field (biofield/aura) that surrounds us. Understanding the emotional nature of the people we interact with is crucial to healthy relationships, as expecting everyone to act and feel the way we do is a surefire way to create bad relations!

When I meet new people whom I feel a connection with, I do the three-card spread below.

HOW ARE WE CONNECTED

For this reading you can use any form of cards you feel drawn to; as a rule, I use tarot, often the deck I keep in my kitchen for long readings, allowing me to focus on the information over a period of days. When you are ready, shuffle your cards and draw three, one for each of the following questions. We can repeat the exercise asking the same questions as ourselves, inquiring about how we perceive and feel about them.

1. **"How do they see me?"** This question is focused on what they perceive of us based on first impressions.
2. **"How do they feel about me?"** This gives you an understanding of how they responded to us emotionally upon meeting. Recognize that this is highly important, as we know that intuition is most accurate as a first response.
3. **"How are we connected?"** This gives us insight into potential past-life connections, as well as foresight into how we are meant to be connected in the future.

I wanted to take a moment here to remind folks of the importance of trusting our first instincts. Many of us have had reminders of this in our everyday lives: times in which we felt immediately off about someone, but saw that others seemed to think they were OK, letting our guard down, and learning the hard way that we should have trusted our first impression. Using cards for this purpose adds a layer of confirmation to the feeling, and often directs us to the areas we need to be careful about.

TELLING TIME

One of the most difficult things to develop in divination, in my opinion, is accurate timing. In fact, many of the big things I foresaw in my own life didn't work out the first time I tried them, as I was ahead of my own timeline. Which brings me to the second piece about telling time: people are constantly changing their timeline! Let's talk about predicting a timeline first, then we will move on to changing it.

Like most things in divination, personal symbolism and intuitive "gut" feelings are paramount to our understanding of timing in a reading. As we approach cartomancy and the tarot as a storyteller, we want to remember that we are tapping into a story that is already created on some level. That we are simply reading the tale of the path the querent is most likely to take, and that being already in existence (according to quantum science) the information is already there for us to glean.

I often use calendars and clocks when telling time; these simple analogies that are already connected to chronological time work well. I also use the images of slide rules and abacuses. These are not images that are on often seen on cards, so I look for these images in my mind, as I gaze at the card in question.

When doing this I simply ask when the event will take place, starting with the number of years and working backward. I usually get the response to this question in the form of a slide rule pushed to the number. Calendars show me seasons, months, and days. Clocks can show me hours, or months.

Another way of getting an idea of timing is to look at the featured seasons on the cards—if there is a majority of one season it is likely telling you something. You can also draw a card while asking about timing and look at the weather featured on the card, as well as its numerological value.

The Wheel of the Year on page 79 is a card spread designed to look specifically at the timeline, breaking down the year into eight points, allowing the querent to see what to expect at different points on their timeline. The same kind of spread can be used to look at five-year and ten-year plans, checking in on them quarterly or annually, something that is good to do when looking at business or investment plans.

My ability to read time accurately developed through practice. The more often you ask yourself "When?" the better you will be at answering. Look for clues in the card, remembering you are telling a story. Trust your gut instinct and the images that come into your mind. Don't be afraid to be wrong, and recognize that timelines can change.

Timelines generally change due to the people associated with them, but sometimes it is due to unforeseen forces. Timelines associated with the military, for instance, are highly flexible as there a lot of players on the field, and they are purposely trying to keep their actions hidden. This makes getting a spot-on date for deployment challenging.

People often change their own timing by rushing ahead or putting the brakes on after a reading. While most people can let things play out, there are those that can't wait—like myself, jumping in before the world is ready for them—and others who get nervous about the change predicted and start pumping their brakes. That is why it is important when doing a reading to let your clients know that timeline is flexible. It is possible to shift timelines, but it is often like bushwhacking through the woods beside the trail. Sometimes that's worth doing, but most of the time it makes for a harder road.

SPREADS AND LAYOUTS

76 ✦ Spreads and Layouts

When developing our ability as a psychic storyteller, it is helpful to have a variety of outlines for doing so. Card spreads or layouts provide the framework for the reading, telling us what questions to ask with each card we lay down. While it is perfectly OK to work without a spread, asking whatever questions pop into our mind, many people find it helpful to have a foundation for their questions.

The most popular spread is the Celtic Cross, which is featured in the booklets that come with most tarot decks. This is a great spread, as it provides a strong storyline, allowing the reader to explore the past, present, and future, as well as how outside people and our emotions influence the situation. In truth, this is the reading most people are looking for when they go to a psychic fair or make an appointment for a private reading. They want to know what is currently happening in their lives, how their past influenced the situation, and what is likely to transpire if they keep following the path they are on.

However, living in a time of psychic evolution many people are seeking a deeper understanding of themselves on a soul level, wanting to know about more than just their current life circumstances and what the immediate future holds. They are looking to explore their expanding consciousness, which makes it worthwhile as a reader to offer a variety of readings geared at helping them do so, and the easiest way to do that is through changing the layout of the reading.

One of the things I love most about working with a variety of spreads is how each layout pushes my psychic mind to look deeper, ask more questions, and look at situations from the view of multiple possibilities. Through spreads we can explore our soul's purpose, the path of this life, and how past/parallel lives are affecting current situations. Spreads can give us an outline of our year, and show us where our gifts are, so that we can nurture them properly. We can look at our career path, and search for the best way to balance our energy in trying times. As a psychic storyteller these questions presented in an orderly fashion are powerful tools that make up the backdrop of the story, much as props support the story being told by players on a stage.

As you explore the spreads featured in this book, I invite you to add and subtract questions to them, reshaping them to be your own. This is something I did early on in my career, by adding additional cards to the traditional Celtic Cross: I used two cards in each position, seeing the additional cards as support players in the story, adding depth to the reading, as I have always wanted more information. I also encourage you to create your own spreads geared toward the questions you want to have answered. You are the storyteller, make the story your own!

Seasonal Card Spreads

WINTER SOLSTICE: THE WHEEL OF THE YEAR

The Wheel of the Year is a modern pagan calendar based on seasonal festivals celebrating the turning of the sun, marking solstices and equinoxes and the cross-quarter points between each. Understanding the collective energy at each point helps us gain a deeper understanding of the psychic story we are reading—as we are Earthlings, and, being such, we ebb and flow like all of the other creatures on the planet!

The Wheel of the Year spread is a psychic map of the year, tuning in at each of these points, designed to give an overview of the querent's year to come, focusing on the most notable situations happening at each of the points. Ideally, I like to begin at the winter solstice, but this spread can be done at any time of the year, starting at the closest holiday. Each point on the map represents a period of forty days, with twenty days on either side of the holiday.

It is important to remember that people change their timelines, with some people speeding it up and others slowing it down, after becoming aware that it exists!

Seasonal Card Spreads ✦ 79

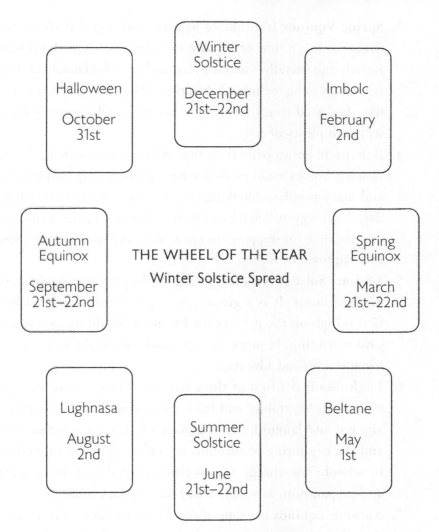

1. **Winter Solstice** is the longest night of the year. For most this is a time of deep introspection, family, and celebration of the returning light.
2. **Imbolc** is celebrated as the first signs of spring, when light is noticeably returning. It is a time of honoring the home and hearth. The energy of the season is one of preparing for the upcoming year and planning how we want to utilize our personal energy.

3. **Spring Equinox** is a time of balance, with equal daylight and darkness. It is a time of fertility and planting seeds—both figuratively and literally—making it a good time for launching projects and placing intentions. As a time of balance people may feel like they need to get a move on, but they will also most likely still need plenty of rest.

4. **Beltane** is quintessential spring! It is a time when juices are flowing, bodies are in motion, trees are blossoming, and animals and many people are looking for love! As a major fertility holiday, the energy at Beltane can manifest in many ways, making it a prime time for stepping into new situations, particularly those that require creative force.

5. **Summer Solstice** is the longest day of the year, hosting the most daylight hours. It is a green, growing time, in which celebration is high on the priority list for many. Weddings, vacations, garden-tending, farmer's markets, and such make it a time of reconnection and adventure.

6. **Lughnasa** is the first of three harvest holidays. It is the time when early vegetables and fruit are in abundance. It is generally hot and languid, holding both a feeling of summer's end and the beginning of autumn, as children prepare to go back to school. The energy at this time is filled with list-making and preparation, as we get ready for the dark months.

7. **Autumn Equinox** is a time of equal light and dark, which holds the energy of going into the darkness. It is the second harvest holiday of the year, carrying a feeling of abundance not only in what is harvested, but also in what needs to be done!

8. **Halloween** is a powerful time of spirit, marking the third and final harvest of the year. It is time of deep thoughts, psychic experiences, and connection to the spirit world. Here people are thinking deep thoughts, contemplating soul-level thoughts, and remembering. It is also a time in which those who are unprepared for winter can feel rushed.

IMBOLC: HEARTH AND HOME

When developing our ability as a psychic storyteller and cartomancer practice is key! Doing seasonal spreads for ourselves and others is a good way of stretching our intuitive mind, and a great way to connect into the energy of the season.

The Hearth and Home spread is designed to take a good look at the querent's home life, including interpersonal relationships, finances, and

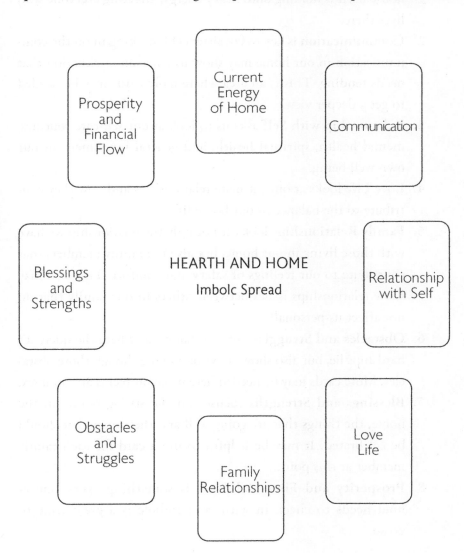

82 ✦ Spreads and Layouts

the general energy of the home, allowing us to look at our obstacles and blessings in a different light. This spread is ideally designed for Imbolc but can be used whenever you like.

1. **Current Energy of the Home** gives us an overview of how the home may feel to any empath entering the space. Checking in with our home vibration is helpful, as we may find that the house itself is holding onto heavy energy, affecting everyone who lives there.

2. **Communication** is key to coexistence! Checking in on the communication in our home may show us a person or situation that needs tending. This is an area where more cards may be needed to get a deeper view.

3. **Relationship with Self** asks us to look at our self-care routines, mental health, spiritual health, and general investment in our own well-being.

4. **Love Life** looks at our intimate relationships and how they contribute to the balance of our home life.

5. **Family Relationships** looks at not only the relationship we have with those living in our home, but also the family members that contribute to our feelings of safety and comfort. This also may show relationships issues between others in our family that do not affect us personally.

6. **Obstacles and Struggles** not only shows us where the querent's hardships lie, but also shows ways of moving though those obstacles. More cards may be needed here if the problems are complex.

7. **Blessings and Strengths** focuses on the strong points in the home, the things that are going well and the things that should be celebrated. It may be helpful to use a card for each family member at this point.

8. **Prosperity and Financial Flow** is something every household needs to check in with, and Imbolc is a great time to do so.

SPRING EQUINOX: BALANCING PERSONAL ENERGY

Balancing our personal energy is something all intuitives should do regularly, but sometimes we can't get a clear sense of how to do it. This is a simple three-card spread designed to give us perspective and direction. While this reading can be done anytime, it is particularly helpful at the equinoxes when our energy is focused on balance. I recommend repeating this spread at the autumn equinox as well. Make sure to record your readings so you can compare.

1. **Head** shows that checking in with our mind clues us in on how we are processing life. Are we overthinking, do we need rest, have we been struggling with focus, or are we running a hundred miles per hour? Sometimes just seeing that we are unbalanced in our thinking can help us redirect our thoughts. This position can also show us what our mind needs to fall into balance. If the first card you draw for this position shows you the state of your mind, you may want to draw a second card showing how you can bring your thinking into balance.

2. **Heart** can show us where our emotions are, or what we need to bring them into balance. We all know that our head and heart

BALANCING PERSONAL ENERGY

Spring Equinox Spread

| Head | Heart | Hand |

84 ✦ Spreads and Layouts

may experience things differently, so this position in the spread focuses on the heart. Again, if the first card you draw in this placement shows where the querent's emotions are, consider a second for balancing.

3. **Hand** shows us what we need to do to bring things into balance, the physical actions we need to take to bring balance into our lives. Sometimes, however, this position may show us what we are doing that is contributing to the imbalance.

BELTANE: RELATIONSHIP READINGS

While Beltane is a great time for relationship readings—as people are generally feeling a bit frisky this time of year—interpersonal relationships are something people seek guidance on all year long. I have included two separate spreads for this reading: one for those looking for love and another for those currently in a relationship.

RELATIONSHIP READING
Looking for Love
Beltane Spread

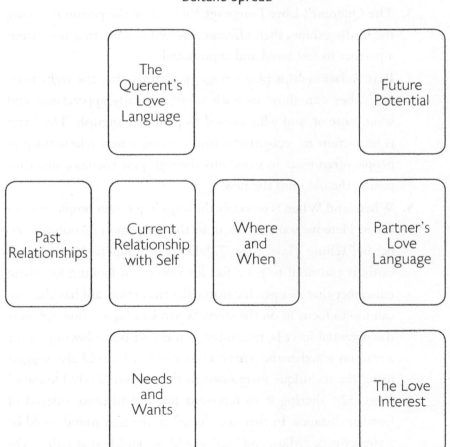

86 ✦ Spreads and Layouts

Looking for Love

1. **Current Relationship with Self** shows how the querent treats themselves, something that is very important before starting a new relationship, as how we treat ourselves affects how we allow ourselves to be treated. This also helps determine whether they are ready for a relationship or still have work to do before setting out in search of love.

2. **Needs and Wants** is the base of the reading, showing what the querent is searching for in a romantic partner. This is a place where a few extra cards may be helpful, particularly if the reading is for someone who has a lot of relationship trauma.

3. **The Querent's Love Language** shows how the person receiving the reading shows their affection, as well as what they need from a partner to feel loved and appreciated.

4. **Past Relationships** play a huge part in finding the right partner. They can show us both what we really appreciated and want more of, and what caused us pain and anguish. The latter is important to recognize before starting a new relationship as people often react to situations through past traumas, superimposing the old onto the new.

5. **Where and When** is probably the biggest question people want to know. Here we want to cue in to the techniques mentioned earlier in "Telling Time" (page 72). Don't be afraid to draw as many cards as you need to get a feel for timing. In looking for where remember that as a psychic storyteller the entire card has clues we can use to focus in on the story. When looking for how far away the potential lover is, remember to use your body dowsing to get a read on whether the person is near or far. I would also suggest using the technique mentioned in the section "Body Dowsing" (page 32), altering it to represent physical distance instead of familiar distance. In this case, "near" in the first round could be a twenty-mile radius, and "far" would be outside that radius. On

the second round, near could be within a hundred-mile radius, and far outside of that, expanding the distance every round until you land on a general distance. From there you can focus your mind on direction and draw a card to see where you are pulled.

6. **Love Interest** is where we focus in on the person the querent is seeking, looking into the story played out on the card for clues to who they are, what they look like, what their energy feels like, what they do for work, hobbies, and so on.

7. **Partner's Love Language** shows us how the potential partner shows love and what they need to feel loved.

8. **Future Potential** shows the direction the relationship is most likely to take. This gives the querent a heads-up on the nature of the relationship, how fast it will progress, and whether it has the potential to be long-lasting.

Current Relationship

1. **Current Relationship** shows the state of the relationship at the time of the reading. This is a helpful place to start because it gives the psychic storyteller an understanding of whether the story unfolding is centered on long-term focus of the relationship, or whether the relationship is struggling and the querent is looking for guidance on how to heal it or end it.

2. **The Querent's Love Language** shows how the person receiving the reading shows their affection, as well as what they need from a partner to feel loved and appreciated.

3. **The Partner's Love Language** shows us how their partner shows love and what they need to feel loved. (In polyamorous relationships use a card for each person.)

4. **Past Relationships** play a big role in our current relationships, both negatively and positively. Understanding these connections is paramount to a healthy love life. I advise drawing cards for all people involved in the relationship, as most people come with relationship baggage of some kind.

88 ✦ Spreads and Layouts

RELATIONSHIP READING

Current Relationship
Beltane Spread

Partner's Love Language		Future Potential

Past Relationships	Current Relationship	Family and Friends	Partner's Relationship Goals

The Querent's Love Language		The Querent's Relationship Goals

5. **Family and Friends** are influential in the longevity of relationships. This card is meant to give us a general feel of whether the relationship is supported or not.

6. **The Querent's Relationship Goals** shows what they are looking for in their heart and dreaming of in their mind both with their current partner and in general, whether they want to get married someday, have children, and so on.

Seasonal Card Spreads + 89

7. **The Partner's Relationship Goals** shows what their current partner is looking for in their heart and dreaming of in their mind both with their current partner and in general, whether they want to get married someday, have children, and so on.

8. **Future Potential** points out the path the relationship is most likely to take. If the outcome is not desired, the querent may ask questions here, inquiring as to whether they can change the trajectory. This is a good time to look for alternate routes, as mentioned in the section on the Web of Fate.

90 ✦ Spreads and Layouts

SUMMER SOLSTICE: BLESSINGS AND BOUNTY

There are times in life when people need to see the blessings life has provided them with, where that bounty comes from, and how to generate more sweetness in their life. This spread is intended to show the beauty that surrounds the querent.

1. **Blessings the Querent Will Receive** shows what goodness is coming into the querent's life, where it comes from, and how to be open to it.
2. **How the Querent Generates Bounty** points out the ways in which the querent can activate abundance in their life.
3. **Blessings the Querent Has to Share** highlights what the querent already possesses and how those gifts are meant to be shared with others, as the feelings of bounty are strongest when we share with others.

BLESSINGS AND BOUNTY

Summer Solstice Spread

| Blessings the Querent Will Receive | How the Querent Generates Bounty | Blessings the Querent Has to Share |

LUGHNASA: CAREER/LIFE PATH

Navigating the Wheel of the Year through cartomancy spreads helps us focus our minds on the things that we are most likely able to influence, recognizing the natural energetic flow of the planet. I encourage you to try these spreads with others, as it is likely to point out to you that others are also capable of making changes and shifting perspective if in alignment with the turning of the wheel.

CAREER/LIFE PATH READING
Lughnasa Spread

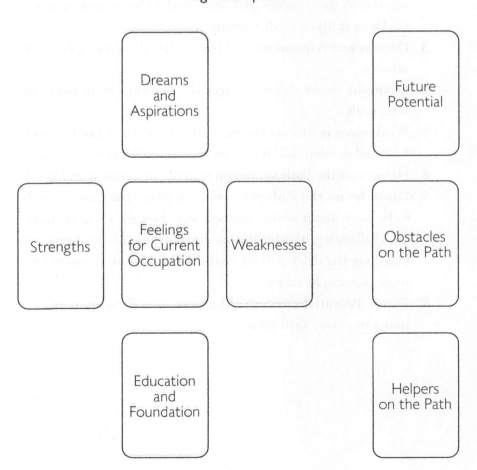

The Career/Life Path is a spread that is useful throughout the year but is particularly handy as summer comes to an end and we begin planning for the dark months of the year. I labeled this reading Career/Life Path as for many people they are separate things. It is helpful for the querent to concentrate on whether they want to look at their job or life path. In writing about this spread, I use the word *occupation* to refer to both career and life path.

1. **Feelings for Current Occupation** shows the querent's level of satisfaction in their job or career and whether they feel successful and appreciated.

2. **Education and Foundation** refers to the training needed to accomplish the querent's goal, and whether the querent currently has those skills or needs training.

3. **Dreams and Aspirations** highlights what the querent hopes to achieve.

4. **Strengths** shows the advantages the querent has in pursuing their goals.

5. **Weaknesses** points out the places the querent will need to work hard and develop skill if they are to accomplish their dreams.

6. **Helpers on the Path** focuses on who can be counted on for aid.

7. **Obstacles on the Path** points out the places the querent needs to be wary, and it advises the best way through. If the obstacles are challenging it is helpful to draw extra cards to determine how long the delay will be, and if there is another alternative route that can be taken.

8. **Future Potential** shows the likely outcome if the querent continues to pursue their path.

AUTUMN EQUINOX:
A YEAR IN REVIEW

The Year in Review is a reflective reading, helping the querent see how far they have come, and all that they have accomplished. All too often people are focused on what they need to do, constantly chasing the next thing on the list. This reading is designed to give recognition to hard work, and closure to difficult situations. This is a reading best done between the autumn equinox and winter solstice but can be useful whenever someone has completed a difficult journey in their life.

THE YEAR IN REVIEW

Autumn Equinox Spread

That
Which was
Overcome

• That
Which was
Celebrated

That
Which was
Learned

1. **That Which Was Overcome** looks at hardships faced by the querent, and the work they did to get there. I think this is important to look at, as often people remember the trauma of hardship but forget to give themselves credit for the hard work that they put into overcoming it.
2. **That Which Was Celebrated** highlights the joyous moments of the past year, the celebrations and accomplishments that make life sparkle.
3. **That Which Was Learned** reminds them of the big lesson the year provided them with.

94 ✦ Spreads and Layouts

HALLOWEEN:
LESSONS FROM GUIDES

While cartomancy is primarily used to tap into our higher consciousness, prophesizing unknown events, we can also use cards to connect with our guides. In this manner we are asking our spirit guides to share messages with us through the cards. It is helpful when doing a reading of this manner to make an extra effort in creating sacred space, treating the experience as if we have a special guest coming for a visit. While we can perform this or any of the spreads whenever we wish, this type of reading is often easier for those new to spirit contact if performed at Halloween, as the veil between the worlds of the living and the dead are thinnest at this time. I recommend performing this reading for yourself until you feel confident in it before doing so for others, as it is helpful to get a good feel for working with your own spirits before engaging with other people's guides.

LESSONS FROM GUIDES
Halloween Spread

What the Head Needs	What the Heart Needs	What the Hands Need

1. **What the Head Needs** asks our guides to show us what we should be focusing our minds on, what puzzles we need to solve, and what mindset we should be working with.
2. **What the Heart Needs** allows our guides to show us what we

need emotionally, where we should focus our personal healing, and how we can generate more love in our life.

3. **What the Hands Need** provides our guides with an opportunity to tell us what we should be doing, what actions we need to take, and how best to perform the task.

Rare Moon Spreads

BLUE MOON: SELF-VIEWING

A blue moon is the second full moon in a month. While it holds no astrological importance, it is notable in that it happens so rarely that we humans place value on it. Where value is placed there is purpose! Blue moons are a great time to do divination focused on our true selves and soul purpose.

BLUE MOON SPREAD
Self Viewing

This spread is designed to look at ourselves from multiple directions: who we are internally, externally, and the essence of our true self. *I prefer to use oracle cards or the Major Arcana from the tarot for this reading.*

1. **Outward Personality** shows us how we present to others. Understanding how others see us helps us communicate better and form better relationships.
2. **True Self** is who we are at our core, the part of us that is connected to our soul. Knowing who we are on a soul level helps us stay true to our life path.
3. **Inner Personality** shows our deep, personal self with all its nuances and sensitivities. Looking at our inner personality helps us prioritize our needs.

98 ✦ Spreads and Layouts

BLACK MOON:
SOUL HEALING

A black moon is the second new moon, or dark moon, of the month. Like a blue moon, there is no astrological importance to this occurrence, but the value placed upon it using our modern calendars makes it a good time for readings focused on the places our soul needs healing.

This spread is designed to help us look at the deep wounding we carry on a soul level, created by trauma from this life and past lives. *I prefer to use oracle cards or the Major Arcana from the tarot for this spread.* As this is a reading focused on healing, oracle cards focused on herbs, crystals, and deities would work well.

BLACK MOON SPREAD
Soul Healing

Healing for the Head	Healing for the Heart	Healing for the Hands

1. **Healing for the Head** shows what we need to heal on a mental level. As the mind is analytical, the card will likely focus on logistical or informational offerings.
2. **Healing for the Heart** shows what we need to heal emotionally; recognizing that we are living in a time of empathic opening, you may want to draw an extra card or two here.
3. **Healing for the Hands** shows what we need for physical healing, showing where our bodies our struggling and what we can do about it.

LUNAR ECLIPSE: HIDDEN POTENTIAL

Lunar eclipses are powerful times of shifting consciousness, in which we humans often find great expansion in our intuitive gifts. Utilize lunar eclipses as a way of exploring our ability to shapeshift. This is a good time for examining our hidden potential.

This spread focuses on our hidden potential, showing hindrances and advantages surrounding us. *I prefer to use oracle cards or the Major Arcana from the tarot for this spread.*

LUNAR ECLIPSE SPREAD
Hidden Potential

1. **Hindrances** shows the obstacles in our path that we must overcome to utilize our gifts to their full potential.
2. **Our Hidden Gifts** focuses on skills and abilities we possess that are unrecognized or underused. Taking them out of hiding we offer them a chance to grow!
3. **Advantages** shows what we have going in our favor: the opportunities, supportive people, and skills that make achieving our gift easier.

Soul-Level Card Spreads

While most people come to psychics looking for information about their near future, and how their past and current actions are affecting their life path, many come seeking knowledge of themselves on a soul level. Soul-level spreads focus on the higher self, exploring the querent's soul purpose, past-life/parallel-life lessons and connections, and what psychic gifts they have and how to develop them. I developed the soul-level spreads to assist people to look deeper into their soul, and I feature them as regular services to my clients. Soul-level readings often help people make sense of the wyrd things in their life, like phobias that have no apparent foundation, and feeling like we have known someone forever upon meeting them.

On the path to becoming a psychic storyteller soul-level readings are a bit more advanced, requiring us to have a strong trust in our skill as a reader, as the information we are looking at—dealing with past lives and the evolution of our soul—is harder to prove and easier to doubt!

As we experience psychic evolution as a species many people are breaking out of that limiting mindset, seeking to understand the nature of their soul, and what it means to be multiple; as they begin to remember versions of themselves from past/parallel lives. In my experience,

Soul-Level Card Spreads + 101

soul-level readings are often a spiritual experience for people, as exploring one's soul requires the querent release dogma that limits their being to one incarnation. It is helpful to see the work you are doing as sacred; create sacred space and hold yourself within the energy of the priest/priestess as oracle!

The soul-level spreads are designed to use both oracle and tarot cards. Each spread starts with one oracle card that represents the foundation of their soul's story. It is important to choose your decks intuitively. I have many decks and often change which ones I am using based on the person sitting in front of me. Remember, use what you have! If you do not have an oracle deck, use a tarot card in the foundational position.

SOUL PURPOSE

When doing this spread it is important to remember that soul purpose and career are not always the same thing! Some people may have careers that align with their soul's work, while others may be connected to developing empathy, or understanding what it means to be cared for (in the case of those who experience life with special needs that require them to rely on others).

1. **Nature of the Querent's Soul (Oracle Card)** creates the foundation of the reading; the card in this position shows core personality traits, as well as desires and skills the querent may have developed in previous incarnations. Example: The querent's soul nature may be that of a healer, in which case they likely work in medicine, social services, or education in this lifetime, and if they don't, they probably have every stray cat or couch-surfing friend crashing at their house.

2. **Querent's Natural Talents** shows the gifts and abilities that have been developed over previous lifetimes, such as being a natural artist, musician, or intuitive. You may feel a need to draw more than one card here.

3. **Psychic Scars and Weaknesses** examines the traumas carried over from previous incarnations. It is normal for a developed psychic to receive past-life information during this spread, in which case you may recognize where the trauma is coming from. Often people who have a soul-level purpose will move onto a past-life reading for more information.

4. **Best Self-Care** shows the best methods for querent to heal, decompress, and grow. We may want to reinforce this lesson throughout the reading, as looking at our soul-level lessons can be challenging.

5. **Lessons the Querent Came to Learn** is the heart of what the querent needs to know. It's important to note here that soul-level lessons are seldom painless.

SOUL PURPOSE
Tarot and Oracle

Querent's
Natural
Talents

Psychic
Scars and
Weaknesses

Best
Self-Care

Nature of
Querent's
Soul
(Oracle Card)

Lessons
the Querent
Came to Learn

Relationships
to Nurture

Best Way
to Connect
with Soul
Consciousness

6. **Relationships to Nurture** highlights the people in the querents life that are worth investing in. While this focuses on one relationship, the querent may have more than one relationship they want to examine here.

7. **Best Way to Connect with Soul Consciousness** shows the practices and techniques the querent should use to develop a deeper connection with their higher self.

WHITE RAVEN

This is one of my favorite spreads. I created it during the pandemic to highlight people's psychic gifts, after recognizing that people needed something good to focus on. While the nature of this reading is light and uplifting, the focus is deep and spiritual. This is a particularly good reading for anyone wanting to develop their psychic ability, as it highlights where their strongest abilities are and the methods for activating them. When doing this reading, I often choose tarot and oracle decks that feel enchanting. This spread is meant to create a sacred circle, as if casting a spell.

1. **Nature of the Querent's Magic (Oracle Card)** represents the querent and the form of magic that comes easiest to them, such as whether they connect with the source or divine through the role of priestess.
2. **Air, Gifts of Communication** begins to cast the circle by looking at the querent's psychic communication skills showing their strength in mediumship and channeling. While intended to look at spirit communication, the querent's magical communication skill may also show up as having a high charisma or being a great public speaker. You may want to draw two cards here, one for natural ability (what we are born with) and one for skill.
3. **How Best to Improve Communication** shows the best ways for the querent to improve their psychic communication skills.
4. **Fire, Gifts of Personal Power** shows the querent's energetic capacity, which includes their willpower, as well as their ability to harness energy through Reiki and other hands-on healing, awakened kundalini, and connection to elemental forces and deities.
5. **How Best to Increase Personal Power** shows the most beneficial practices and techniques the querent should use to improve their energetic capacity.
6. **Water, Gifts of Healing** shows the querent's natural ability and

106 ✦ Spreads and Layouts

trained skill in the healing arts. You may want to draw additional cards here to look at a variety of healing modalities, in which case you would draw one card for each modality you want to look at. This position may also show that the querent needs healing, in which case you could draw cards to see which modality is most beneficial for them to receive.

WHITE RAVEN

Psychic Gifts

How Best to Increase Healing Ability

Earth Gifts of Manifestation

How Best to Improve Manifestation

Water Gifts of Healing

Nature of the Querent's Magic (Oracle Card)

Air Gifts of Communication

How Best to Increase Personal Power

Fire Gifts of Personal Power

How Best to Improve Communication

7. **How to Increase Healing Ability** shows the practices and techniques that will be most effective for the querent on their path of healing or being a healer. The information that comes through here may not be directly connected to healing but, nevertheless, is needed for them to move to the next level.

8. **Earth, Gifts of Manifestation** shows the querent's most effective forms of spell work and prayer for manifesting. This may show up as a mundane skill, as Earth is solid and rooted.

9. **How Best to Improve Manifestation** focuses on the skills and techniques that will make the querent's manifestation more successful.

PAST-LIFE READINGS

Connection to past incarnations is something most people are curious about, recognizing that some skills, phobias, and memories do not make sense when only looking at their current lifetime. The belief in past lives has shifted a bit in the last decade with many people seeing life progression as sideways or parallel, with all lifetimes existing in unison, making it possible for a past version of ourselves to be aware of us in our present incarnation, something I have experienced personally. Past-life/parallel-life readings can help us understand much about ourselves, creating a map of sorts of us to explore! As past-life exploration is quite popular, I have created three spreads for examining past lives.

In developing our ability to do past-life readings it is helpful to study history, particularly in the form of anthropology. I have always been a history buff, with my favorite topic being the study of people, and how they have shaped the world through religion, culture, art, and war. I mostly watch documentaries, which add imagery to my symbolic language that can be easily triggered during a reading to give more precise information. What's more, I often find myself unlocking information about my own past lives in the process of watching them!

I recommend using decks that carry a feeling of placement, but do not blatantly place themselves in a particular culture or time. Using an Egyptian deck, for example, would not be advised unless you were looking at a life you already knew was in Egypt.

Past Life

This spread helps you discover a past/parallel life and explore its deeper meaning.

1. **Location in Time and Space (Oracle Card)** shows where and when the past life takes place. Pay close attention to the feel of the card, colors, depth, and symbolism. Close your eyes periodically, allowing the images you see with your eyes to be interpreted through your third eye. It may help to imagine a video screen in the middle of your mind featuring the images you saw on the card. Focus first on location, feeling it out. Examine the climate, landscape, and population, noting anything that comes to mind. Once you feel like you know *where* you are, it's time to look for *when* you are. Draw an extra card here if you feel you need it. To determine timeline, I look for signs of technology, religion, art, and war: all things easily learned through documentaries. Intermittently open and close your eyes, allowing the card to lead your mind into a story.

2. **What the Querent Was Born Into** shows social class, and family reputation, as well as the jobs and roles our parents held. In sitting with this card, we can feel our relationship with our parents in that lifetime, determining how close we were and whether we know them in this lifetime. Feel free to pick extra cards.

3. **Early Childhood Gifts** looks at what we learned and were given in the early years of our life, such as talents, titles, freedom, wealth, and adoration.

4. **Early Childhood Obstacles** shows the hard things we endured in this childhood, and how we got through them.

5. **Young Adulthood** focuses on adolescence and coming of age, noting anything relevant in the person's life at that time.

6. **Profession/Life Path** shows what role and/or occupation the querent played in this life.

110   +   Spreads and Layouts

PAST LIFE

Tarot and Oracle

Location
in Time and
Space
(Oracle Card)

What the
Querent
Was Born Into

Early
Childhood
Gifts

Early
Childhood
Obstacles

Young
Adulthood

Profession
Life Path

Personal
Relationships

Family
Relationships

Accomplishments

End of Life

Soul-Level Card Spreads + 111

7. **Personal Relationships** focuses on influential relationships in this life, including romantic ones. The querent may want to go deeper here; to do so draw a few more cards and focus on details of the relationship. For those wanting to look specifically at romantic connections through past lives, use the Past-Life Relationship spread.

8. **Family Relationships** speaks of children and grandchildren as well as extended family, focusing on relevant information. You can also use this position to see if there are people in the querent's life who are present in both the life being examined and their current life.

9. **Accomplishments** focuses on the things the querent learned, created, and achieved.

10. **End of Life** looks at when and where the lifetime ended.

Past-Life Relationship

As human consciousness expands, many people will experience the intensity of past-life connections, including meeting a stranger and feeling as if you already know them. In the case of romantic interests—where the person is sexually attractive to us—the feelings can often be overwhelming, particularly if we are not looking for a relationship! Understanding the nature of the connection is helpful, as the attraction is not always a sign that we should throw caution to the wind. The Past-Life Relationship spread is designed to give us an overview of the karma that is pulling us together, helping us to fully see the nature of our connection. This spread can be used for platonic past-life connections as well.

1. **Location in Time and Space (Oracle Card)** shows where and when the connection took place. Close your eyes periodically, allowing the images you see with your eyes to be interpreted through your third eye. Focus first on location, feeling it out. Examine the climate, landscape, and population, noting anything that comes to mind. Once you feel like you know where

112 ✦ **Spreads and Layouts**

PAST LIFE RELATIONSHIPS

Tarot and Oracle

Location
in Time and
Space
(Oracle Card)

The Querent's
Background

Obstacles
and
Advantages

The Querent's
Lessons

Meeting

Nature of
the
Relationship

Gifts and
Lessons
of the
Relationship

The Partner's
Background

Obstacles
and
Advantages

The Partner's
Lessons

the connection took place, it's time to look for when it occurred. Draw an extra card here if you feel you need it. To determine timeline, look for signs of technology, religion, art, and war. Intermittently open and close your eyes, allowing the card to lead your mind into a story.

2. **The Querent's Background** shows who the querent was at the time of the shared life. Lean into the card, allowing your psychic mind to explore details of who the querent was.

3. **Obstacles and Advantages** focuses on what obstacles or advantages the querent faced in having the relationship. More cards may be helpful here to represent family, finances, and health.

4. **The Querent's Lessons** highlights the querent's soul path in the lifetime.

5. **Meeting** focuses on how the couple were introduced to one another.

6. **Nature of the Relationship** is the most important placement in the reading. Often people assume that meeting someone we have a karmic connection to is a sign of being destined to be together; however, there are many reasons why we remember someone from a past relationship, and most of them are complicated! Look deep, draw more cards if you need to as you feel this one out.

7. **Gifts and Lessons of the Relationship** clues us in on why the relationship has reemerged, showing us the essence of our life together and the nature of our relationship going forward.

8. **The Partner's Background** shows who the past-life partner was at the time of the shared life. Lean into the card, allowing your psychic mind to explore details of who the querent was.

9. **Obstacles and Advantages** focuses on what obstacles or advantages the past-life partner faced during the relationship. More cards may be helpful here to represent family, finances, and health.

10. **The Partner's Lessons** highlights the partner's soul path in the lifetime.

114 ✦ Spreads and Layouts

Past-Life Triangulation

Past-life triangulation focuses on two lives that are currently affecting the querent. This is a spread I created many years ago that I still work with regularly. I like that it looks for the shared lessons triangulated between the lives, and how as a soul we are learning from multiple perspectives. This reading leans deeply into the concept of parallel lives, acknowledging that we can communicate and share wisdom between incarnations.

One of the interesting things that has transpired since people started doing ancestry work is seeing how many of us have lived lives within our own family tree. One of the most notable past-life readings I did was for a woman who had a life in Boston just after the American revolution. In that life she was a man who had come to this country with his family. The unusual thing about the life was that she was born into a family of blacksmiths but stepped away from the family trade to become a doctor. When I told her this, she exclaimed, "Oh my God! That was my great-great-great-grandfather!" having found the information in her family's genealogy. In another reading the querent recognized the lives she was triangulating as members from both sides of her family tree: one life being an ancestor of her mother's and the other her father's.

When doing past-life triangulation, it is helpful to see the stories as parts of the whole instead of individual readings, for the lives featured are clearly connected. Triangulation can change throughout our lives, as it focuses on the lives that are currently affecting us. The lives we related to when we were twenty may be different than the lives we triangulate with at fifty, making this a good reading to repeat for ourselves every few years or whenever we go through a major life change.

This spread is aligned with the concept of parallel lives in which time runs progressively forward when we are living: we are four before forty, but outside of physical form it is not limited to a linear time-

Soul-Level Card Spreads   ✦   115

line. This makes it possible for people to have lives with very little time between incarnations.

1. **Lessons of Triangulation (Oracle Card)** shows the life we are currently living and the major lesson being explored between the two lives featured in the spread.

2. **Location in Time and Space: First Life (Oracle Card)** is the placeholder, showing when and where the life took place. Focus first on location, feeling it out. Examine the climate, landscape, and population, noting anything that comes to mind. Once you feel like you know where it took place, it's time to look for when. Draw an extra card here if you feel you need it. To determine timeline, look for signs of technology, religion, art, and war. Intermittently open and close your eyes, allowing the card to lead the mind.

3. **What the Querent Was Born Into** shows social class and family reputation, as well as the jobs and roles our parents held. In sitting with this card, we can feel our relationship with our parents in that lifetime, determining how close we were and whether we know them in this lifetime. Feel free to pick extra cards.

4. **Early Childhood Gifts** highlights the soul-level strengths and abilities the querent incarnated with, as well as physical world blessings such as land, title, wealth, and so on.

5. **Early Childhood Obstacles** looks at the hardships the querent was born with, such as health problems, lack of finances, and trauma carried on a soul level.

6. **Young Adulthood** shows what was happening in the querent's early adult life.

7. **Professional Life Path** looks at how the querent made their livelihood, and the skills they developed. Exploring this area often explains natural abilities in their current life. It also provides the querent with areas they may want to explore. For example, after remembering a past life I had in Egypt in which I used my voice

116 ✦ Spreads and Layouts

What the Querent Was Born Into	Early Childhood Gifts	Early Childhood Obstacles
Young Adulthood	Professional Life Path	Personal Relationship
Family Relationships	Achievements	End of Life

Location in Time and Space (Oracle Card) First Life

Location in Time and Space (Oracle Card) Second Life

Soul-Level Card Spreads + 117

PAST LIFE TRIANGULATION
Tarot and Oracle

Lessons of
Triangulation
(Oracle Card)

What
the Querent
Was Born Into

Early
Childhood
Gifts

Early
Childhood
Obstacles

Young
Adulthood

Professional
Life Path

Personal
Relationship

Family
Relationships

Achievements

End of Life

in healing and magic, I began doing so in this lifetime. Sacred singing/vocal toning has been a vital part of my magical skill set for over twenty years now!

8. **Personal Relationships** highlights the querent's romantic relationships and close friendships. More cards may be helpful here if you feel there are multiple relationships to look at. If you feel like the querent has connected with these relations in this lifetime, make sure to draw another card and look for where/who they are now.

9. **Family Relationships** examines the querent's immediate family, spouse, and children, as well as their close biological family and community.

10. **Achievements** looks at accomplishments made by the querent.

11. **End of Life** shows the circumstances surrounding the querent's death.

Repeat steps 2–11 for the second life, making note of how they approach the same lesson from different perspectives, and reflect on how both have similarities with our current life circumstances.

Thinking Outside the Spread

The availability of tarot and oracle cards has changed over the last decade with new decks coming out regularly, making it easy to find one that appeals to any aesthetic. From angel cards to witch oracles, there is something for everyone, and many people have multiple decks, including some they have never used.

Not every deck is meant to be used in the same way! Some decks are great for everyday divination, looking at the mundane situations of life, some are better for readings geared toward psychic opening, while others we keep for our hands only, marking them as sacred to our deep spiritual work. Taking the time to get to know our decks helps determine how they can best be used.

Any card can be used for self-reflection, working as a mirror for the soul, giving us the opportunity to describe our feelings through the layered symbolism of its imagery. Look at any card long enough and we will see how its story relates to us, even if the connection appears as a minute detail in the background.

Using our cards in unconventional ways helps us develop a deeper understanding of their symbolic nuances. Incorporating cards into our spells and prayers gives our intuition a reference point. Seeing the familiar cards, we remember the stories they told in our magical workings and recognize how those stories pertain to the current situation we are reading. Similarly, journeying with our cards through guided meditation inlays a deeper understanding of the card's meaning into our subconscious mind, where it can be retrieved easily by our intuition. Exploring cartomancy beyond traditional card spreads offers our psychic minds another avenue to develop, one in which we are actively opening parts of our mind and programming it with symbolic language. I encourage you to think outside the spread!

LONG-TERM DRAW

This spread is designed to be looked at over a longer period, such as a week or month. Placing the cards on your altar, or top of your dresser where you can see them often, they are meant to be looked at daily, allowing our minds to ponder the message they are presenting. This is a helpful personal reading that is beneficial for looking at big problems we struggle to understand, as well as questions related to our spiritual development. I always have cards on my working altar for this purpose, changing them out every two to four weeks. Here we will use the head, heart, hand spread—keeping it simple. If you don't have a specific question, you can ask "What do I need to know right now?" while shuffling your cards.

LONG-TERM DRAW

What the Head Needs	What the Heart Needs	What the Hands Need

1. **What the Head Needs** highlights how we should focus our mind.
2. **What the Heart Needs** shows us our emotional needs regarding the subject.
3. **What the Hands Need** indicates what we need to do about the situation.

CARTOMANCY IN ACTIVATED PRAYER

Cartomancy is out of the broom closet; no longer set aside for those who identify as witches, there are decks designed with faith-related imagery and symbolism for every spiritual path, making it easier for people to receive messages from their higher self and spiritual allies. By choosing cards that reflect our personal spiritual beliefs we will likely understand the symbolism better, and as a bonus have a great tool for activating our prayers!

Activated prayer, also known as active prayer, has physical actions that help us focus more fully and direct our will. The action can come in the form of a posture, for example kneeling or crossed-legged yoga poses such as lotus or *sukahasana* (easy pose); through walking prayer on your favorite trail or labyrinth; by repeating mantras, working with prayer beads or witch's knots; focusing on an image of our Gods/Goddesses and gurus; or by creating or gazing at a picture representing our desired outcome. Oracle cards work well for the latter, as each deck is like a book and every card a stand-alone story.

Along with setting up our altar, it is advisable to prepare ourselves as well, acknowledging that we will be standing before our Gods/Goddesses and ancestors. Just as people get dressed up for church, we prepare ourselves for activated prayer!

Thinking of oracle cards as books helps us pick the right deck for the working, recognizing that an angel deck or herbal oracle is well suited to prayers of healing, whereas a witch's oracle or elemental deck is better suited to prayers of self-growth and psychic development. That being said, work with what you have! Remember, it wasn't too long ago that there were only a few styles of tarot decks on the market, and they were hard to come by. While having a variety of cards is helpful, they are simply tools for our intuitive mind to work with. Tools do not determine our psychic potential!

Thinking Outside the Spread ✦ 123

◇◇◇◇◇◇◇◇◇◇◇◇

TECHNIQUE

ACTIVATED PRAYER WITH ORACLE CARDS

Activated prayer is a sacred act and should be treated as special. I recommend setting up an altar, decorating it with symbols of your faith, statues of the deities you work with, photos of your ancestors, candles, and incense, as well as things that represent your need, such as medical bills, help wanted ads, and symbols of love for those seeking romantic relationships. The act of setting up a shrine or altar for our work is part of active prayer!

—————————————— **You Will Need** ——————————————

An oracle deck of your choice (tarot and playing cards are also acceptable), a small bowl of sacred water (moon water, water collected from sacred well, holy water, or bottled spring water in a pinch), scented oil for anointing, incense, candles, and personal items for the altar, and your Book of Shadows.

1. Begin by preparing yourself and your altar for the work at hand, including sacred practices of your religion in the setup.
2. Light your candle and take a seat in front of the altar. You may choose to incorporate a seated posture here, such as kneeling, or lotus pose.
3. Reach out to your God/Goddess through the traditional methods of your religion. If you are not particularly religious you may invoke God/Goddess/Universe by saying, "Divine one, beloved creator of the universe, I ask that you join me and hear my prayers," as you light the incense.
4. Using your index and middle finger purify your heart, third eye, and crown chakras with sacred water, asking your God/Goddess to clear away any emotions that do not serve us in the moment, such as fear, shame, and doubt.
5. Anoint your heart, third eye, and crown with fragrant oil, taking a moment to recognize the sacred in yourself.
6. Picking up your cards, begin shuffling as you speak of your need. It is

124 ✦ Spreads and Layouts

important that you do this from the heart: do not hold back, activated prayer is vulnerable and filled with truth.

7. Focusing on your prayer, pull a card from the deck to represent your need. You can draw a card randomly or pick one from the deck that speaks of your need, placing it in the center of the altar where you can clearly see it.

8. While gazing at your card, focus on the essence of your need, breaking it down to a simple, abbreviated form, such as "I am healthy and strong" to represent all the things that need to happen to make that so.

9. Continuing to gaze at your card, begin repeating your consolidated prayer, adding imagery to your words. Spend at least five minutes on this step. *In this way the images featured on the card add to the prayer, similarly to how a picture adds to the story of a book. This is particularly helpful for those of us who are visually oriented.*

10. If you are praying for guidance, do a three card pull to determine what is needed by your head, heart, and hand. Take time viewing them, closing your eyes periodically to view them with your third eye, noting that one of the powers prayers grants us is focus and connection with a higher power. Time is needed to receive such!

11. When you are finished give thanks to your God/Goddess/Guru for acknowledging your prayers. You may leave your altar up or dismantle as you choose.

12. If you break down your altar after prayer, move the card representing your prayer to your working altar, or near your bedstand, where you will see it regularly.

13. Whenever you see the card representing your prayers, take a moment to repeat the abbreviated prayer. This should ideally be done daily!

14. Make sure to document your experience in your Book of Shadows.

We don't always have the time or space for rituals, including long drawn-out prayers. Sometimes our need is acute and our surroundings unhospitable to sacred works, such as praying for our loved ones as we

Thinking Outside the Spread + 125

sit in the hospital waiting room or dealing with anxiety during a turbulent flight. In these cases, we can rely on oracle cards to help us focus our intention discreetly, even if we forgot our deck at home.

This is where technology really is our friend, as there is a plethora of card images just a Google search away, as well as tarot and oracle apps. I recommend The Fool's Dog tarot app as it features a variety of decks, with decks being under five dollars. There are also a handful of great oracle deck apps out there, making it easy to find one that fits your needs. While tarot and oracle apps lack the tactile goodness of physical cards, they do provide us access to our cards in spaces where pulling out a deck is inconvenient. Whether you carry the real deal in your purse or choose to use an app, oracle and tarot cards are helpful for activated prayer in a pinch!

◇◇◇◇◇◇◇◇◇◇◇◇

TECHNIQUE
ACTIVATED PRAYER IN A PINCH

1. Find a quiet place where you can get a moment to yourself, noting that privacy is more important when using actual cards.
2. Take a few deep breaths as you center yourself, remembering that emotional upheaval can influence our work.
3. Invite your God/Goddess/Guru to join you where you are, silently or out loud depending on your environment.
4. Using an app or deck of cards, draw a card to represent your prayer, either randomly or by choosing the one you feel best suits your needs.
5. Gaze at your card as you pray, closing your eyes periodically to focus on your third eye, seeing your need in the card.
6. Break down your prayer to a few words, such as "safe travel" or "healthy and happy."
7. When you are finished give thanks to your deities and take a photo of your card so you can access it whenever you have need or wish to reinstate your prayers.

126 ✦ Spreads and Layouts

CARTOMANCY SPELLS

For most of history divination has been connected to magic, and psychic abilities were taken as a sign that the purveyor of information was a witch! Now, through the help of science, cartomancy and other forms of viewing the unseen and unknown are recognized as naturally occurring experiences that happen for some people. What was once reserved for darkened parlors and obscure metaphysical shops is now mainstream, with readers offering services in hair salons, restaurants, parties, and fundraisers. Just like divination the worldview of magical manifestation is also changing, with many people recognizing the similarities between activated prayer and spell work.

Spell

A magical formula designed to use energetic force to manifest the wielder's will, often activated by words of power and the use of natural components with magical attributes.

Spells and prayers are both ways of shifting the energy around our needs. Both require a deep level of dedication on the part of the user, and a level of belief in a supernatural force having the ability to make change. How we view the force we are reaching out to is often the determining factor in whether we call it a spell or a prayer. *As a practicing witch for most of my life, with strong relationships to deities, I use the words interchangeably, as both apply to the way I manifest.*

Some people like to keep their spells simple, others prefer elaborate rituals and precision timing and control, and still others perform their spells while in an ecstatic trance state. The best way to do spell work is to recognize yourself and how you like to do things. I'm personally not a big ceremonial magic kind of girl. I work spells simply and intuitively throughout the day, adding magic to everything I do; however, I love nature, a good altar, and dressing up, so my personal spell work is a combination of unstructured instant magic and evening-long tributes to manifestation. Whatever form of spell worker you are, cartomancy fits nicely.

The foundation of all spell work comes down to the will and the way. Will is the ability to focus our intention; it is our personal power, and performing magic requires us to channel that will some way! The way is the method we use to do so, be it through belief in a higher power, working with elemental powers, or focusing on your psychic abilities.

Cartomancy is a form of spell work in which we focus our will on manifesting answers from the unseen/unknown; interpreting cards is the way in which we create the spell.

Just as we can use a photo as a representative of someone we are sending healing to, we can use cards to represent hard-to-find magical components, animal spirits, elemental energies, and deities. Cards can also represent the purpose of a spell, featuring images that focus our will on the intended outcome. Using cards in this manner can turn Pinterest boards and social media posts into powerful manifestation altars.

PLAYING CARD CHARMS

Blessing spells are crafted to bestow beneficial magic on people, places, and circumstances, such as babies, marriages, and homes. Much like fairy godmothers grant blessing in folktales, beneficial charms and enchantments have been woven into secular traditions with the idea of bestowing love, bounty, and health on the receiver. In magical traditions blessings often come in the form of a lucky charm.

Charm

An item that has been bestowed with blessings.

Card charms can be crafted using tarot, oracle, and/or playing cards, and they can be created as a permanent blessing for weddings,

128 + Spreads and Layouts

babies, and homes, or as a situational charm for an event. They are made by punching holes in the upper right- and left-hand corners of each card, and then stringing them together with ribbon to make a garland of cards. If you don't want to punch holes in the cards, you can use clothespins to attach the cards to the ribbon.

Playing cards are recommended for these spells as playing cards are innocuous, making them appear harmless on public display. There are unique playing card decks available on Amazon and Etsy if you want to customize your charms.

◇◇◇◇◇◇

SPELL

SOUL MATE CHARM

The Soul Mate Charm is an energetic want-ad meant to bring a soul-level, loving relationship into our life. In preparation for crafting the charm it is wise to know what we are seeking. But note that it is **not** OK to do love magic on another person against their will! Place the charm above the outside door of your home, or bedroom door if you share space with others. If you prefer to have friendships online, place the charm above your computer. This spell can be used for both romantic and platonic relationships (as a means of calling in a good friend).

There are three cards in this charm. The Knight of Hearts represents the action of love coming to us. The second card we choose as it represents the relationship interest. Choose a Queen if you are seeking a woman, a King if you are seeking a man, a Joker for nonbinary, and multiple cards for polyamorous relationships. Use your intuition when choosing this card and use the Court cards starting on page 250 for reference. (The suits vary between tarot cards and playing cards, so use the following equivalents: Pentacles/Diamonds, Cups/Hearts, Wands/Clubs, Swords/Spades.) The third card is the Ace of Diamonds, representing the relationship solidly manifesting in our life.

Thinking Outside the Spread ✦ 129

——————— **You Will Need** ———————

A yard of quarter-inch red ribbon, a hole punch, the Knight of Hearts, Ace of Diamonds, and card/s representing your relationship interest, a white candle, a red candle, incense, and your favorite perfume.

1. Light the white candle on your altar. It is your working candle, representing the purity of your intentions in your work. Welcome your spiritual allies (ancestors, guides, elementals, and deities) into your sacred space, envisioning the light of the candle creating a protective sphere of white light around you.
2. Light the incense and the red candle, representing passionate love, off the white working candle.
3. Punch holes in the top right- and left-hand corners of each card. Shuffle the cards a few times as you think about the blessings that you wish to bestow on your soul mate.
4. Bless the Knight of Hearts as you pass the card over the flame of the red candle, saying, "The Knight that my love will quickly find their way to me."
5. Bless the Queen/King/Joker of your choice as you pass the card over the flame, saying, "The Queen/King/Joker to represent the soul mate that I call to my side."
6. Bless the Ace of Diamonds as you pass the card over the flame, saying, "The Ace of Diamonds that our relationship will manifest, solidify, and grow."
7. String the cards onto the ribbon, knotting each card in place.
8. Spray yourself and the charm with your favorite perfume, that your love may recognize your scent.
9. Thank your spiritual allies, and blow out your candles. Make sure to record your experience in your Book of Shadows. Hang your charm above your door or computer.

130 + Spreads and Layouts

◇◇◇◇◇◇◇

SPELL

MARRIAGE BLESSING CHARM

I have always loved weaving magic into gifts I give at bridal showers and weddings. The marriage charm uses the Queen of Hearts and the King of Hearts as representatives of the bride and groom; use two Queens or two Kings for same-sex marriages (use other suits or buy two sets of playing cards). I prefer the suit of Hearts as it represents love! Use the Ace of Clubs to represent growth and fertility. *Blessings of fertility can come in many forms; when working fertility into blessings for others, our focus is on the fertility of their choice.* I recommend getting cards with a nice pattern on the back as we will be alternating the side of the card facing up.

Make your Marriage Blessing charm in sacred space, during a full moon. Full moons are connected to emotions and are known for enhancing romantic feelings.

―――――――――― **You Will Need** ――――――――――

A yard of quarter-inch red ribbon, a hole punch, the Queen of Hearts, the King of Hearts, the Ace of Clubs, six cards to represent the month, year, and day of the wedding (for example, using a Joker for zero, the date 02/20/93 would be a Joker, a Two, a Two, a Joker, a Nine, and a Three), a white candle, a blue candle, incense, a tablespoon of rose water, and your Book of Shadows.

1. Light the white candle on your altar. It is your working candle, representing the purity of your intentions in your work. Welcome your spiritual allies (ancestors, guides, elementals, and deities) into your sacred space, envisioning the light of the candle creating a protective sphere of white light around you.

2. Light the incense and the blue candle, representing fidelity, off the white working candle.

Thinking Outside the Spread ✦ 131

3. Punch holes in the top right- and left-hand corners of each card. Shuffle the cards a few times as you think about the blessings that you wish to bestow on the couple.
4. Bless the Queen and King of Hearts with fidelity as you move the cards above the flame of the blue candle.
5. Dip your fingertips in the rose water (for love), and anoint the red ribbon, representing love and passion with it.
6. String the cards together from left to right making a simple knot after each card. Place two cards for their wedding month facing up.
7. Place either the Queen or King of Hearts next, facing down.
8. Place the first card of the wedding day facing up.
9. Place the Ace of Clubs facing down.
10. Place the second card of the wedding day facing up.
11. Place the other partner card (King or Queen) facing down.
12. Place the two cards representing the last two days of the wedding year facing up, using a Joker for zero. *When your charm is complete it should have the date on one side in numbered cards, and the King and Queen of Hearts and the Ace of Clubs on the other.*
13. Your charm is now ready to be given as a bridal shower or wedding gift. Be sure to record your experience in your Book of Shadows.

◇◇◇◇◇◇

SPELL

House Blessing Charm

All blessing charms in this book are made in similar fashion, creating a garland of cards strung on colored ribbon. The house blessing version is a great charm for new homes, and spaces that need energetic rebalancing, and are *charming* enough to be used yearlong as a decoration! The House Blessing charm uses the four Aces. The Ace of Diamonds for prosperity, the Ace of Spades for protection, the Ace of Hearts for love, and the Ace of Clubs for creativity.

132 ✦ Spreads and Layouts

────────────── **You Will Need** ──────────────

A yard of quarter-inch green ribbon, a hole punch, the Ace of Diamonds, the Ace of Spades, the Ace of Hearts, the Ace of Clubs, a white candle, incense, a teaspoon of cinnamon, evergreen needles, rose petals (fresh or dried), and a plate or tray.

──

1. Light the white candle on your altar. It is your working candle, representing the purity of your intentions. Welcome your spiritual allies (ancestors, guides, elementals, and deities) into your sacred space, envisioning the light of the candle creating a protective sphere of white light around you.
2. Punch holes in the top right- and left-hand corners of each card. Shuffle the cards a few times as you think about the blessings that you wish to bestow upon the house/space.
3. Pass the Ace of Diamonds over the flame of the candle, saying, "The Ace of Diamonds for fertility and abundance," then place the card on the tray.
4. Pass the Ace of Spades over the flame, saying, "The Ace of Spades for clarity and protection," then place it on the tray.
5. Pass the Ace of Hearts over the flame, saying, "The Ace of Hearts for love and emotional balance," then place it on the tray.
6. Pass the Ace of Clubs over the flame, saying, "The Ace of Clubs for creativity and growth," then place it on the tray.
7. Sprinkle cinnamon, evergreen needles, and rose petals over the cards, saying, "Cinnamon for prosperity, evergreen for renewed growth, and roses for sweetness."
8. String the cards together facing the same direction, knotting the ribbon after each card, as you direct energy into each with Reiki, chanting, toning, or deep breathing.
9. When you have finished thank your spiritual allies, and write about your experience in your Book of Shadows.

Thinking Outside the Spread ✦ 133

When making house charms as a gift I like to share a bit of the process with the home owner. I list the meanings of the cards and herbs used and the intentions I added to the cards.

<><><><><>

SPELL

PROSPERITY CHARM

Blessings of prosperity are great when we need to increase our personal cash flow. They are also helpful for blessing gardens and businesses. Prosperity charms are designed to bring wealth, success, and affluence into our lives. I like to make prosperity charms at the winter solstice and give them as gifts to friends and family. These simple charms use only one card, making them compact enough to slip into your wallet.

You Will Need

A quarter-yard of gold and green ribbon, the Ace of Diamonds, a white candle, a gold candle, incense, and a pinch of cinnamon.

1. Light the white candle on your altar. It is your working candle, representing the purity of your intentions. Welcome your spiritual allies (ancestors, guides, elementals, and deities) into your sacred space, envisioning the light of the candle creating a protective sphere of white light around you.
2. Light your incense and give thanks for the prosperity you already received in your life.
3. Light the gold candle to represent the prosperity and abundance you desire.
4. Punch a hole in the top center of the card. Spend a few minutes meditating on the card imaging what prosperity will look and feel like.
5. Pass the Ace of Diamonds over the candles, saying, "The Ace of Diamonds for prosperity and abundance."
6. Place the green and gold ribbon through the Ace of Diamonds and tie it. Direct energy into it with Reiki, chanting, toning, or deep breathing as you move the charm through the incense smoke.

134 ✦ Spreads and Layouts

7. When you are finished thank your spiritual allies, document your experience, and hang your prosperity charm in a place where you can see it or place it in your wallet.

INTUITIVE HEALING BOARDS

It is important to remember that spells and prayer are not an alternative to professional medical and mental health treatment; instead, they are meant to be a collaboration, used to strengthen our resolve, reduce stress, and engage that part of the existence that cannot be explained—like miracles!

> *I have always approached healing through intuition, as I was a professional psychic for ten years before finding my way to the healing arts. Through my study of Reiki, rune galdr, and vocal toning I noticed a significant increase in my capacity to receive psychic information. I also found that my psychic ability made me a far more effective healer, particularly when dealing with emotional traumas, as I could often see the wounding like a movie in my mind. Working in both fields I blended my experiences, and I began seeing how the tools and techniques could be woven together. If you are skilled as an intuitive healer, you will likely see the crossover quite quickly when developing your intuition.*

Most people are familiar with vision boards; traditionally this meant cutting out pictures from magazines and gluing them to a piece of cardboard with the intention of creating positive change, and now we also have the modern, digital equivalent of Pinterest. The intuitive healer's vision board is the same idea, only utilizing the magical symbolism of cards.

Intuitive healing boards are visual spells created with images chosen for inspiration: in this case, playing cards, tarot, and oracle cards. They can be created quickly for instant need, or lovingly over time, using physical or digital means. Like all vision boards they work best if we come into regular contact with them, as part of the magic happens on the subliminal level, showing us that the changes we are manifesting are possible.

Intuitive healing boards are created around need. How we make them and what we put on them is dependent on the situation. We can draw cards at random or intentionally pick through multiple decks; either way, our psychic intuition will guide the choosing.

Instant Need Healing Boards

Instant need healing spells are great for acute medical and emotional situations, like the flu, emergency surgery, mental breakdowns, natural disasters, and social violence. It is the magic we work when we have no time to gather components or create lyrical incantations. Lacking time and privacy we must do much of the work in our mind. This is where digital technology shines!

Instant need boards are best done digitally, using a tarot or oracle card app, or Pinterest board. They can also be made by taking a photo of your spell board with the camera on your phone quickly. For those who are not technology savvy I recommend carrying a deck of cards in your purse or jacket (mini tarot decks work great for this). Instant need spells do best with repetition: once you have chosen a method, stick with it! Those who like to be prepared can create the board ahead of time and store it in their phone.

Instant spells work best if they are not complicated and we don't have to do a lot of thinking. For this reason, I created a Mental Health Instant Need board and a Medical Instant Need board with recommended tarot cards. Each board works with four cards, weaving a bit of numerology into the spell, adding the strength and stability. Those who like to be prepared can create the board ahead of time and store it in their phone. *People who are in emergency medical or mental health situations often through their work or family can reuse their instant need healing board by storing it on their phone.*

136 ✦ Spreads and Layouts

SPELL
MENTAL HEALTH INSTANT NEED

Cards

Strength, the Hanged Man, Ace of Cups, and Eight of Cups.

1. Close your eyes and take a few deep breaths. Call in your spiritual allies (ancestors, guides, elementals, and deities).
2. Creating a square, begin with the Strength card; as you place your card, think or say, "Strength for stability."
3. Place the Hanged Man next to the Strength card and say, "The Hanged Man for a change of perspective."
4. Place the Ace of Cups above Strength and say, "The Ace of Cups for Emotional Healing."
5. Place the Eight of Cups above the Hanged Man, completing the square, and say, "The Eight of Cups for continued growth."
6. Save the board in your camera photos or on an app of your choice.
7. Once the board is saved you can look at it often to reconnect with the healing magic you are sending. To amplify your work, repeat the words spoken for each card in your mind like a mantra.

SPELL
MEDICAL INSTANT NEED

Cards

Strength, Ace of Cups, Ace of Pentacles, and Three of Pentacles.

1. Close your eyes and take a few deep breaths. Call in your spiritual allies (ancestors, guides, elementals, and deities).
2. Creating a square, begin with the Strength card; as you place your card, think or say, "Strength for stability."

3. Place the Ace of Cups next to the Strength card and say, "The Ace of Cups for Emotional Healing."
4. Place the Three of Pentacles above the Strength card and say, "The Three of Pentacles for skillful medical treatment."
5. Place the Ace of Pentacles on top of the Ace of Cups and say, "The Ace of Pentacles for physical health."
6. Save the board in your camera photos or on an app of your choice.
7. Once the board is saved you can look at it often to reconnect with the healing magic you are sending. To amplify your work, repeat the words spoken for each card in your mind like a mantra.

Long-Term Healing Boards

Long-term healing boards are created over time and tended at a sacred altar, adding cards to them over time to represent our need. They can be created as digital vision boards using Pinterest, or the old-fashioned way by gluing images to posterboard; both are powerful. The Pinterest board option is convenient and space saving, allowing us to access it wherever there is Wi-Fi. Creating a physical board can become a magical work of art, especially if you are using real cards on the board. Whichever you choose, the key is to see it as a continuous healing stream that you are contributing to energetically as you add to it and watch it grow. Continuing to develop our long-term healing altars we can add cards that represent herbs and crystals whose healing properties we wish to access, as well as cards to represent deities and spirits we are working with.

Digital Boards. There are many options for cards and decks when creating a long-term healing board using Pinterest and other social pinboards. When creating your board, I recommend looking for an aesthetic that resembles the person it is created for. Incorporate oracle and playing cards with similar style along with the tarot. Digital boards can be accessed anywhere, including hospital waiting rooms, allowing us to magically utilize the hours spent on watch when our loved ones are undergoing tests and treatments. Not only can we

138 ✦ Spreads and Layouts

look at what we have already done, but we can invest what would be wasted time into our healing spell.

Physical Boards. When creating physical healing boards, we can use printed images of cards from downloaded images, cutting them out old-school, or we can create our healing board with tarot, oracle, and playing cards from decks we have not found our way to using. This is a great way to use old cards that have lost their wax coating due to use. Long-term healing boards are visionary altars and should be pleasing to the eye. Take a photo of your board before heading out to long doctors' appointments and testing, so that you can look at it periodically during the wait. If heavy-duty treatment is involved (such as chemotherapy) consider bringing the physical healing board with you to the hospital.

When creating a long-term healing board, we build the base with six cards. The number six represents dutiful action and healing, sympathy and love, all beneficial things when dealing with chronic illness.

◇◇◇◇◇◇

SPELL

LONG-TERM HEALING MENTAL HEALTH

This board for long-term mental health healing uses six cards, which may be arranged in the form of a six-sided star or a rectangle.

Cards

Strength, the Hermit, Justice, Ace of Wands, Ace of Cups, and Eight of Cups.

1. Close your eyes and take a few deep breaths. Call in your spiritual allies (ancestors, guides, elementals, and deities).
2. Creating a six-sided star (or rectangle), begin with the Strength card; as you place your card think or say, "Strength for stability."

Thinking Outside the Spread + 139

3. Place the Hermit to the left of the Strength card and say, "The Hermit to learn of one's self."
4. Place the Justice card to the right of the Strength card and say, "Justice that they may know what is true."
5. Place the Ace of Wands above the Strength card and say, "The Ace of Wands for soul growth."
6. Place the Eight of Cups above the Hermit completing the square and say, "The Eight of Cups for continued growth."
7. Place the Ace of Cups above Justice and say, "The Ace of Cups for emotional healing."
8. Save the board in your camera photos or on an app of your choice.
9. Once the board is finished take a picture on your phone so you can reconnect with the healing energy when needed. To amplify your work, repeat the words spoken for each card in your mind like a mantra.

◇◇◇◇◇◇◇
SPELL

LONG-TERM HEALING PHYSICAL HEALTH

———————————————— **Cards** ————————————————

Strength, Ace of Cups, Ace of Pentacles, the Magician, Nine of Pentacles, and Six of Wands.

1. Close your eyes and take a few deep breaths. Call in your spiritual allies (ancestors, guides, elementals, and deities).
2. Creating a six-sided star (or rectangle) begin with the Strength card; as you place your card, think or say, "Strength for stability."
3. Place the Ace of Cups to the left of the Strength card and say, "The Ace of Cups for emotional healing."
4. Place the Ace of Pentacles to the right of the Strength card and say, "The Ace of Pentacles for physical health."
5. Place the Magician above the Strength card and say, "The Magician so they may have all the components of healing."

140 ✦ Spreads and Layouts

6. Place the Nine of Pentacles to the left of the Magician and say, "The Nine of Pentacles for quality of life."

7. Place the Six of Wands to the right of the Magician and say, "The Six of Wands that they may find the best treatment."

8. Save the board in your camera photos or on an app of your choice.

9. Once the board is finished take a picture on your phone so you can reconnect with the healing energy when needed. To amplify your work, repeat the words spoken for each card in your mind like a mantra.

HOUSE OF CARDS
TRAVEL ALTAR

Strange noises, unfamiliar house spirits, and emotional tension can make unwinding challenging when traveling, as sleeping in hotels, rental homes, and visiting family often involves managing psychic and emotional energies we are not used to. Learning how to create a sacred environment when away from home is a lifesaver if you enjoy your sleep, and taking up minimal space doing so is always a plus!

The House of Cards spell is designed to give you everything you need for a portable altar. Any deck can be used, but if you travel a lot, I recommend having a deck that is solely for this purpose, as tools used repetitively for the same purpose become acquainted with their purpose, making working with them easier. Additionally, if we have many decks, we can craft a personal deck specifically for this purpose from other decks that we have. Customizing our magical tools helps us develop a deeper connection with them.

The House of Cards spell is a warding spell designed to create a sacred protective space wherever we are. Cards are chosen to stand guard in each of the cardinal directions, assist in clear communication, and bring good health. Feel free to add additional positions to your deck to suit your needs.

Thinking Outside the Spread ✦ 141

◇◇◇◇◇◇◇◇◇

PROJECT

CHOOSING YOUR HOUSE OF CARDS

New tarot and oracle decks come out all the time making it easy to develop a collection, but one deck is truly all that is needed to do readings and magic! Using the same deck for all our magical purposes is convenient while traveling, taking up minimal space, while providing us with the opportunity to create sacred space and consult our intuition for ways to deal with any situation that may arise, like family members who communicate poorly.

This project was designed to be used with a tarot deck. If you only have an oracle deck, you can use this as an outline for creating your own protective House of Cards. As you develop your skills in magic you may want to assign cards to your spiritual allies, adding to the level of protection they offer.

———————————— **You Will Need** ————————————

One tarot deck and your Book of Shadows.

1. As the House of Cards is primarily a protective warding spell, the most important positions in the house are the Guardians. Each of the four directions will be guarded by a Knight. The Knight of Wands guards the east, the Knight of Swords guards the south, the Knight of Cups guards the west, and the Knight of Pentacles guards the north. (If you feel strongly that the suit of Swords represents the east, and the suit of Wands represents the south, feel free to shift their directions.)

2. Choose the Speaker of the House, the card that will represent clear communication. Think about the way you want to come across: If you are traveling for business and want to come across as skilled and confident, the King of Pentacles is a good choice. If, instead, you are expecting to keep the peace at a family gathering, the gentle messenger the Page of Cups is well suited. You can pick a different card for Speaker of the House for different situations.

142 ✦ Spreads and Layouts

3. For the position of Healer, the Queen of Cups is a natural pick to aid us in restful sleep and good health. If we are traveling for medical reasons, we may want to step this up a notch and put the Strength card in this position.

4. If you choose to represent the God and Goddess in your House of Cards, I recommend using the Emperor and Empress cards, as they are also referred to as the Lord and the Lady, common names given to the God and Goddess.

5. Make note of what cards you have chosen to represent your House of Cards in your Book of Shadows, noting any additional positions you have added.

◇◇◇◇◇◇

SPELL

ACTIVATING THE HOUSE OF CARDS

When traveling, use the top of a dresser or a nightstand to set up your house of cards shortly after arrival, noting that the sooner you do, the smoother your stay is likely to go.

——————————— **You Will Need** ———————————

Your House of Cards and your Book of Shadows.

1. Using the compass on your phone, begin by placing the Knight of Wands in the east, calling in the Guardians of the east, and asking for protection as you do. How elaborate you are in doing so is completely up to you; it is perfectly fine to perform this spell silently. Here is a simple example: "Guardians of the East, I welcome you to this circle. I ask that you protect me and this space from hurtful communication for the duration of my stay."

2. Placing the Knight of Swords in the south, call in the Guardians. "Guardians of the South, I welcome you to this circle. I ask that you protect me and this space from anger and hurtful actions for the duration of my stay."

3. Placing the Knight of Cups in the west, call in the guardians. "Guardians of the West, I welcome you to this circle. I ask that you protect me and

Thinking Outside the Spread ✦ 143

this space from emotional and physical pain for the duration of my stay."

4. Placing the Knight of Pentacles in the north, call in the Guardians. "Guardians of the North, I welcome you to this circle. I ask that you protect me and this space from financial misfortune for the duration of my stay."

5. Welcome the Speaker of the House by placing the card of your choice next to the Knight of Wands in the east, saying, "I welcome the Speaker of the House to this circle. I ask that you aid me in clear communication, that I may be here and speak, and be heard and spoken to with compassion and respect for the duration of my stay."

6. Place the Queen of Cups or Strength card in the position of Healer, next to the Knight of Cups in the west. Welcome the Healer by saying, "I welcome the Healer of the House to this circle. I ask that the Healer protect me from illness and injury, and aid me in restful sleep for the duration of my stay."

7. Place the Empress in the north, next to the Knight of Pentacles, and welcome the Goddess by saying, "I welcome the Goddess/Lady (or name of your personal goddess) to this circle. I ask that you bestow blessings of love and prosperity upon me and this space for the duration of my stay."

8. Place the Emperor in the south, next to the Knight of Swords, and welcome the God by saying, "I welcome you God/Lord (or name of your personal god) to this circle. I ask that you bestow blessings of strength and wisdom upon me and this space for the duration of my stay."

Leave your altar up for the duration of your stay, and make sure to make note of how the trip goes in your Book of Shadows. When you are packing up to leave, take a few moments to give thanks as you break down your House of Cards. A simple farewell is often enough, but you may want to officially thank and dismiss each member of the house.

Here is what I do: Before picking up the cards I close my eyes and say, "Guardians of the house, Knights of the East, South, West, and North,

144 ✦ Spreads and Layouts

I thank you for your blessings, go in peace. Speaker of the House, I thank you for your blessings, go in peace. Healer of the House, I thank you for your blessings, go in peace. Lord and Lady, God, Goddess, I thank you for your blessings, go in peace."

∞∞∞∞∞∞∞∞

PROJECT

CREATING YOUR OWN DECK

This is a project designed for people who have multiple oracle and tarot decks and are not afraid to create something entirely their own. The House of Cards using one deck is a powerful aid, but when we begin to mix and match our cards, choosing them for the resemblance they have to our spiritual allies, they become infused with the essences of our spirits and guides. Creating this deck takes time and will likely change as our magical relations develop.

We can add to the potency of this protective ward by keeping the cards together once they have been assigned a job. Just like programming a crystal for a particular type of healing, we can program our magical tools for specific tasks. The more they are used exclusively for this purpose the stronger the programming.

When creating a custom House of Cards, the positions in the circle remain the same: Guardians in the four cardinal directions, the Speaker of the House, the Healer, and cards representing the God and Goddess. You are free to add cards and positions as you see fit.

──────────── **You Will Need** ────────────

Tarot and oracle decks that you are willing to dissemble, and your Book of Shadows.

1. Choose a card for Guardian of the East to protect you from hurtful communication. When choosing a card, first think of which of your spiritual allies (spirit guides, ancestors, deities, or elemental spirits) is best

Thinking Outside the Spread + 145

suited for this position. Once you know who the Guardian of the East is, choose a card to represent them.

2. Choose a card for Guardian of the South to protect you from anger and chaos. Determine which of your spiritual allies is best suited for this position. Once you know who the Guardian of the South is, choose a card to represent them.

3. Choose a card for Guardian of the West to protect you from emotional and physical harm. Determine which of your spiritual allies is best suited for this position. Once you know who the Guardian of the West is, choose a card to represent them.

4. Choose a card for Guardian of the North to protect you from financial hardship. Determine which of your spiritual allies is best suited for this position. Once you know who the Guardian of the North is, choose a card to represent them.

5. Choose a card for Speaker of the House to aid you in clear communication. Determine which of your spiritual allies is best suited for this position. Once you know who the Speaker is, choose a card to represent them.

6. Choose a card for the Healer of the House to support your physical and emotional health. Determine which of your spiritual allies is best suited for this position. Once you know who the Healer is, choose a card to represent them.

7. Choose a card to represent your Goddess; if you work with more than one, find a card for each.

8. Choose a card to represent your God; if you work with more than one, find a card for each.

Once your House of Cards is complete, store them in a box or bag together along with any traveling charms you may have. Use the spell Activating the House of Cards when you arrive at your destination and get settled in your room. You can create similar decks by assigning cards to spiritual allies for aid in your magical workings.

146 ✦ Spreads and Layouts

JOURNEY OF THE ORACLE

Spiritual journey work is a form of meditation in which you are guided to a place where your intuition, memories, and emotions are more accessible. It is a form of lucid dreaming in which the dreamer enters the dream state while awake. Such meditations help develop our intuition, as the dream-like state overrides our hypercritical thinking mind, allowing us to accept what we see without our analytical mind getting in the way.

Unlike guided mediation, journey work does not rely being directed where to look; instead, it uses intention and sound to bring us into liminal space where we can receive information from our intuition. Such meditations rely heavily on entrainment, requiring rhythmic music that coaxes the brain into a light-to-medium trance state.

Journey work is a form of divination that combines well with cartomancy, particularly when using one- and three-card draws. Asking our question, we focus our mind on the cards before beginning our journey. The images seen on the cards transform in our mind's eye, and begin to tell a story, as our mind is brought into a deeply relaxed state through the music. When we surface from our journey into the physical world, we remember highlights of our experience.

The key to developing our intuition through journeying is to reexamine the key elements of our experience, by reentering the journey multiple times, going deeper into the message each time. In this way we are thinking like detectives, examining the clue from every angle until it has revealed all the information it holds. The key to getting the most out of an intuitive journey is to make return trips!

Music is a key factor to journey work, as it is the vehicle our psychic mind rides into the astral realm of dreams. Many people explore journey work within group settings—with someone using singing bowls, drums, or vocal toning—often with great results. The problem with this is that such sessions are usually led by someone who has designed their own working for the music, making it difficult to use it for a cartomancy journey. Those who want to practice more regularly can do

Thinking Outside the Spread + 147

so with recorded music via apps such as Spotify, YouTube, and Apple Music, making it easy to create a regular practice.

Oracle cards are great for doing personal divination, particularly when it comes to our spiritual development. Decks are like books telling a story, with each card a chapter contributing to the tale being told, much like the Major Arcana. (We'll explore the story of the Major Arcana in much more depth starting on page 154) In fact, the Major Arcana can be used for journeying if you do not have an oracle deck to work with. Each card holds a story of its own, detailed and layered. In this technique we will zoom in on the details that stick out to us, looking for the story told between the layers.

Picking the right music is often the most challenging part. You want to pick something that has a relaxing, trance-inducing rhythm. Binaural beats, singing bowls, and shamanic drumming are good choices. If you like the sound of the human voice, go for music that is in a language you don't understand, as the words will often take our minds astray. One of my favorites is the album *Daudra Dura* by Forndom. Using the same music every time we do journey work helps us slip into trance state quicker and deeper. I have worked with the latter album for years as my primary trance music. Doing so has made it so I can slip into the betwixt and between almost instantly when listening to it. The key is to find something you like that puts you in a deeply relaxed state without putting you to sleep.

I recommend doing this work in sacred space. Journey work divination of this kind is deeply personal; creating ritual around it helps us focus our mind and take our work seriously. You may choose to invite in your spiritual allies to stand witness and help you navigate the journey.

◇◇◇◇◇◇◇◇◇◇

JOURNEY

ONE-CARD JOURNEY

A one-card journey is best done when you have a specific question. If you have multiple oracle decks, choose a deck that shares a story style with

148 ✦ Spreads and Layouts

your question. For this journey focusing on our spiritual path, we will ask the question, "What should I do next on my spiritual path?"

——————————— **You Will Need** ———————————

An oracle deck or the Major Arcana of the tarot, trance-inducing music of your choice, your altar, a white candle, incense, and your Book of Shadows.

1. Sitting in front of your altar, light the candle and incense, and invite your spiritual allies in if you choose.
2. Put on the trance music and shuffle the cards, asking "What should I do next on my spiritual path?" Take a few moments to examine the cards, draw a card, and then close your eyes.
3. Holding the image of the card in your mind, repeat the question silently to yourself, "What should I do next on my spiritual path?" Allow the images in your mind to shift and change. If you struggle to receive information through imagery, remember as much of the card as you can, as the details you remember are important.
4. Spend the length of a song in your journey (approximately five minutes).
5. When you come out of the journey at the end of the song, write down the messages your received in your Book of Shadows.
6. Look at the card again briefly, and then go back into the journey for a second song. This time focus your mind on locating the detail that stood out to you in the first journey.
7. When you have located the item of your interest examine it from all possible directions, looking for clues that reveal further details.
8. Come to the surface again at the end of the song, and write down your new details.

You may go into the same journey as many times as you need. In most cases two or three times is enough.

Thinking Outside the Spread + 149

⋄⋄⋄⋄⋄⋄⋄⋄⋄⋄

JOURNEY
THREE-CARD JOURNEY

For this journey we will focus on the question "What do I need in my life right now?" by drawing three cards: one for the head, one for the heart, and one for the hand. This journey can be adapted to look at any situation that needs a three-part perspective, which is most situations in my opinion. Like the one-card journey we will be going in multiple times to get a clearer view.

──────────────── **You Will Need** ────────────────

An oracle deck or the Major Arcana of the tarot, trance-inducing music of your choice, your altar, a white candle, incense, and your Book of Shadows.

1. Sitting in front of your altar, light the candle and incense, and invite your spiritual allies in if you choose.
2. Put on the trance music and shuffle the cards. Draw your first card and place it in front of you while asking, "What does my head need at this moment?"
3. Draw your second card and place it next to the first while asking, "What does my heart need at this moment?"
4. Draw a third card and place it next to the others, asking, "What does my hand need at this moment?"
5. Take a few moments to look at the cards, taking in as many details as you can.
6. Holding the image of the card in your mind, repeat the question silently to yourself, "What does my head need at this time?" Allow the images in your mind to shift and change. Ask your second question, "What does my heart need at this time?" and your third, "What does my hand need at this time?"

150 ✦ Spreads and Layouts

7. Spend the length of a song in your journey (approximately five minutes).

8. When you come out of the journey at the end of the song, write down the messages you received for all three questions in your Book of Shadows.

9. Look at the cards again briefly, and go back into the journey for a second song. This time focus your mind on locating the details that stood out to you in the first journey. The answers to one question may show up more clearly than another.

10. When you have located the item of your interest examine it from all possible directions, looking for clues that reveal further details.

11. Come to the surface again at the end of the song, and write down your new details.

You may go into the same journey as many times as you need. In most cases two or three times is enough. You may find it easier to ask one question at a time, instead of all three at once. Feel free to make adjustments where you like.

◇◇◇◇◇◇◇◇◇◇

JOURNEY

STORYLINE JOURNEY

Another way to use oracular journey work is to journey through the story as it evolves. To do this we draw cards as we go, letting each one take us deeper into the story. You can use any deck for this journey, but the tarot works best in my opinion.

—————————— **You Will Need** ——————————

A card deck of your choice, trance-inducing music of your choice, your altar, a white candle, incense, and your Book of Shadows.

1. Sitting in front of your altar, light the candle and incense, and invite your spiritual allies in if you choose.

Thinking Outside the Spread + 151

2. Put on the trance music and shuffle the cards. Draw your first card and place it in front of you while asking your first question, "What is my current situation really like?"

3. Holding the image of the card in your mind, repeat the question silently to yourself, "What is my current situation really like?" Allow the images in your mind to shift and change. If you struggle to receive information through imagery, remember as much of the card as you can, as the details you remember are important.

4. When you come out of the journey at the end of the song, write down the messages you received in your Book of Shadows.

5. Look at the card again briefly, and go back into the journey for a second song. This time focus your mind on locating the detail that stood out to you in the first journey.

6. When you have located the item of your interest examine it from all possible directions, looking for clues that reveal further details.

7. Come to the surface again at the end of the song, and write down your new details.

8. Draw your second card, asking "What do you contribute to the story?" Place this card in front of you next to the first.

9. Holding the image of the card in your mind, repeat the question silently to yourself, "What do you contribute to the story?" Allow the images in your mind to shift and change.

10. When you come out of the journey at the end of the song, write down the messages you received in your Book of Shadows.

11. Look at the card again briefly, and go back into the journey for a second song. This time focus your mind on locating the detail that stood out to you in the first journey.

12. When you have located the item of your interest examine it from all possible directions, looking for clues that reveal further details.

13. Come to the surface again at the end of the song, and write down your new details.

14. Repeat the purpose a third time, asking "What do you contribute to the story?"

15. Holding the image of the card in your mind, repeat the question silently to yourself, "What do you contribute to the story?" Allow the images in your mind to shift and change.
16. When you come out of the journey at the end of the song, write down the messages you received in your Book of Shadows.
17. Look at the card again briefly, and go back into the journey for a second song. This time focus your mind on locating the detail that stood out to you in the first journey.
18. When you have located the item of your interest examine it from all possible directions, looking for clues that reveal further details.

You can use this method of journey work with any spread. Working with the cards in this manner helps us build personal memories around the cards, making it easier for cards to trigger stories in our mind.

THE TAROT

THE CHARIOT.   DEATH.   THE EMPEROR.   THE EMPRESS.   THE FOOL.   THE HERMIT.   THE HIEROPHANT.   JUDGEMENT.

The Major Arcana

The Major Arcana are the trump cards of the tarot, representing bigger issues that carry more force around them. While the Minor Arcana are broken into four suits that each contain Court cards and number cards much like playing cards, the twenty-two Major Arcana cards have stand-alone meanings that are more potent than the Minor Arcana cards. When a reading features many Major Arcana cards, the reader can expect situations surrounding the querent will be more intricate; usually many hands are affecting the outcome, and changing the path will be more challenging.

When I am doing a reading, I weave stories that are similar in nature to the querent's situation, personalizing the experience so that it is easier to remember. As we have mentioned, in cartomancy images are used to trigger the mind of the psychic that they may retrieve information through supernatural means. The images on the card are interpreted through the psychic's personal experiences and the knowledge they have obtained through study, which in turn translates into the information relative to the situation. The more personal experiences we have with a card, the broader our viewpoint.

Therefore, it is helpful when building a relationship with the tarot to explore each card individually, moving through them as personal stories. This journey begins with the Fool and evolves through the Major Arcana, creating memories that—like images of old friends—

trigger stories in our memory that are relevant to our reading. In this chapter I'll provide information that will serve as a starting point for your personal journey. We'll explore each card of the Major Arcana in depth: its attributes and imagery, what it might mean when it comes up in a reading, and some of the details that might stand out and why.

In addition, I have provided twenty-two guided meditations on the Fool's journey. Take the time you need moving through Major Arcana, making sure to document your experience as you go. Much like adventurers setting out on the trail, this journey will have unexpected obstacles and brilliant treasures, as discovering ourself is one of the most interesting things we can do! The journeys are meant to be done in order, as each prepares you for the next. *The bold are recommended to do one journey a day for the next twenty-two days, as such dedicated practice creates an energetic familiarity much like an attunement.*

Some people can journey simply by reading along with and breathing deep, but most people need a bit more. Most phones have a voice recorder app already installed. Hit record and read the journeys in a slow, even pace. It is helpful to take a few moments to study the card before beginning your journey! When you are finished find a comfortable spot, close your eyes, and guide yourself through the cards.

If you find that you fall asleep during guided meditation, I suggest sitting instead of lying down.

The Major Arcana in many ways represents the journey of one's soul, the sacred pilgrimage of development that the seeker must journey. In fact, we can use the path of the Major Arcana in our personal journey work as meditation tools for our personal development. This is a great practice for anyone really wanting to develop a deeper understanding of themselves and the cards, as utilizing them as tool to understand our personal journey helps us remember them more intimately. If you are choosing to do this, I suggest meditating on the Major Arcana cards in order, ideally choosing one to work with for a week, making sure to jot down our experience in our Book of Shadows.

✦ The Fool ✦

0. The Fool is generally depicted through the image of a young, carefree person stepping off the edge of a cliff. With a rucksack slung over their shoulder, and their dog in tow, the Fool shows us that the journey has begun! Dualistic in nature—representing both the beginner's mind and the resting consciousness of the wise—the Fool reminds us of the bravery and faith needed to make the first steps. The Fool being numbered "0" allows for the card to be placed at either the beginning or the end of the Major Arcana, implying the secret all adepts know: what we do

out of sheer gumption in the beginning is the same thing we naturally do through experience.

To the beginner, the Fool is the invitation to begin, regardless of the fears that may threaten to hold us back. To the adept, the Fool is the quantum ignition card, reminding us that we are co-creators of our own reality and that we must believe in our dreams for them to manifest. Regardless of whether the querent is new to their path or highly experienced, when the Fool shows up in readings it is a reminder that the path must be navigated with faith—believing in oneself, higher powers, and the magic of creation.

When encountering the Fool in a reading, whether for yourself or others, it is important to note what stands out about the card upon first viewing. Do you feel excited or intimidated by the action taken by the Fool? Which did you notice first: his bag filled with provisions or the daunting cliff? Did you notice his companion, the dog, when looking at the card, or did you overlook it entirely? Remember we must look with the eyes of a storyteller; we are seeking clues, which means all details that stand out to us are relevant!

What did you notice?

The Cliff. Representing the unknown, noticing this first means the querent will most likely have to go through the situation without a guarantee of the outcome.

The Bag. Representing being prepared with the bare necessities—provisions and a basic map, perhaps written in crayon or some archaic script—this shows that while the querent is facing unknown factors, they do so with the vital bits necessary to begin the endeavor.

The Dog (Animal Companion). This shows that the querent is not alone, that they will have support along their path.

The Vast Expanse. Noticing the background first, with its high peaks and great openness, shows us that the journey will be long, with much distance covered (emotionally, physically, or spiritually).

158 ✦ The Tarot

MEDITATION
THE FOOL

Take a few moments before closing your eyes to look at the card in front of you, allowing yourself to take in as many details as you can. Close your eyes and bring your attention to your breathing. Focus on your inhalation and exhalation as they become balanced and rhythmic, inhaling and exhaling evenly through the nose.

Continuing to breathe deeply, imagine you are outside on a beautiful sunny day. The sun is warm on your back and you feel buoyant, as if lighter with every breath. You are preparing to set off on a journey of self-discovery. You have prepared a small bag for the journey holding items you will need along your path. Open the bag and look inside.

Take a few breaths here, allowing your mind to focus on the items you are taking on your journey. Examine the items one by one, making note of whether they are something you own in the waking world or something you will need to collect. (Pause for a few breaths.)

Placing the items back in the bag, you swing it over your shoulder, and call out to your companion: the animal spirit that will accompany you on your journey. Make note of what animal appears for you. Is it an animal, a bird, or insect? Does the animal feel familiar to you? Have you worked with this animal spirit before? (Pause for a few breaths.)

Focusing your mind, you notice you are standing on a groomed garden path, one created by stories of your past. You know that must leave the garden and that your journey will require bravery, and faith. You pick a rose from the garden and start down the path, your animal companion following along behind you.

Looking at the vista you see vast mountains, and you feel a deep surge of excitement. The sun is still high in the sky, and your steps are light. Traveling with a light and open heart you soon find yourself at the edge of a cliff. As you turn and look back the path behind you has disappeared. To continue your journey, you must progress from here! How do you prog-

The Major Arcana ✦ 159

ress? Do you walk boldly off the cliff? Do you look for a way down? Pause for a few breaths and make your decision!

You make your way down to the valley below, either by jumping or climbing down. Having completed this quest, you are rewarded with a pentacle, a sword, a cup, and a wand. Place the items in your bag and return to your breath.

Continuing to focus on your breath, focus your mind on your physical body, wiggling your toes and fingers, moving your consciousness back into your physical form with every movement. Open your eyes and take a few moments to record your experience.

✦ The Magician ✦

I. The Magician holds the tools of empowerment necessary to continue the journey of self-discovery. Whether using the cards in divination or as a meditative tool for personal growth, the Magician shows us we are no longer a beginner; we have skills and tools. Looking at the Magician we see his confidence and dedication. Where the Fool gave us the courage and faith to begin our journey without much knowledge of the road ahead, the Magician is a skilled manipulator who knows the path will be filled with obstacles and opportunities and therefore does a bit of planning to make the process easier.

When looking at the symbolism of the Magician card we see he has implements of each of the four Minor Arcana suits—Pentacles, Cups, Wands, and Swords—on the table before him. His hands are often stretched out before him with one hand facing the sky and the other facing the Earth, mimicking the old saying "As above, so below," showing his connection to God/Goddess/Universe. He is depicted in the act of performing magic (sacred activation/prayer), in which he is standing before the powers that be saying, "I am worthy of this venture, and I call upon my tools to help make it so!"

One of the things I love best about the Magician is his connection with infinity. The lemniscate (infinity symbol) represents his ability to move between timelines, looking into the past and future for answers as well as the present. He exists not only in his current incarnation but traverses his reality through multiple lifetimes and dimensions with an awareness that his answers may not come from this moment alone. This is an important lesson when using the tarot for divination, as we must let go of our belief that the future is unknown or that the past is behind us to truly see—for in truth life is a woven thing of memories, dreams, and active moments. When we begin to see this, we—like the Magician—will be ready to take our place at the altar of life as co-creators.

With co-creation in mind, I often relate the Magician to the saying "What we believe we create!" Now that may seem like a glossy, glitter-coated statement, but what it really means is that with com-

mitted effort and a strong intentional mindset we can accomplish our goals. Real magic is not waving a magic wand over something and saying "abracadabra"—and all our problems are gone. Real magic is work, dedication, and knowing how to use your tools. The Magician requires us to hold a belief that you are capable of the work ahead.

If the Magician is showing up for you in your readings it is most likely that you are being asked to gather your tools, get serious about the goals in front of you, and see yourself as the bridge between heaven and Earth who is here to make manifest those dreams. Note that the Magician is where we set our intentions and call upon our Gods and ancestors to support us. It is the intentional beginning of our journey; where we intuitively stepped onto the path as the Fool, the Magician is where we begin the creation of our map. Stand in your power, recognize it, and see yourself as the co-creator you are. The work ahead of you may be hard, but you have the tools and the inner power, so step forward as a co-creator and get to work!

What did you notice?

The Lemniscate. This symbol represents no-time/no-space, the existence of past, present, and future simultaneously. In a reading it is a reminder that you have done this before in another incarnation, lifetime, the past, or even in the future.

The Magician's Arms. One hand extended to heaven and one pointing down to the Earth show the importance of calling in our guides, deities, and ancestors in our working.

The Tools. Make note of how you feel upon seeing them. If you are filled with trepidation, it may be a reminder to gather your tools, whereas feeling calm upon seeing them is a reminder you have what you need to proceed.

The Foliage. The foliage of the Magician card is flourishing, showing success and ease. Noticing it first is a sign that the endeavor you are undertaking will be fruitful.

162 ✦ The Tarot

◇◇◇◇◇◇◇◇◇◇◇◇

MEDITATION
THE MAGICIAN

Take a few moments before closing your eyes to look at the card in front of you, allowing yourself to take in as many details as you can. Close your eyes and bring your attention to your breathing. Focus on your inhalation and exhalation as they become balanced and rhythmic, inhaling and exhaling evenly through the nose.

Continuing to breathe deeply, imagine you are outside on a beautiful sunny day. The sun is warm on your back and you feel buoyant, as if lighter with every breath. Focusing your mind, you find yourself in a familiar garden, your garden, the garden you picked the rose from, your garden! As you look around you see an altar surrounded by rose bushes and lilies. Notice any details of the garden that stand out to you. (Pause here for a few breaths.)

Looking down at yourself you notice that you are dressed for ceremony in robes and a shawl, with a circlet upon your head. You step up to the altar and open your bag, the bag you carried as the fool. You pull out a chalice, a metal pentacle, a long sword, and a wooden wand. You may also place on the altar any personal items found in the bag. (Pause here for a few breaths.)

Another item on the altar catches your eyes. A cylindrical white wand, which is tapered on both ends. Holding it, you feel power surge through you. You realize that the wand is a conduit for energy. You turn it over and examine it, noting what it is made of, or whether there is an inscription.

Holding the white wand in your right hand you raise it to the sky, and you instinctively drop your left hand. With one hand reaching to the sky, and the other pointing to the Earth, you say "As above, so below!" You feel a surge of energy run through you as you become the conduit between the heavens and the Earth.

Continuing to breathe, focus on your crown as you begin to feel energy moving through your body. There you see a glowing lemniscate—the infinity symbol—illuminated above your head, and you recognize that you are standing in no-time, no-space. This is your initiation, showing you have the tools and skills needed to continue. Stay in this place for a few moments, breathing rhythmically.

Continuing to focus on your breath, focus your mind on your physical body, wiggling your toes and fingers, moving your consciousness back into your physical form with every movement. Open your eyes and take a few moments to record your experience.

✦ The High Priestess ✦

II. The High Priestess asks us to move through our life thoughtfully, reflecting on the knowledge our intuition brings to us. This is a powerful feminine card embodying the receptive knowledge we all have within us, and the need to prepare our body to use the knowledge. She

reminds us that we must live our life consciously, contemplating events and ideas as they are presented to us in a calm, thoughtful manner. She asks us to see ourselves as holy and to engage with the world around us as if all life is sacred. She recognizes that the world around her is much more complicated and layered than it appears, and so are the obstacles and inconveniences that appear on her path. Everything holds an opportunity to connect more deeply with oneself and divine consciousness.

She does not take things at face value; instead, she questions and meditates knowing that things are not always as they seem and that every story has a backstory that plays into the main. In the process of seeking enlightenment, she must become softer, more fluid, and open to otherworldly contact. She desires an understanding of any situation that she may know it in its truest fashion and make her decisions from a place of clarity. Often the High Priestess can seem aloof, as if she is beyond the problems of others; in truth, she has learned to empathically protect herself, so that she may be of service to others without drowning in the emotions of others.

The High Priestess represents the feminine in the singular, uncoupled form. This does not mean she cannot/will not/does not have an intimate relationship; it more accurately refers to the need to show herself as both an individual and the figure of authority for a much higher calling.

When the High Priestess shows up in a reading, she is asking us to embrace our higher self, so that we can become thoughtful in our actions and deeds. It is a time to work on our composure and boundaries that we may reinforce our ability to stay balanced and grounded while simultaneously opening our consciousness to receive more. This is a tricky thing, as often people feel overwhelmed when their psychic knowledge begins to open, as they are bombarded by emotions and knowledge that do not necessarily belong to them. The High Priestess reminds us that through ritual and repetitive practice we can strengthen our inner being and learn to navigate the flow of knowledge with grace. She asks us to step back from the situation and examine it from a higher perspective, and most of all she shows us that we are holy in our own right!

The Major Arcana ✦ 165

We must honor and value ourselves if we are to evolve. We must strengthen our boundaries and acknowledge that we are co-creators of our reality. Where the Fool gave us the courage and faith to step onto the path, and the Magician showed us we had gathered the tools to truly begin, the High Priestess reminds us we are worthy of the path!

What did you notice?

Ceremonial Dress and Composure. Robed, crowned, and adorned with holy symbols, the ceremonial clothing of the High Priestess represents the need to see our endeavors as sacred, worth preparing ourselves for, and the need to interact with our temple (body) as a sacred thing. Holding herself with the strength of one who knows themselves and their importance, letting no judgment pass her visage, the High Priestess's composure reminds us to remain centered and calm, empowered in the knowing of who we truly are.

The Pomegranates. Often associated with the underworld, the land of the dead, the pomegranates represent the ability of the querent to think deeply and enter the unseen world. Having this image catch your gaze first is a reminder to look beyond the obvious, and often it is a reminder that the querent perceives reality beyond the seen realms.

The Black and White Columns. These remind us of the duality of the situation: the negative and positive, magical and mundane, projective and receptive. If this image catches your eye first, you must remember that there are two sides to every story.

Holy Documents. The High Priestess is seen holding the Torah, which is a religious document sacred to the Hebrew people. The type of religious document held by the High Priestess may change between decks, but the symbolism is the same. It represents the written agreements of religion and spirituality, showing that the High Priestess follows a well-worn path with rules and procedures. Seeing this first suggests that the querent may, like the High Priestess, need to follow a structured path to progress.

166 ✦ The Tarot

MEDITATION
THE HIGH PRIESTESS

Take a few moments before closing your eyes to look at the card in front of you, allowing yourself to take in as many details as you can. Close your eyes and bring your attention to your breathing. Focus on your inhalation and exhalation as they become balanced and rhythmic, inhaling and exhaling evenly through the nose.

Continuing to breathe deeply, imagine you are sitting on a small platform; on one side of you is a black pillar, and on the other side a white one. The pillars are ancient and marking the entrance to the temple! You are the priestess, dressed accordingly in a ritual gown. Upon your head you wear a triple-goddess crown, and there is a crescent at your feet, recognition of your right to be seated upon the dais. Examine your dress, noticing the details of your gown and the jewelry you wear. (Pause here for a few breaths.)

You are the High Priestess dedicated in your study. You have found yourself here after your initiation as the Magician, proving that you are capable of being a bridge between the heavens and the Earth. As High Priestess you have come to gain knowledge, to deepen your understanding of reality.

Upon your lap you hold mystical scrolls, filled with ancient magic. An equal-distance cross lies upon your chest: a mark of balance among the four elements of Earth, Air, Fire, and Water. Behind you lies a tapestry of pomegranates marking your journey into the betwixt and between. Like Persephone, your path will take you into the world of spirit. (Pause here for a few breaths.)

You are between the worlds. You are the High Priestess, ready and open to the messages of the universe. You are the seeker, and the dedicated, on your path to a higher consciousness. You are attuned to the mysteries, having made the leap of faith as the Fool and channeled universal energy from the heavens as the Magician. You are the embodiment of mystery, sensuality, and intuition. Open yourself to receiving messages from the divine. Stay in this place for a few moments, breathing rhythmically.

Continuing to focus on your breath, focus your mind on your physical body, wiggling your toes and fingers, moving your consciousness back into your physical form with every movement. Open your eyes and take a few moments to record your experience.

✦ The Empress ✦

III. The Empress represents the fertile seed of femininity. She is potent and ripe, abundant, and juicy, a soon-to-be mother carrying the glowing light of new life. The Empress represents potential and abundance, for she sits upon her throne with all of the symbols of new life surrounding her. She is the Goddess as Mother, and she is the very land itself. Three is the number of creation, something the Empress clearly represents with full belly and cornucopia of abundance!

168 ✦ The Tarot

The journey through the Major Arcana to this point has led us from our brave beginnings as the Fool, who walked off the cliff believing the path would open before him, through the incarnation of the Magician, gathering our tools, and the lessons of composure and dedication gifted to us by the High Priestess. Now as the Empress we are fertile and abundant, filled with potential.

The fertility of the Empress is not limited to human fecundity, although it is often a card that comes up when someone is pregnant or soon to be. Instead, it represents fertility on the broader spectrum, marking potential and abundance in all forms. The reader must determine how they feel that fertility will unfold, something easiest done by taking in the story of the cards surrounding the Empress into the reading.

I love the potential the Empress represents, as she is a container of growth: literally as a pregnant mother, and figuratively as she is often surrounded by symbols of fertility and abundance. In the latter form, she can be a representative of land or project as well as human potential. When she shows up in a reading, we must ask these questions, "What is being created?" "Who is the querent becoming?" and "What is being creating with this fertile, juicy soup inside of them?"

Another form the Empress takes on is that of sovereign leader, for she is the queen of queens! Carrying the creative force of the universe, she is the mother of nations, communities, and family. She holds space with regal grace, knowing that she must nurture and guide those in her charge. Often those drawn to community leadership will find themselves connecting with the Empress card, as they recognize that their personal fertility and spark is best used in service to the greater good. The best part of this is the Empress does so without sacrificing herself. She is well cared for and relaxed, taking responsibility without overwhelming herself; she knows her own well-being is paramount to her ability to be of service.

If the Empress shows up in a reading, ask yourself what projects you are dedicating yourself to, and if you are caring for yourself properly. The Empress is a sacred vessel of potential, and as an aspect of self she

The Major Arcana + 169

shows us that we are carrying that spark; we have the potential inside us to accomplish our goals. Know yourself, do not be afraid of your potential, give over to the idea that your light is bright enough to illuminate your dreams and that of others. The Empress is a team player, she is the mother after all, and being so she knows that supporting her community supports her own potential.

Where the High Priestess serves the community from a point of aloofness—seeing herself as separate or individual—the Empress does so in partnership, for she is generally seen as having a partner with whom she shares rulership. In this form, the Empress represents the empowered feminine who has moved beyond needing solitude to hold herself so, making her a representative of the divine feminine in a healthy intimate relationship (hence the pregnant belly). For many, she shows that they have found the inner strength they needed in the High Priestess and are now ready to share the world with another.

What did you notice?

The Pregnant Belly. If you get a strong hit on the pregnant belly of the Empress, this can be an indicator of a current or soon-to-be pregnancy. As a rule, it is not good to just blurt that out to folks as it can be a sensitive topic, and if you are new to tarot or unsure of your skills it is not an area you want to be wrong. Instead, you may say something like, "I see fertility around you, and a high likelihood of pregnancy." If you are not wanting to get pregnant currently, there is no room for error (don't forget your birth control). It is important to note that the strong attraction to the belly of the Empress can also be referring to the fertility and birth of a project, so feel into it. Test your intuition through body dowsing (or with a pendulum).

Stars and Pomegranates. The pomegranates of the Empress's dress—like those of the backdrop behind the High Priestess—represent the querent's the ability to enter other dimensions of reality, particularly that of the dead. The stars represent the heavens, connecting her to both the underworld and the celestial realms. If you are strongly

170   ✦   The Tarot

drawn to this imagery in a reading, note that the connection to the other realms is important. Combining this with the pregnant belly, infused with the light of life, the card can be interpreted as being fully connected to the realms of life and death and infused with the potency of light! Creation waiting to happen . . .

Venus and Heart Shield. The symbol of the Goddess (female sign) inside a heart-shaped shield beside the Empress is symbolic of love, fertility, and relationship. Being drawn to this symbol often indicates an intimate relationship, as the Empress is a strong person in a healthy relationship.

Golden Wheat and Cornucopia. Noticing the foreground and background of the Empress card we see harvest in its full glory: golden wheat and fruitful abundance. Noticing this in a reading is an indicator that the results of hard work will pay off, that abundance surrounds the querent or question at hand.

◇◇◇◇◇◇◇◇◇◇◇◇

MEDITATION
THE EMPRESS

Take a few moments before closing your eyes to look at the card in front of you, allowing yourself to take in as many details as you can. Close your eyes and bring your attention to your breathing. Focus on your inhalation and exhalation as they become balanced and rhythmic, inhaling and exhaling evenly through the nose.

Continuing to breathe deeply, imagine you are seated on a cushioned throne in your garden. The same garden you started your journey from as the Fool, and channeled the heavens from as the Magician. It is rich now with wheat and bountiful fruit trees. Like your garden you are radiant in your beauty. Luminous and ethereal you are ripe with fertility; creative energy flows from you like the stream you sit next to.

The stream is filled with the knowledge of the universe accessed through the intuitive mind. Trained and initiated as the High Priestess, you

The Major Arcana ✦ 171

know how to listen to your intuition. Take a few moments here to breathe and receive messages. (Pause here for a few breaths.)

A crown of twelve stars rests upon your head, one for each month of the year. As Empress you are Gaia, Mother Nature, Queen of all growing things. The phallic scepter you hold in your hand shows your life-giving power and the gentle confidence you rule from. A heart embossed with the symbol of Venus; you are the embodiment of love! Take a few moments to feel the bounty of the Earth and your connection to it.

What once was held between the gateway of betwixt and between for the High Priestess you now embody as the Empress! You are the gateway between life and death, the fertile mother passing souls from spirit into life. Imagine, like the Empress, creativity and life force flows from you. What you touch grows and prospers. What does that creative force look like? Where does fertility take root in your life? How does it manifest? (Pause here for a few breaths.)

Continuing to focus on your breath, focus your mind on your physical body, wiggling your toes and fingers, moving your consciousness back into your physical form with every movement. Open your eyes and take a few moments to record your experience.

✦ The Emperor ✦

IV. The Emperor is more than a king; he is the king of kings, ruler of all! He is in control and capable of managing his vast world. Having followed the road before him, he has braved the unknown, stepping boldly off the cliff as the Fool, gathered his tools as the Magician, stepped into his own sacred self as the High Priestess, and gathered his bounty as the Empress. Now as Emperor he must learn to navigate his own sovereignty and truly become ruler of his own path.

To many, the Emperor can come across as rigid, as in most cards he is seen armored with an ankh scepter in one hand, representing eternal life, and a globe in the other, representing domination. His background is often stark, and his body language speaks of the ability to move suddenly if need be. He oozes command!

The Emperor is in control. He has a quick mind and a broad vision allowing him to take on the world (or his world at least). Often seen as warlike or willing to engage in battle, the Emperor is a force to be reckoned with, one that seldom needs to use his power directly as knowledge of his power precedes him. He can accomplish great plans and is ready to sacrifice in order to do so.

The Emperor is the embodiment of discipline, self-control, and stability. While it is true that he can be rigid and controlling, it is important to remember that such things lie within the Emperor's shadow, not in his true light. *Duality is a key component to all things; the tarot is no exception, which is one of the reasons it's so important to develop your psychic knowledge.*

The Major Arcana ✦ 173

When the Emperor shows up as a representative of the querent it is often to remind them that they need to recognize their own *sovereignty*, which means "the authority to self-govern, supreme power or authority." But what does it mean to self-govern? Can we truly oversee our own boundaries? How can working with the Emperor help us do so? What stories does he have to share? While we cannot truly self-govern, as we all must obey the laws of the land, the Emperor reminds us that we must honor ourselves and our own boundaries as much as we honor those of others. He speaks of self-importance and self-governance. The Emperor holds his position because he has great discipline, recognizes his boundaries, and is willing to work hard for the things he believes in. He is not a spoiled brat who inherited the crown from his daddy; instead, he is a strategic mastermind who landed upon his throne through his own doing. If he shows up as a representative of where we are on our path we must be prepared to work hard, stay focused, and stand up for what we believe in, for it is through the development of structure, repetition, and boldness that we will achieve our goals.

If the Emperor shows up in a reading it is important to ask how honor and sovereignty can be found. Has a structured plan been created? Have clear boundaries been set? Are those boundaries enforced? Is there repetition and discipline in the work involved? These are the requirements of the Emperor.

What did you notice?

Armor, Robes, and Crown. Armor represents protection, and the Emperor's sure is fine! Noticing the armor is a sign that there is a solid plan involved, one that shows the querent or question has a strong defense. The robes covering the Emperor are of the finest quality and in the richest of colors, showing that he is a person of authority. His crown is strong and solid showing he has "a good head on his shoulders" (strong mind); the golden color shows his mind holds arcane knowledge or illumination.

The Ankh and Sphere. As I said above, the ankh is a representation

174 ✦ The Tarot

of eternal life and the sphere a sign of dominion. These symbols connect the Emperor with the sovereignty of the querent on a soul level, showing that such skills come to them naturally, and in the case of a situation, it shows that the very essence of the project or situation is going to have solidly set rules.

The Rams. Representing strength, determination, and male virility, the ram is symbolic of the offensive nature of masculine leadership. Masculine can be determined as "the manly man," or as the projective energy, straightforward approach, depending on the context.

The Throne and Background. The Emperor's throne is carved of stone, and his background is the chiseled remains of industrialization and progress. Being drawn to this imagery shows that the querent did not get into the situation they are in haphazardly. Situationally it shows that hard work and overcoming the obstacles created the situation.

◇◇◇◇◇◇◇◇◇◇◇◇

MEDITATION

THE EMPEROR

Take a few moments before closing your eyes to look at the card in front of you, allowing yourself to take in as many details as you can. Close your eyes and bring your attention to your breathing. Focus on your inhalation and exhalation as they become balanced and rhythmic, inhaling and exhaling evenly through the nose.

Continuing to breathe deeply, imagine you are sitting upon a stone throne adorned with rams: the symbol of Aries, Greek god of war. Your body is heavily armored, and your presence radiates power. Red velvet cloaks your shoulders, a sign to the world showing the power of your will and passion. Sit with your power for a moment, examine your ego, look at your rage. Do you hold grudges? Do you seek revenge? How do you carry power? (Pause here for a few breaths.)

In your right hand you hold an ankh, symbol of reincarnation and eternal

The Major Arcana + 175

life, a sign of your divine self, and in your left hand you hold a globe symbolizing your power over the world and your ability to influence outcomes. You have earned your place here, having begun your journey boldly as the Fool, proven yourself worthy of channeling divine energy as the Magician, passed the right of passage as the High Priestess, and embodied life-giving force as the Empress. Now you wield power!

Take a few moments to examine the balance of power in your life. Are there areas that you are in full control? Do you use that control with authority? Are you fair and balanced? Does your ego hold you back or do you dominate others? Are there places where you feel disempowered, in need of the Emperor's strength? Do you feel outside forces are controlling your life? Take a moment to sit with your feelings around authority, recognizing that the Emperor represents the highest secular power in life.

Bringing your consciousness back to your throne, and how it feels to sit upon it, allow yourself to feel the power and authority that you have over your life in this form. Notice the protection the armor offers you; imagine that armor being absorbed into your body like a protective shield. Feel the crown that rests upon your head; recognize it as a sign that you have earned this seat, and with it comes a responsibility to sit on your throne with fairness.

Continuing to focus on your breath, focus your mind on your physical body, wiggling your toes and fingers, moving your consciousness back into your physical form with every movement. Open your eyes and take a few moments to record your experience.

+ The Hierophant +

V. The Hierophant is a card of tradition, rules, and law, thick with religious teachings and a feeling of control. In truth, this is a card I have struggled with on a personal level, as I am not a fan of heavy regulations, particularly when it comes to what I should think and believe. The image of the card often shows a priest sitting above his followers, dressed richly in the vestments of his religion, crowned to show he is closer to God than those who kneel beneath him, visually demanding that we heed his word.

The Hierophant represents the societal view of right and wrong, and a need to follow the path as instructed. It is a card filled with judgment and a feeling of needing to earn wisdom and God's good grace.

I admit to being a bit roguish and acknowledge that my own disdain of religious overlords can be tainting my opinion of this card. I often feel the Hierophant shows up in readings as a representative of society's expectations, which can be either good or bad depending on the society and one's ability and desire to blend with it. In short, the Hierophant is the face of societal norms, particularly when it refers to religion and ethics.

In the beginning of my working with the tarot, I had only the Rider-Waite deck, which depicts the Hierophant in his heavy robes and

crown, sitting upon a dais. This image was cumbersome and restrictive to me, representing all the reasons church did not work for me. But as my exploration of the tarot continued, I met other images of the Hierophant, in which the image of High Priest wore the face of Druid, shaman, and mystic. I began to understand that this card was malleable, and the rules of engagement that are enforced through spiritual belief change according to the culture and community being represented.

The Hierophant is a representative of our collective view of God's will; the changing of his robes and spiritual adornment between card styles echoes the many ways we approach the divine. He is the overseer of tradition and the teacher of religious and cultural norms, and our relationship with him depends on how well we fit into a particular society. If he is showing up in readings for you, he is most likely asking that you examine your connection with your community and whether the belief system you surround yourself with is right for you. It is important when working with the Hierophant to ask yourself if the message he is sharing feels restrictive or more like advice on how to follow the path.

I used to be triggered by the way the Hierophant sat above his followers in what looks like a holier-than-thou position: a view tainted by my own personal beliefs of organized religion, no doubt. But then I started thinking about him as a mystic and realized that many of the things the Hierophant experiences in his personal search for God are truly above the comprehension of most people. Like the shaman, he is a voyager of time and space, both of this world and not. His station as a spiritual leader is one earned through his experiences in the unseen world of spirit, and through such his vision is greater. With this alternate view of the Hierophant as a wyrd mystic, navigating the physical and spiritual world, I now see that his appearance may also be a sign to go deeper, asking that I look between the lines and find the understanding behind societal rules and norms. He knows that not everyone can understand the greater workings of the universe and that rules are meant to keep the simpler folk safe. He reminds me that people often make judgments based on what they can understand and that those of

178 + The Tarot

us who see far beyond the veil must learn to communicate in a way that is understood by those with less knowledge.

I invite you to explore this side of the Hierophant. Look at the card from his perspective, and explore not only what he looks like and represents to others, sitting there on his throne of godliness, but who he is! See yourself as the Hierophant: What would such a position require of you? What goes on inside the mind of such a person? What does it mean to be an intermediary of God/Goddess/Universe?

What did you notice?

The Hierophant's Position. The Hierophant sitting on a dais above his partitioners is representative of authority and guidance. When drawn in by this imagery, make sure to ask yourself if the card feels repressive or helpful.

The Keys. The crossed keys below the Hierophant's feet are representative of their access-granting capability. Symbolically keys in general grant us access to doorways, whether they be physical, emotional, or spiritual. As the Hierophant is a religious figure, noting the keys in this card shows that the querent may gain access to that which they seek through following the rules and guidance of their higher selves, religious leaders, deities, and spiritual allies.

The Columns. Much like the columns seen in the High Priestess card, the columns the Hierophant sits between show the forces that influence his decisions, in this case it is often seen as law and freedom, or obedience and disobedience.

Crown and Scepter. The Hierophant's crown (often golden and triple layered) and scepter are both symbolic of his station. The crown shows he is close to God, enlightened, and holds rulership of God's domain in the physical world. The scepter shows he rules over the multiple levels of God's domain; he is often seen as the ruler, through militant force, of the realms of angels and archangels. There is a powerful force behind the card, which may or may not be in the querent's favor.

MEDITATION
THE HIEROPHANT

Take a few moments before closing your eyes to look at the card in front of you, allowing yourself to take in as many details as you can. Close your eyes and bring your attention to your breathing. Focus on your inhalation and exhalation as they become balanced and rhythmic, inhaling and exhaling evenly through the nose.

Continuing to breathe deeply, imagine you are sitting upon a platform much like you were as the High Priestess. You are dressed in heavy, red robes adorned with religious signs. You are a member of the clergy, with petitioners kneeling at your feet, looking to you for guidance. Feel the responsibility of the office you hold, the soul-guiding authority that others look to you for. Examine how this plays out in your life, the people and situations that rely on you for guidance. How does the mantle of wisdom feel upon your shoulders? (Pause here for a few breaths.)

Upon your head rests an ornate three-tiered crown. The layers of the crown refer to the three realms of knowledge understood by the Hierophant: the common knowledge of everyday thinking, the deep knowledge known on a soul level, and the unexplained wisdom that comes from contact with God/Goddess/universal consciousness. Feel the heaviness of the crown; weigh your wisdom against the weight of the crown, determining how fit you are to wear it. Take a few breaths here as you do.

Your right hand is raised with two fingers pointing toward the heavens and two toward the Earth in the form of a blessing. As the Hierophant you channel celestial energy, siphoning it through your body from skyward raised hand to the petitioners at your feet, your training as the Magician making you a powerful conduit.

Feel the energy move through you, and imagine you are bestowing blessings on those who are in need. In your left hand you hold a golden staff, which you recognize as a sign of authority. You are the representative of godly power and authority to the petitioners, a judger of souls, something

180 + The Tarot

reinforced by the keys to heaven that are just below your feet. Take a few moments to sit with that. Breathe deep, and sit with the heaviness of the role, the responsibility that comes with the crown of wisdom. (Pause here for a few breaths.)

You began your journey as the Fool bravely leaving your garden in search of self-knowing. Becoming the Magician you were attuned to divine power, a sign that you are worthy and ready for growth. As the High Priestess you were initiated into the intuitive arts, piercing the veil between the worlds that you may see into the unknown. Initiation led to fruitfulness and abundance through the feminine power of the Empress. As the Emperor you took command and created structure, leading to this moment where, as the Hierophant, you share your wisdom with others, guiding them on their soul-level journey. Take a few moments here thinking about the ways you lead others, and how you could do that job better.

Continuing to focus on your breath, focus your mind on your physical body, wiggling your toes and fingers, moving your consciousness back into your physical form with every movement. Open your eyes and take a few moments to record your experience.

+ The Lovers +

VI. The Lovers is a swoon-worthy card, filled with intimate connection that has the potential to go deeper than our libido. While the Lovers is a passion-filled card it is also one of emotional connection and expansion of consciousness. It speaks of relationships that elevate our minds and push us into expanded consciousness.

In many decks we see this potential for elevated consciousness represented by the angel in the background. In such images, the man representing ordinary consciousness is looking at the woman who represents the subconscious, who in turn looks to the angel representing our superconscious or higher self. The snake in the apple tree and burning bush are reminders of the wisdom and temptation that lies within the complexity of such relationships.

The Lovers ask people to examine their relationship's full potential, seeing not only communication but sexual intimacy as a way of expanding consciousness. Any of you who have had the fortune of having an extended sexual orgasm will know exactly what I am talking about, as the ecstatic state it creates is often a gateway to higher consciousness, for in such moments our kundalini is awakened and we are able to perceive situations with greater clarity and understanding. While it is not a controlled state of questions asked and answered, it is often one in which a deeper understanding of oneself and psychic abilities can be perceived.

While most people getting a reading will experience the Lovers in their more mundane form—speaking of the connection between intimate partners and how it can help them to grow and expand as a

182   ✦   The Tarot

person—there are those for whom the card is referring to spiritual evolution and the ability to use our sexual potential as a tool to do so. In this latter form, the partner does not necessarily need to be another person; it may instead refer to our multifaceted self or the spirits we work with, and our ability to reach higher consciousness through an ecstatic state. *Sex is not the only way to reach an ecstatic state: dance, breathwork, yoga, and vocal toning are some of the other ways such a state can be achieved.*

When working with the Lovers as part of our soul evolution, following the path of the Major Arcana, we have reached a point in which our growth of consciousness has asked us to explore temptation. It asks us to harness our potential and move beyond carnal lust, moving beyond our loins so that we may truly embrace our lover. This means stepping fully and deeply into a relationship, whether it be for the short-term or long-term, to embrace the experience consciously that we may bring our mind and soul into the experience of lovemaking and the foundational structure of how we live our lives. In such acts we are not required to be "in love" with someone, but it is necessary to trust them and care for them. In truth, that's pretty good advice in general. If we wouldn't trust the person to be in our home without us being there, we may not want to let them into our being so easily!

What did you notice?

The Angel. In many decks the angel takes up a big portion of the card making it hard not to see, but there is a difference between seeing and *seeing*. If your attention is drawn to the angel, make note that the card is more likely connected to querent's soul growth, spiritual passion, and connection to a higher power.

Burning Bush and Serpent Tree. This one plays upon the Christian beliefs of the serpent as tempter in the Garden of Eden and Moses's burning bush as communication with God; both speak of wisdom. Being drawn to the trees of lore shows that there is much to learn in the relationship. Feel it out! Notice which trees you are more drawn

The Major Arcana ✦ 183

to. Please remember that the snake in the tree is not a messenger of evil, but more symbolic of hidden and occult knowledge; whereas the burning bush is more the knowledge that is most acceptable for the masses.

The Lovers. Noticing the lovers (naked before one another, sometimes entwined in the act of lovemaking) one naturally connects the card with a romantic relationship. Once your attention has been drawn so, use your body dowsing to feel out the card. Each card has a slightly different story to tell every time it appears.

The Environment. The Lovers are often depicted outdoors, speaking of the primal nature of the card. Most often the landscape is fruitful and lush, featuring blue skies and sunshine. The landscape shows that which supports the Lovers. Make note of how you feel looking at it. *Landscapes can also be used to feel out time in a reading; paying attention to them often helps develop our ability to determine when something is likely to take place.*

◇◇◇◇◇◇◇◇◇◇◇◇◇

MEDITATION
THE LOVERS

Take a few moments before closing your eyes to look at the card in front of you, allowing yourself to take in as many details as you can. Close your eyes and bring your attention to your breathing. Focus on your inhalation and exhalation as they become balanced and rhythmic, inhaling and exhaling evenly through the nose.

Continuing to breathe deeply, imagine you are standing naked in an orchard with your lover. You are open and vulnerable in your nudity, and you are aware of a higher power present in your union. The presence feels beneficial as if offering a blessing upon the union. Take notice of how you feel. Do you recognize your lover? Is it someone you know? Are they in your life presently? Think on these questions as you take a few deep breaths.

184 ✦ The Tarot

The orchard behind you holds much temptation and choice. A snake moves through one of the trees reminding you of the untasted fruit, representing other possible lovers. The other tree is on fire, representing the burning passion that exists between you and your lover. The way they stare at you shows you they not only desire you but admire you, see your wisdom, and hold you as kindred.

You look to the heavens and the spirit that watches over you. Through this relationship you grow, becoming more than you are alone. Imagine the love that you desire. Allow yourself to sit in the energy of being both admired for your wisdom and desired for your beauty. Take a few breaths here.

Now reverse the viewpoint, allowing yourself to feel admiration and desire for another. Let yourself sit with that feeling of longing and the power it carries with it. Take a few moments here focusing on your current lover. If you are looking for love, allow yourself to imagine the lover you desire. Take a few moments here.

Continuing to focus on your breath, focus your mind on your physical body, wiggling your toes and fingers, moving your consciousness back into your physical form with every movement. Open your eyes and take a few moments to record your experience.

✦ The Chariot ✦

VII. The Chariot is a card of stability, growth, and accomplishment. The Chariot comes after we have gathered our tools as the Magician, dedicated ourselves as the High Priestess, acknowledged our sovereignty as the Emperor, and activated our connection to source through the Lovers. Having come this far in our development we are now ready to turn up the speed! The valiant warrior crowned in victory and parading their might, the charioteer stands tall, showing they are ready for action.

When the Chariot shows up in a reading it states that you are prepared, and able, to handle the challenges ahead. This is a card of strength and willpower! The black and white sphinxes (as seen from the original Rider-Waite deck) or horses represent duality and choices, showing the way is determined by the driver alone, and that the power of one's mind is paramount. In readings, this shows we are ultimately the ones steering the way to our goals, and therefore we must be centered and in control to reach our destination; this is well within our potential, as is portrayed through the confidence of stature and facial expression of the rider. The Chariot reminds us that victory comes through hard work and determination!

Numbered card seven of the Major Arcana, the Chariot shows the confidence that comes from a deep connection with God/Goddess/higher power. In numerology seven is a number associated with contemplating God and the need to find a deeper meaning in life. While the Chariot often portrays a victorious display of power (often seen as a

warrior in a victory parade) the body language of the charioteer shows that this is not just some brute who's good with a weapon; instead, we see a confident leader who contemplates reality. This is important, as it shows us that our success is not determined by physical prowess alone, but instead requires us to think bigger, look at the whole picture, and question our very existence. Success as seen through the Chariot comes from using all our resources, including our spiritual faith.

In many readings, the Chariot is interpreted as a sturdy foundation earned through the querent's hard work and clever thinking, reassuring the querent that with continued dedication and contemplation they will move through their obstacles. It is a reminder to stay aware of the road ahead, but that they may do so with a level of confidence.

For the spiritual seeker, the Chariot can have a deeper meaning, one that reminds us we are following a path we have planned, either in this life or another. It asks us to use all our resources; in making our plans we must consult our higher self, guides, and gods, as we are working through lessons connected to our soul's work. This is where I usually meet the Chariot! It shows up when I am working through karmic lessons or interacting with something that is bigger than me alone. It reminds me that I am the driver of the vehicle, and therefore I am in control, which means I need to keep my thoughts focused on the outcome I am seeking. This brings in the quantum "what we think we draw to us" philosophy of co-creating our existence.

The Chariot is a great card to focus on in challenging times, as it reminds us that while we may not know the way in front of us, we hold the skill, knowledge, and connected intuition to maneuver the path as it unfolds. If you are struggling with the changes being thrown at you, remember you are the charioteer and you hold within you what is necessary to survive and thrive!

What did you notice?

The Charioteer. Standing confidently at the reins, the charioteer is often seen in armor inscribed with magical writing, showing they

The Major Arcana ✦ 187

still work with the tools of the Magician. Their stance is confident, strong, and a bit relaxed. Noticing the charioteer is a reminder to the querent that they possess these traits, and that they are prepared to face the road ahead.

The Sphinxes. While some decks have horses instead of sphinxes, I believe the sphinx holds a stronger resonance to the meaning of the creatures that pull the Chariot. Like the High Priestess and the Hierophant, the sphinx represents duality and opposing forces. Noting the sphinxes when observing the card shows that the situation ahead will experience both help and hindrance. Here it is important to remind the querent that they are the charioteer, and they can remain in control of the situation.

Wings and Scepter. Finding oneself drawn to the wings, which are often featured on the chariot itself, we get a feeling of swift movement. The scepter held by the charioteer is a reminder that we control the speed of our movement.

The Environment. The background and framework of the Chariot card is often one of opulence, reinforcing the idea that victory is at hand. The stars draped through the background connect the charioteer to the heavens, showing that God/Goddess/Universe stands with the charioteer, and the lush city background shows that the earthly world does so as well. As always, feel into the environment and trust your intuition!

MEDITATION
THE CHARIOT

Take a few moments before closing your eyes to look at the card in front of you, allowing yourself to take in as many details as you can. Close your eyes and bring your attention to your breathing. Focus on your inhalation and exhalation as they become balanced and rhythmic, inhaling and exhaling evenly through the nose.

188 ✦ The Tarot

Continuing to breathe deeply, imagine you are paraded in a chariot led by two sphinxes: one black, one white. You wear armor inscribed with symbols of ceremonial magic, and an eight-pointed star crown adorned with laurel, representing your success and the evolution of your soul. A square is embossed in the center of your armor showing that you are solid and logical. Take a few moments to feel the weight of your armor energetically. Crescent moons adorn your shoulders, representing the phases of the moon, that which is yet to come, predicting your future successes. Feel the magical inscriptions and the weight of the starred crown. Feel your solidness, recognize how your intuition has been sharpened by an analytical mind. (Pause here for a few breaths.)

The sun is high in the sky and brightly shining. You are sheltered from the heat by the star-covered canopy, showing that your path is celestially influenced. Pulling your chariot are two sphinxes: the black represents the night, femininity, the unconscious mind, and the moon; the white represents masculinity, the conscious mind, and the sun. You are being influenced and watched over by celestial powers. Take a few moments to receive any information or experience coming through at this time.

Your hands wear gauntlets of protection, and you hold a wand in your right hand showing you are a master channel. You are victorious and successful with a strong foundation. Allow yourself to feel the adoration that comes with your success. Having experienced intimate love through the Lovers, now let yourself feel the praise of triumph. Take a few breaths here noting your comfort level with being recognized for your success, and how it feels to be admired by colleagues and strangers.

Continuing to focus on your breath, focus your mind on your physical body, wiggling your toes and fingers, moving your consciousness back into your physical form with every movement. Open your eyes and take a few moments to record your experience.

✦ Strength ✦

VIII. The Strength card is generally seen as representing the internal vigor, durability, and resilience of the querent, often with a focus on the manner in which they face personal trials and tribulations, showing when the situation at hand must be navigated with determination and grace.

Most often depicted with the image of a woman laying her hands on a lion (or bear or wolf) in a way that shows she has gently overcome the beastly nature of the creature, Strength shows us that while the larger-than-life problem the querent is struggling with may seem overwhelming, it is not impossible! Through gentle persistence and a true desire to understand the situation, they hold the power to overcome such trials.

Often in our society we confuse strength with bravado. Bravado is the act of boldness meant to impress or intimidate. Strength is the

190 ✦ The Tarot

state of physically being strong, as well as the capacity to withstand great force or pressure. It is the latter that is most often depicted in the Strength card. Strength is persistent, resilient, and expansive. It does not need power over a situation; instead, it is the force that allows us to resist the pressure, to keep our mind balanced and our thoughts agile when we are facing adversity. It is the determination to succeed even when the odds are against us. Strength does not require us to be rigid; in fact, many of the strongest natural materials, such as spider silk, are flexible, gaining their power from their ability to move with the force instead of being destroyed by it. What's more, strength can come in the form of kindness, something well represented in the card.

When the Strength card shows up for you, ask yourself how best such a force should be worked with. What beast needs overcoming? Study your situation, not from an analytical perspective but from a receptive, empathic perspective. Ask yourself what the burden you face is trying to teach you. If Strength is presenting itself to you as a reminder of old trauma, do not run away from it; instead, move slow, taking your time to examine the situation as it unfolds.

As a Reiki Master, the Strength card often shows up in readings to indicate that the querent or situation may require healing, as the hand positions used by the woman in the card upon the beast are reminiscent of those used in Reiki and other forms of hands-on healing. Tune in to your intuition and really feel this one out. If you feel it is speaking of a wound, ask what there is to gain from exploring it, and perhaps suggest they consider getting some healing done. I have no doubt that I am energetic. Hands-on healing is a powerful tool of Strength, whose gentleness often allows us to face the beast of our mind with a feeling of safety and comfort. Not all battles need to be furious, as many of our biggest life battles take place in the dark, quiet space of our minds. Choosing to approach our wounding with love and compassion is often a far more effective way to face our obstacles than through anger and rage. We must be kind to ourselves, gather our strength, and go gently.

The Major Arcana + 191

What did you notice?

The Lady and the Beast. The symbolism of the woman with her hands upon the lion (bear or wolf) show the ability of the meek to overcome the mighty. Noticing this imagery shows that the querent can overcome a daunting situation through their steadfast inner strength.

The Laying on of Hands. Noticing the action of the woman as an act of hands-on healing shows that the querent or situation need healing. Feel into this one, and don't be afraid to add additional cards to your reading if you need more information.

The Lemniscate. The infinity symbol above the woman's head is symbolic of her ability to tap into her higher self and the eternal energy of the universe. Being drawn to this image often indicates that the person has been through this before, perhaps in another lifetime, and that they have the ability to connect with the part of themselves that already knows how to navigate the situation.

Laurels and Landscape. If you find yourself drawn to the flowers that adorn the woman, the lush green landscape, and bright sky, then the situation will move forward with ease and flow, as you are already seeing the success.

◇◇◇◇◇◇◇◇◇◇◇◇

MEDITATION
STRENGTH

Take a few moments before closing your eyes to look at the card in front of you, allowing yourself to take in as many details as you can. Close your eyes and bring your attention to your breathing. Focus on your inhalation and exhalation as they become balanced and rhythmic, inhaling and exhaling evenly through the nose.

Continuing to breathe deeply, imagine you are filled with the energy of the heavens. Having learned how to channel it as the Magician and honed your skill as the Hierophant, you now hold the Strength to do so at will.

192   ✦   The Tarot

Through your travels you have developed an understanding of the power that lies in internal strength, courage, and patience. Take a few moments to sit with the energy, feeling the peace, calm, and balance that it brings with it. (Pause here for a few breaths.)

You are dressed simply in white and adorned with a garland of flowers. The sun is warm and comforting and the ground beneath you cool to your bare feet. You are deeply connected to the Earth. Above your head energy moves in the form of an infinity symbol, showing that you are experiencing a state of no-time, no-space. Feel into the experience, allowing your senses to fully explore the moment.

A great beast approaches you; it may appear as a lion, a wolf, or another predator. You are not afraid; you stand in your power as the beast approaches you. You place your hands upon its head and begin to channel universal energy to the animal before you. The beast has come to show you how strong you are and that you are capable of achieving great things. Take a few moments here to let the energy of the universe run through you, imagining you are channeling it into the beast that presented itself to you. Feel the power that moves through you, taking a few breaths here.

Continuing to channel energy to the beast, take a moment to focus on how you utilize your internal strength in your life. How have you overcome unlikely odds? How do you utilize healing energy in your life? In what way does bravery manifest in you? (Pause here for a few breaths.)

Continuing to focus on your breath, focus your mind on your physical body, wiggling your toes and fingers, moving your consciousness back into your physical form with every movement. Open your eyes and take a few moments to record your experience.

✦ The Hermit ✦

IX. The Hermit is the ninth card of the Major Arcana (as the Fool is 0, seen as both the beginning and end of the Major Arcana). Nine is a number associated with completion as it is the last single-digit number. It is a number that is filled with the culmination of our experiences, oozing wisdom and potential, perfect for the nature of the Hermit.

I began my fascination with the Hermit as a young child when I first saw it on the inside cover of Led Zepplin IV. I understood immediately that the character portrayed in the photo was on a sacred journey, one that would require him to seek solace and silence. I would stare at his image, imagining his journey; he was a wise old sage, a wizard or priest contemplating the depths of the mind, and oh the places he would go!

The Hermit represents our journey inward, the introspective examination of what makes us tick. Seeking growth, we begin the adventure of knowing ourselves—in which we examine our life, mind, and consciousness under the metaphorical microscope, identifying the building blocks that have made us who we are. In terms most of us can relate to, the Hermit is the representation of shadow work.

194 ✦ The Tarot

Shadow work has become a common thing to hear, as the challenging times of recent years have made many of us take a good look at what makes us tick and whether we want to continue to engage with the thoughts and actions that have brought us to this point. It is also a necessity for those who are seeking to develop psychically, as true personal power requires us to know ourselves! In truth, everyone can benefit from some self-reflection, but those who are on a magical path have no choice but to look at themselves, lest their way be blocked by their own flaws and insecurities.

Those who identify as spiritual seekers—regardless of whether the seeking be through psychic development, religion, or ceremonial magic—must at some point enter the shadow of their soul. Like the Hermit, we must enter with bravery, determination, and the understanding that the way will be challenging. Notice his walking stick and lantern: he is prepared for the road to be unstable and filled with darkness. He does not walk in unprepared, but rather he chooses to bring light into the darkness. (Plus, I bet that walking stick could be used as a staff if it was necessary to defend himself.) Going into the shadow is not a journey of self-defeat; instead, it is the journey of the wise sage who is going into the dark to take back what he has lost.

In practical terms, this card asks us to look deeply at ourselves, to face our fears and misgivings, deal with our trauma head-on, and see who we truly are!

While most decks depict the Hermit as being alone on his journey, in some decks he is accompanied by an animal companion, showing he is not truly alone on his path but accompanied by his spiritual allies. I feel this is an unspoken fact when we see the Hermit alone, that we are never truly alone as we are assisted by our guides! For many of us it is within the shadows that we discover who these guides are and how we can work better together in the future. It also feels a lot easier stepping into the shadow of our soul knowing we are supported. The journey is still singularly ours, but we are not truly alone in doing so. This is much

The Major Arcana ✦ 195

like how the ring was Frodo's burden to carry in the *Lord of the Rings*, but he was never truly alone in the mission. If you are being called to deeply examine your own being, do so knowing that you are never truly alone.

Remembering that the Hermit is numbered nine in the Major Arcana, it often represents an ending of the life we have lived; no longer able to stay the same, we must change! The Hermit offers us a way to do so that is truly healing, because instead of running and avoiding the darkness of our story, we gather our tools and spiritual allies and head into the darkness, facing it head-on, with an awareness that we are carrying the light.

What did you notice?

The Hermit's Posture. Back straight and head bowed, the Hermit's posture shows us the humbleness that is needed to face ourselves. We must go into our journey with the desire to discover, understand, and make peace. Noticing the posture in a reading shows that the querent must remember that to heal and grow they must be both the observer and the observed.

The Lantern. Symbolically being drawn to the lantern is a reminder that the querent brings the light into the darkness with them, and that they need not be afraid.

The Staff. Noticing the staff means it is important to check in with your internal knowing, asking whether the staff feels like it is there for stabilization, meaning the road will likely be rocky, or as a potential weapon, meaning the querent may need to defend themself.

The Terrain. The Hermit's terrain is often barren, ice covered, and grey. Snow and ice are symbolic of frozen emotions, showing that the querent will likely find many hidden emotions and memories along their path.

196 ✦ The Tarot

◇◇◇◇◇◇◇◇◇◇◇◇◇

MEDITATION
THE HERMIT

Take a few moments before closing your eyes to look at the card in front of you, allowing yourself to take in as many details as you can. Close your eyes and bring your attention to your breathing. Focus on your inhalation and exhalation as they become balanced and rhythmic, inhaling and exhaling evenly through the nose.

Continuing to breathe deeply, imagine it is a cold winter night. The air is still, and the sky dark, the clouds hiding moon and star alike. You are heading out into the night. There is a feeling of anticipation as the journey you are departing on is of the soul. Take a few moments here to think on your soul's desire; what is the knowledge you seek?

Cloaked in gray robes from head to toe you are a part of the night. You carry a staff as a sign of your wisdom, and your lantern is lit by a single six-pointed star, representing your mantra "As above, so below!" Like the Fool you set out on your journey bravely, not knowing what the path will reveal. Take a few breaths here, feeling the weight of your cloak upon your shoulders, offering its protection against the night's chill—and outside influence. Your journey is yours alone, and your mind must be clearly focused on its own thoughts.

Your journey is one of the soul, a deep voyage into the recesses of your being. You are going to the Hermit's cave, a place of solitude and spirit where you will be tested and tried by the things you bring with you. Have no fear, the shadows that haunt you hold no power against the light you carry with you. Your star-powered lantern will show you truth where there is deception. You enter the cave and a voice inside your mind asks you, "What are you seeking?" Take a few minutes here, quietly meditating on what it is you seek, continuing to breathe deeply as you do.

Continuing to focus on your breath, focus your mind on your physical body, wiggling your toes and fingers, moving your consciousness back into your physical form with every movement. Open your eyes and take a few moments to record your experience.

✦ Wheel of Fortune ✦

X. The Wheel of Fortune is the essence of luck itself! It represents the collective energy of possibility that always swarms around us. When the Wheel of Fortune appears in a reading, it is important to notice the cards that surround it as well as the feelings you, the reader, get while looking at it, as this greatly determines how that luck will play out. In the simplest terms, spinning the Wheel of Fortune is much like gambling, as it shows that one's fate, in this situation, is not determined by merit; instead, it is filled with the mystery of chance. Some people are luckier than others and the wheel always seems to spin in their favor, while others have a history of bad luck, noting that random opportunities seldom fall in their favor. Most of us, however, fall somewhere in

198 ✦ The Tarot

the middle with experiences on both sides of the wheel, knowing her blessings as well as her bane.

I often imagine the Wheel of Fortune as a sentient being, a collective consciousness of opportunities granted and destroyed, with a sophisticated understanding of what is really needed in our personal realities. In truth I don't believe the Wheel of Fortune is completely random, just as luck itself is not! While it can appear to be random and outside of fate, destiny, and predetermined plans, it is in fact more of a free agent with the ability to push us in the direction we need go in as opposed to the direction we seek. For even when the Wheel of Fortune seems to be spinning out bad luck in our direction, following the path further down the way it is often revealed that what we saw as shit luck actually helped us get out of situations that were not truly in our favor.

When the Wheel of Fortune shows up in your readings this is often a sign that what the querent desires, plans, and plots for is under the viewing eye of fate. If the Wheel of Fortune is upright or is accompanied by a feeling of optimism, *take heart because luck is in your favor*! However, if the Wheel of Fortune is spinning in opposition to your desires (reversed or carrying a feeling of restraint), instead of bullying your way forward, ask more questions, such as Why is luck working against my desired outcome? Is there something I can change to make it spin more favorably? Is there another path?

The Wheel of Fortune helps us to remember that we are part of a bigger plan, even if we are just cogs! While few of us will have lives that play an obvious effect on the greater world, all of us affect the world around us. The randomness of the Wheel of Fortune looks far less random. The Wheel of Fortune is a powerful card, representing that which can make a change and create opportunity where it is least expected. If the Wheel of Fortune is showing up in your readings, take some time to really meditate on it. Ask how it is trying to steer you, and what direction is it leading you in? If luck keeps coming up in opposition to your desired goal, look for the side doors—the

The Major Arcana + 199

opportunities you are missing while focused on that which you want. If it's coming up in your favor . . . well, hot damn! Get on that shit because the universe is behind you, and luck is adding her blessing to your path.

What did you notice?

The Letters on the Wheel. Inside the wheel we see the letters TARO—which on a spinning wheel would repeat themselves, spelling TAROT—as well as letters from the Hebrew alphabet that translate to YHWY or Yahweh/God. If the letters catch your eye, then know that God/Goddess/Universe is lending its favor to the luck of the querent.

Beings in the Corner. In each corner of the card there is a winged creature sitting on a cloud: man, ox, lion, and eagle. These creatures generally have fixed astrological correspondence, which in turn means elemental connections: man/Aquarius/Air, ox/Taurus/Earth, lion/Leo/Fire, and eagle/Scorpio/Water. Make sure to take note of which of the beings stands out to you and ask yourself how that element and its astrological traits are influencing the situation.

Creatures around the Wheel. Just as there are beings in the clouds, there are also mysterious creatures, originally seen as a Typhon/snake god, Anubis, and a sphinx. All are seen as gatekeepers of a sort, with connections to death and the mystery. Being attracted to these mythical beings shows that there is likely an otherworldly element to the situation. If you feel this is the case it means the situation is likely out of the hands of the querent, and that there is an element of fate involved.

The Intensity of the Card. The Wheel of Fortune is generally a card of strong contrast, the colors boldly sitting against each other in representation of the outcomes that can take place when the wheel appears in a reading. If you find it is this contrast that catches your eyes, there is truly an element of random chance involved in the situation.

200 ✦ The Tarot

◇◇◇◇◇◇◇◇◇◇◇◇

MEDITATION
WHEEL OF FORTUNE

Take a few moments before closing your eyes to look at the card in front of you, allowing yourself to take in as many details as you can. Close your eyes and bring your attention to your breathing. Focus on your inhalation and exhalation as they become balanced and rhythmic, inhaling and exhaling evenly through the nose.

Continuing to breathe deeply, imagine you are standing in front of a large disc covered in mystical symbols. Walking up to the ornate wheel you give it a spin, as if playing a game of luck. As the Wheel of Fortune spins, you begin to see mythical creatures surrounding it, coming forward as if riding on clouds. In the top left you see a human, the top right an eagle, the bottom right an ox, and the bottom left a lion. As you continue to study the Wheel of Fortune you notice Anubis, a snake, and a sphinx riding the wheel itself. Take a few moments here to sit with the images, allowing your psychic mind to imagine the story behind such an unusual sight. (Pause here for a few breaths.)

As you watch the wheel the mystical writing draws your attention, the Hebrew letters spinning and flashing in your mind, spelling out the sacred unpronounceable name of God: "Yahweh." Suddenly the wheel changes its direction, spelling out TORA in English, referring to Hebrew scripture. As the wheel continues to spin, you realize that the name of God is unspoken because it has so many variations. Take a few breaths as you watch the spinning wheel, allowing yourself to sit with the message it is spinning out.

Bringing your attention back to the full story taking place, you focus on the creatures riding the wheel: Anubis, the Egyptian god of death; the Typhon-like serpent, representing luxury; and the sphinx reminding you of mystery and the unknown. The Wheel of Fortune is spinning between fate and luck, God's will and chaos. The angel, lion, ox, and eagle now come back into view through mist and clouds reminding us of how outside influence affects the outcome.

The Major Arcana ✦ 201

Focusing on the Wheel of Fortune, you remember the Strength you hold within yourself and how you have been trained and tempered by your transition through the Major Arcana so far. You reach out to the faith of the Fool, and channel the heavens through the Magician, and hold your will intact through the training of the High Priestess. You remember the feeling of growth and luxury experienced as the Empress, and the chiseled determination of the Emperor. Continuing to breathe, you remember you wear the heavy mantle of wisdom that comes with the Hierophant, and the joy and ecstasy that comes through your journey with the Lovers. You have been victorious in your endeavors and celebrated upon the Chariot, and you know that your Strength comes from channeling celestial energy and your own will. You have faced your shadows in the darkness as the Hermit, and you now have the ability to influence the spinning of the Wheel of Fortune.

Call upon the energy of the Universe, and reaching out to the heavens imagine that you are combining it with your personal will. Now direct the energy at the wheel, seeing it spin good fortune into your life. Recognize that you have the power within you to influence random chance and chaos, directing it in your favor. Take a few moments here visualizing this.

Continuing to focus on your breath, focus your mind on your physical body, wiggling your toes and fingers, moving your consciousness back into your physical form with every movement. Open your eyes and take a few moments to record your experience.

✦ Justice ✦

XI. Justice is blind! The old statement holds much truth when it comes to the Justice card. This card is meant to enforce the idea that the truth is not something we come to by casual glance and surface observations, but instead justice is achieved through logical investigation and the use of all our senses. There is a difference between what is fair and what we believe ourselves and others to deserve, as emotions and feelings of rightness often taint our view of the truth. Justice is a card of truth, representing the balance point between differing views, the place where we weigh the facts!

The Justice card carries the vibrations of empathy and psychic knowing, showing that the decisions made are done so with a heightened sensitivity to the truth. Being the eleventh card of the Major Arcana, it resonates as a master number—meaning it has an enhanced vibration, carrying more impact. This is depicted in the imagery of the card as the judge is seated upon a dais holding the scales of justice in their left (receptive) hand, showing they are ready and able to listen and observe to make the fairest decisions. In their right hand is a sword, meant to represent clarity, as well as symbolizing that their decision will be enforced.

Justice is void of emotions, holding itself above the feelings that surround the situation to find where the truth lies—and what is fair. The

The Major Arcana ✦ 203

appearance of Justice in a reading is meant to tell us that the fairest decision will be made. Fairness does not mean getting what we want; it truly means getting what is best and fair for all parties involved. It represents decisions based on facts and requires us to put aside all the "he said, she said" bullshit and look at the truth of the situation. Justice cares little for our feelings and is instead focused on what is right and fair. When the Justice card is reversed—or comes in carrying an uncomfortable, irritating feeling—it is likely that there will be something unfair about the situation. *Developing our relationship with the tarot as a storyteller, we learn to follow the story as we are led into the web of wyrd by fate.*

Justice seldom shows up in a reading unexpectedly. In most cases, we are aware of the situation that needs balancing. If it shows up for you personally it can be a sign that you are too emotional about the situation and need to look at it from an outside perspective. Take the time to see it through the other lens, placing yourself in the consciousness of the opposing force. Often, we experience injustice through the cloudy lens of self-importance, seeing every wrong that is done to us as purposeful. Justice asks us to take time, sit with the situation, allow ourselves to see it from all sides. Remember that the truth is often three-dimensional: our truth, the truth of the other, and the balanced truth that lies between the two!

What did you notice?

The Scales. Noticing the scales shows that the question at hand is complicated, and the decision cannot be made without weighing all the factors.

The Sword. Being attracted to the sword in the card often shows that the decision will be clear and absolute. It also indicates that a relationship or situation will have a clean cut, ending it completely.

The Pillars. Again the tarot offers us pillars. In the case of Justice, the judge sits equally between the two, a hand stretched out in front of each holding the symbols of the office: the sword and scales. This

204 ✦ The Tarot

depiction shows the opposing forces that are influencing the querent and/or situation. If this stands out it is likely speaking of the heaviness of the decision.

Robes and Backdrops. Often the judge wears the same color as the backdrop, showing that they do not exist personally in the decision but stand as a representative of Justice itself. If this piece draws your attention in a reading, it suggests that the querent may want to seek an unbiased ear to help them solve their problem, such as a counselor, lawyer, or friend capable of remaining neutral.

◇◇◇◇◇◇◇◇◇◇◇◇

MEDITATION
JUSTICE

Take a few moments before closing your eyes to look at the card in front of you, allowing yourself to take in as many details as you can. Close your eyes and bring your attention to your breathing. Focus on your inhalation and exhalation as they become balanced and rhythmic, inhaling and exhaling evenly through the nose.

Continuing to breathe deeply, imagine you are once again sitting upon a dais, wearing a red robe of authority. In your right hand you hold the sword of Justice and in your left the scales of balance. Upon your head you wear a golden crown engraved with a simple square, showing that your thoughts and actions are based on solid facts and analytical thinking. You are the judge holding court as a representative of justice, truth, fairness, and the law! Take a few moments here to allowing yourself to feel the weight of your office—and the balance of the unbiased mindset that is required to hold such.

Take a few moments here to think on how Justice applies to situations in your life. What areas are in need of balance, where does the truth need to be revealed, and in what areas are you making judgment based on bias? Are the scales of Justice balanced in your life? If not, how can they be brought into balance? As a psychic are you approaching your readings from a place of unbiased judgment?

Continuing to focus on your breath, focus your mind on your physical body, wiggling your toes and fingers, moving your consciousness back into your physical form with every movement. Open your eyes and take a few moments to record your experience.

✦ The Hanged Man ✦

XII. The Hanged Man is a powerful card that asks us to step outside of our normal view of reality and look at the situation from a different perspective, stating quietly that we may have to turn our world upside down to understand the situation.

The posture of the Hanged Man in the traditional Rider-Waite Tarot, which influences so many other decks, shows a man hung upside

206 ✦ The Tarot

down by one ankle, with his hands bound. This form was commonly used in *pittura infamante*, a type of artwork created to debase criminals, particularly those seen as traitors to the crown of Italy (hanging by one foot was a prolonged and excruciating form of death, reserved for traitors). Knowing this image, we could see how this card was representative of wrongdoings, but in fact it is more interested in telling us that the man hanging or those who receive this card need to consider things in a way that is unlike what they have believed before—metaphorically hanging upside down!

The Hanged Man is a card of surrender, of allowing one's mind to open to possibilities beyond the knowing of our day-in, day-out lives. Even in the earlier decks that depict the Hanged Man as hanging by one foot and bound, you will notice that his head is illuminated in some way, such as a glowing halo or oak leaves in his mouth. This halo is representative of the expansion of our mind that happens when we surrender (or are forced) to look at our situation from a different perspective. It is important to see that his eyes are open, showing that while he has surrendered to his fate, he is there to learn what he can!

As a follower of Odin, I cannot help but be reminded of how he hung himself from Yggdrasil, the World Tree, to attain the wisdom of the runes. Sacrificed to himself, by himself, Odin hung suspended for nine days with no food, no water, and a spear in his side. At the end of his ordeal, he was rewarded with the knowledge of the runes. While I don't believe I need to physically hang myself, I do understand the sentiment. As a god of war, Odin needed to change his perspective drastically to become what he was not yet, a poet and magic user. After his time suspended from the World Tree he could no longer return to his regular life; in fact, he had come to the tree to surrender himself so that he may be transformed.

When the Hanged Man presents itself in our life, we are being asked to choose a different perspective, one that may be far out of our normal way of thinking. Often this change is unexpected—and earthshaking—making it hard to avoid. Most of us can think of moments when we

The Major Arcana ✦ 207

were forced to surrender to the will of the Universe: our lives were completely thrown about; we had no choice but to surrender. It is through this surrender that our perspective is changed, and our consciousness is opened.

When the Hanged Man shows up in a reading, the querent should prepare for things in their life to take an alternative path, one in which their way of seeing the world will be challenged. What kind of change it brings depends on the situation. We all experience the Hanged Man in ways that are in alignment with our own growth. With this in mind, we must remember that, like Odin, we in some way went searching for this growth. Even if we look at the Hanged Man as a traitor to the crown, such as his body positioning depicts, we must ask ourselves, What crown is he traitor to? By the look of contemplation and acceptance on his face, I would suggest he is *a traitor to ways that no longer serve*, turning his back on what was, to find a new way of understanding the world. Many great thinkers were persecuted as traitors for sharing thoughts that proved to be true, yet lay outside of the accepted norms of the time.

What did you notice?

The Halo. The space around the Hanged Man's head is illuminated in a golden halo. This is symbolic of enlightenment and soul growth, showing that through this challenge of thinking and seeing differently, the Hanged Man gains wisdom and spiritual awakening. Being drawn to this image often signifies that the experience will hold spiritual growth for the querent.

Body Binding. If you were drawn to the pittura infamant, the concept of *traitor* needs to be looked at. What loyalties no longer feel comfortable to the querent? How do they feel they are betraying their way of life? What things must they turn their back on in order to help their soul evolve?

The Tree. Symbolically, the tree the Hanged Man is suspended from is connected to the World Tree that is prominent in many spiritual

208 ✦ The Tarot

practices. The World Tree is said to connect our reality to other realms. Being drawn to this suggests that the situation the querent is in will most likely hold spiritual growth and mind-expanding experiences.

The Hanged Man's Expression. It is important to point out that the Hanged Man generally does not look distressed. His eyes are wide open, and he appears serene in an otherworldly way. It is generally obvious when looking at the card that the Hanged Man is not suffering. If you feel drawn to this imagery, note that the querent may need reassurance that they will be able to traverse the situation safely.

◇◇◇◇◇◇◇◇◇◇◇◇◇◇

MEDITATION
The Hanged Man

Take a few moments before closing your eyes to look at the card in front of you, allowing yourself to take in as many details as you can. Close your eyes and bring your attention to your breathing. Focus on your inhalation and exhalation as they become balanced and rhythmic, inhaling and exhaling evenly through the nose.

Continuing to breathe deeply, imagine you are hanging upside down, suspended by one ankle, your arms bound behind your back. Take a deep breath here as you feel the unease of your position.

Coming back to center through your breath, you remember that you are the one who suspended yourself so, placing yourself in a position of discomfort that you may shift your perspective and see the world from a different viewpoint. Much like the god Odin, you have sacrificed yourself to yourself in the search of knowledge. Take a deep breath here and allow yourself to remember the joy of standing on your head as a child, or in yoga class, and give over the discomfort in trade for a deeper understanding. (Pause here for a few breaths.)

Relaxing into your new perspective you realize you are suspended from a living tree; like Odin on the Tree of Life you have the ability to look into

The Major Arcana + 209

the multiple realms of reality. Your crown chakra begins to open, and in your mind's eye you can see there is a halo surrounding your head, much like illustrations of saints and bodhisattvas. You feel your consciousness expanding out, allowing you to become one with all things. Take a few moments here to receive visions and thoughts from the collective consciousness.

You are in the betwixt and between suspended between worlds, neither here nor there. Take a moment to examine your relationship with this space. Do you feel comfortable in this space? Do you seek to disappear or are you seeking the wisdom of the universe? What has brought you to this place?

Coming back to your breath, focus your mind on something in your life that puzzles you. Looking from your new unbiased viewpoint, influenced by your time as Justice, spend a few moments examining the problem with a different viewpoint. Are there other ways to approach it? Change roles with the other people in the story, imaging yourself in their shoes. Can you understand their point of view more clearly? What is the most beneficial way to rectify the situation? (Pause here for a few breaths.)

Like the Hermit, the Hanged Man asks us to explore the uncomfortable, the silence of self-dedication, and the expansiveness of multiple perspectives. Continuing to focus on your breath, focus your mind on your physical body, wiggling your toes and fingers, moving your consciousness back into your physical form with every movement. Open your eyes and take a few moments to record your experience.

+ Death +

XIII. Death is notably the most misinterpreted card by those who are new to the tarot. The appearance of the Death card in a reading can cause hearts to race with a mild case of panic as it is often seen as the harbinger of, well, Death! While the card certainly can show up as a sign of someone's impending voyage into the spirit, it is more commonly a representative of big change, in the form of endings and beginnings.

Death's story is one of transition. While the card features a skeletal figure—most often depicted as a version of the Grim Reaper, sickle and all—it is a card about rebirth just as much as it is about dying. For the trained eye, this is perceivable in all depictions of the Death card, including the original Rider-Waite Tarot, which features the image of the rising sun of dawn through the towers in the background. In many newer cards, the rebirth is depicted more clearly, with images of the spirit rising out of the fallen body, helping to enforce the idea that this card is so much more than the end of one's physical life.

Life is filled with little deaths; endings of relationships, jobs, and life situations all force us to change. This is the profound change that the Death card speaks of: moments in our life in which we can look back and say, "I changed there!" Many of us fear change, especially the life-altering change that the Death card speaks of. Even when life is

The Major Arcana + 211

miserable many will stay in their shit simply because they are afraid. It is natural for people to be taken aback by the Death card.

When the Death card shows up it is in many ways liberating, as it takes away the decision of change, showing us that time is up, this change is coming whether we want it or not, so best be prepared! The kind of change Death speaks of is often profound, changing our lives in a way that there is a definite before and after to the scenario. If Death shows up in your readings, remember it is also a card of rebirth. Do not dwell solely on what is ending; instead, look for where the light of the rising sun takes you. Draw a few supporting cards if you are confused about the new direction that is presenting itself through the death of the old. Expect things to be a bit unstable as things are shifting and growing.

Take some time to meditate on the Death card, and think about the transitions you have experienced personally. What pieces of your life story needed to die so that you may become the new improved version of yourself? When fear comes up, remember not to dwell on it for it will eat away at your soul. Instead, step bravely forward, look at the change that is inevitable and ask what tools you will need on the way—a perfect time for drawing a few more cards. Dance with death; see it as the harbinger of growth that it truly is. Understanding your transitions with Death will help you understand it better in future readings.

What did you notice?

The Skeleton. It's hard not to see the skeleton when looking at the Death card as it is the most common interpretation, and it gets its point across easily. Note how you feel when looking at it. Does it feel welcomed or guarded against?

The Rising Sun. Noticing the rising sun shows that there is rebirth, growth coming out of the old. When this pulls you strongly, the rebirth will likely come quickly and be worth the pain of transition.

The Fallen and the Risen. Noticing the dead lying on the ground, and the spirits rising from them, brings our attention to the rebirth,

212 ✦ The Tarot

renewal, reincarnation bit. It brings in a feeling of having experienced this before and offers strength from knowing you will do it again. In fact, some people move through their life in a series of death/rebirth, ending relationships and stories of their lives to recreate themselves again and again.

The Holy Figure. Often we see a form of the Hierophant or High Priest in the Death card; this symbolizes the sacredness of the transformation.

<><><><><><><><><>

MEDITATION

DEATH

Take a few moments before closing your eyes to look at the card in front of you, allowing yourself to take in as many details as you can. Close your eyes and bring your attention to your breathing. Focus on your inhalation and exhalation as they become balanced and rhythmic, inhaling and exhaling evenly through the nose.

Continuing to breathe deeply, imagine you are standing in a battlefield. The battle past, you look upon what remains. On the ground in front of you a king lies dead, his crown fallen from his head. The Hierophant in all his wisdom prays over the scene, as a child waits in the wings: his heir come to claim the crown and begin the cycle again.

Continuing to breathe deeply, you notice a skeletal figure dressed in dark armor, upon a white horse, carrying a black flag with the Tudor rose fluttering in the wind. Your mind is brought back to the rose garden that began your quest as the Fool. You remember the feelings of love and peace that came from that garden, and you intuitively understand that the white rose on the flag speaks of better times coming. Death itself has come to this moment, come to bring an ending and beginning into motion; transformation is in motion.

Expanding your view to include the vista, you see that it is dawn and that the sun is rising between two towers, which you recognize as the gates that separate the living from the dead. The darkness has passed, giving way to the light of a new day and the clarity it brings. New beginnings are on the horizon, for the old has been slain, overcoming that which was. From here you must go forward anew. The towers of mercy and severity in the distance remind us that new beginnings can either be hard or easy. How do you feel in seeing them? Are you filled with hope or fear?

Take a few moments to think on what is dying and transpiring in your life. What have you laid to rest? What pieces of your life have come to an end? Are you struggling to let go? Are you focused on the ending or the beginning? You have gained so much in your journey through the Major Arcana, learning through the Wheel of Fortune that you can influence your luck; take a few moments there to focus on the new beginning you want to come out of this ending.

Continuing to focus on your breath, focus your mind on your physical body, wiggling your toes and fingers, moving your consciousness back into your physical form with every movement. Open your eyes and take a few moments to record your experience.

✦ Temperance ✦

XIV. Temperance invites us to stand between the worlds, with one foot in ordinary reality and the other in the fluid waters of our higher consciousness, where we connect with the divine in its many incarnations. While it is traditionally connected to taking the middle road—choosing balance, patience, and moderation—I have always seen it as a card of manifestation and alchemy!

Alchemy is the act of transforming one substance into another: transformation in action. Like the Magician, Temperance carries the teachings of "As above, so below," representing the act of co-creation, in which we manifest ourselves into being through our actions and beliefs. Notice how I said *actions* and beliefs! That's because we cannot simply wish something into being; we must also take actions that support our new way of being. Without action, our dreams fail to alchemize, leaving us treading water in our own life.

Temperance is deeply connected to the element of Water, with most depictions showing a winged being standing with one foot in the water and one foot on land, representing the querent's ability to connect to both ordinary reality and the realm of spirit. In this state of betwixt and between we are more fluid, represented by the abundance of water in this card, and capable of allowing the divine source of the universe to move through us. Through this connection, we can begin the alchemy of becoming. The foot on the ground speaks of our need to apply the structure of ordinary reality to that which we are manifesting, showing that we must connect our dreams to reality, and we must put real effort into supporting them. Here we find the balance point, the middle ground between the physical and incorporeal!

The Major Arcana + 215

I often refer to Temperance as the Witch Card, as witchcraft is all about manifestation and co-creation. One of the interesting things I have noticed about this card is how it shows up repeatedly for some people, making an appearance in most of their readings at some point. These people are naturally good at manifestation and co-creation, having a natural understanding of how important our thought process is and the need to put action behind our dreams. For those who identify as manifesters and co-creators, Temperance is a reminder to be careful what we think as we just might make it happen! This is something to really take note of, as many of us spend an awful lot of time thinking about all the bad things we don't want to happen. Magic is afoot when Temperance shows up—and, more truly, a Magic-Maker is afoot! If Temperance is showing up for you, ask yourself how you are utilizing it.

What did you notice?

The Foot in the Water. Symbolically, noticing the partial submersion in water shows that the co-creation of Temperance will be strongly experienced in the astral realm, through dreams and journey work. This happens more often when the querent is experiencing growth in their spiritual life. This can also happen when the querent is too wishy-washy in their approach to change. Use your intuition to help you determine which applies.

The Road to the Rising Sun. Noticing the path shows that the querent is moving toward that which they are manifesting.

Chalices of Water. The Angel holds two chalices pouring water between the two. This often feels supernatural, as the water is illuminated and sometimes appears to defy gravity. Symbolically this stirs thoughts of generating and passing the essence of life, prana, mana, energy. If this draws your attention, it often shows the querent can generate energy both magically and in ordinary life.

The Illuminated Third Eye. The Angel has a glowing symbol of the Sun, self, and center located in the middle of their third eye. A circle with a dot in the center is in recognition of the third eye, and

216   +   The Tarot

our ability to utilize it in manifestation through focus and practice. If this draws your eye it shows that the querent can develop a stronger relationship with their own ability to manifest through working with their third eye.

◇◇◇◇◇◇◇◇◇◇◇◇◇

MEDITATION
TEMPERANCE

Take a few moments before closing your eyes to look at the card in front of you, allowing yourself to take in as many details as you can. Close your eyes and bring your attention to your breathing. Focus on your inhalation and exhalation as they become balanced and rhythmic, inhaling and exhaling evenly through the nose.

Continuing to breathe deeply, imagine you are standing on the edge of the water. It's dawn, and you feel the heat of the sun as it crests the mountains behind you. You found your way here via the path through the towers of mercy and severity presented by Death, and you are reborn, tempered by the experiences of your past.

The shore you stand upon is lush green, with yellow irises and reeds. You recognize the water as sacred, a spring or well, where water flows to the surface from within the ground. You place one foot into the water and feel its vitality. Take a moment here to connect with the water, opening your mind to its presence.

Having opened yourself to the water you feel your third eye open, giving you clearer vision. Take a moment here to acknowledge the opening of your visionary chakra, making note of anything you see, feel, or know.

Continuing to breathe you feel your crown chakra open, expanding out, creating a halo around your head, as you experienced during your time as the Hanged Man. As you breathe out the halo expands, and you start to feel a pressure in your shoulder blades. Taking a deep breath in and out, wings unfurl from your shoulders, expanding out over the water. You feel luminous, your light expanding out over the water and land.

The Major Arcana + 217

You pick up two chalices you find sitting on the shore and begin pouring water from one to the other, charging it with celestial energy. You are peaceful and calm, channeling the energy of water with its ability to calm, clean, and purify. You recognize yourself as a powerful manifester in this moment, with the ability to co-create your own reality, and you recognize your ability to spread blessings wherever you are. You are patient and calm, knowing that what is meant for you will find its way.

With one foot still firmly on the ground you feel your connection to the Earth, and you chose it by placing an upward-facing triangle on your chest as a sign of your duty to the Earth, your choice to be in this physical world, firmly grounding your intentions in the earthly realm.

Continuing to focus on your breath, focus your mind on your physical body, wiggling your toes and fingers, moving your consciousness back into your physical form with every movement. Open your eyes and take a few moments to record your experience.

+ The Devil +

XV. The Devil is another showstopper of a card, one whose arrival in a reading often causes those who know nothing of the tarot to be a bit anxious. As depicted in decks based on the Rider-Waite Tarot, the Devil is seen sitting on a pedestal as judge or warden over the man and woman who are chained in front of him. Naked and unremorseful, the couple wear chains around their necks that appear to bind them to the Devil. But upon close examination, we see the chains are loose and could easily slip over their heads.

The Devil card shows us the dance we play out with our consciousness and the choices we make. It speaks of our shadow and what vices we carry. In some decks there is a more passionate feel in connection to the Devil, as the naked couple are lovers lounging sleepily in their satiated pleasure, while the Devil—the untamed horned god of wild things—looks on. In this form the Devil is titillating and intoxicating, like a curse we place upon ourselves through addiction and poor choices. The Devil speaks of forbidden fruit, and the price we pay for partaking of it!

When the Devil shows up in a reading it asks us to examine the same old song and dance we keep performing. Our actions, habits, and thoughts are being called in for examination. What bad habits and relationships do we keep repeating? How are we contributing to our own hell? From another perspective it asks us to question why we keep feeding it: What purpose is it serving in our lives? By recognizing that we are living in a reality we are creating, and caretaking, we can choose how we want to engage with it. This may lead us to disengage from destructive behavior, or it may lead us to reexamine the stories we tell and how cultural and religious dogma influence our beliefs.

Our minds are mighty, and the stories we tell ourselves about good and evil, and bondage and freedom will often create tense dra-

matizations within our consciousness. The Devil is our creation, the illusion of a demented overlord, created through our thoughts and actions. When the Devil shows up it is important to remember we are the ones controlling the beast, the chains are ours to remove, and we are our own liberators. We need to change the dance and move in a direction that frees us!

What did you notice?

The Chains. The chains are symbolic of bondage; some decks use cages instead of chains, but either way they speak of our captivity. Noticing how the chains appear to rest while doing the reading will help you to see whether the querent is able to remove the chains.

The Inverted Pentagram. The upside-down star on the head of the Devil brings up an immediate connection to dark magic for some. The symbol is, however, far more complex than that; it also has connections to gods such as Baphomet and organizations such as the Eastern Star (a Masonic organization). Either way it is connected to hidden knowledge, and noticing it in a reading often directs the querent to look for such: whether it be through revealing deceit or finding knowledge deep within their consciousness. Which is being played out in the card is up to the reader to determine.

Flaming Tails and Grapes. The prisoners of the Devil in many decks have tails tipped in grape bunches and flames. This is symbolic of vice, the things that keep us in our own prison. When this stands out to you, it is likely that the querent or person being inquired about is imprisoned by their own habits, particularly those that can be deemed addictions.

The Stark Background. The background in the Devil card is often similar to depictions of hell, with black and foreboding imagery. If this catches your attention it is wise to advise the querent that they will need to change their background, and the people they associate with, if they want to break the habits that are holding them back.

220 ✦ **The Tarot**

◇◇◇◇◇◇◇◇◇◇◇◇

MEDITATION

THE DEVIL

Take a few moments before closing your eyes to look at the card in front of you, allowing yourself to take in as many details as you can. Close your eyes and bring your attention to your breathing. Focus on your inhalation and exhalation as they become balanced and rhythmic, inhaling and exhaling evenly through the nose.

Continuing to breathe deeply, imagine darkness surrounding you, and you have a feeling of tightness. Your body is naked, and the air hot and humid. You feel a weight around your neck and realize it is a collar of sorts, attached to a chain. It feels heavy and burdensome. Take a few moments here to breathe rhythmically, remembering that you are OK, and that like the Hanged Man there is a lesson here.

The area around you is dimly lit and you can see fires burning in the distance. The chain around your neck is connected to a large black pillar, and you are not alone. Beside you stands another also chained to the pillar, and looming over you both is a bat-winged beast of a man with ram's horns, the Devil. Around you are signs of indulgence and intoxication, and the fires burning about remind you of lustful passion. The inverted pentagram above his head a sign of banishing in witchcraft, showing that the things represented are baneful to our well-being. Vice is the story to the Devil, but so is fear, false judgment, and self-loathing. The Devil asks us to look at our shadow, the parts of ourself we don't feel comfortable with, that keep us chained. Take a moment to sit with any fear that comes up at this moment, and any thoughts on what would place you here, chained. (Pause here for a few breaths.)

Quieting your mind through deep breathing, you notice that the chain around the other person's neck is quite loose, and that they could take it off anytime they wanted. You then reach up and feel the chain around your own neck, to find the same. Realizing that you are the one keeping yourself bound, you remove the chains. Take a few moments to see how removing the chains you have bound yourself with will enact change in your physical world.

Continuing to focus on your breath, focus your mind on your physical body, wiggling your toes and fingers, moving your consciousness back into your physical form with every movement. Open your eyes and take a few moments to record your experience.

✦ The Tower ✦

XVI. The Tower is the card of the times! Most people have become familiar with it thanks to COVID-19. Having a pandemic is a surefire way for people to get a close-up view of what it means to be living in Tower Times. In short, the Tower represents catastrophe or unexpected

222 ✦ The Tarot

trouble of a life-rearranging kind. When the Tower shows up it is inevitable that things are going to change; the only thing we can do is determine how we are going to react.

The Tower card depicts a tower being struck by lightning, perhaps having caught on fire or crumbling to the ground. In most cards two people are falling from the tower: one is fretting and fighting the whole way, and the other has given over to the experience, realizing there is nothing for them to do but surrender. This to me is the question that the Tower asks us, "How are you going to manage the transition?"

The Tower rearranges our life because the change it ushers in is something we cannot avoid. No side-stepping the issue, no sticking our heads in the sand, the Tower forces us to pay attention and to choose how we are going to experience the inescapable challenge that is before us. Have no doubt, no matter how you choose to interact with the Tower you are going to be uncomfortable! But that does not make the Tower a bad card, for the disruption it brings can just as easily bring us to a better place as it can destroy. It simply is a messenger that these things we have been holding onto are no longer stable. It has been hit by lightning and is on fire—we can't ever go back to the way things were!

The Tower forces us to change the way we have been living, as it is no longer sustainable. The truth is we will all face our own personal Tower card at some point in life. It is a difficult card, but—in truth— the destruction it depicts was a ticking time bomb to begin with. The systems that collapse under such adversity are broken to begin with; the destruction of the Tower just makes the move for us, throwing us out of the broken tower that no longer serves us. The Tower is not a house-wrecker that comes in and destroys all that we love. Instead, it is a flood-light shining on the broken bits we have been holding together with duct tape. When things start to fall apart, we are not really surprised by what part of the system fails, for there have been telltale signs for ages.

When the Tower comes up in a reading, we need to forget about stopping the change, and instead decide how we want to weather it.

The Tower is a chance to evolve! By really looking at the things that are falling away, we can choose to create ourselves in a healthier more functional way. It is important to remember that the difficulties we face in life, and the lessons we learn through them, are often the very things that define us—for they present opportunities to gain experience! In many ways, we humans are like swords . . . we need tempering to create the sharpest, most developed version of ourselves.

What did you notice?

The Two Falling People. The falling people show us the diverse ways we can maneuver the unraveling of the situation. Like riding a roller coaster, they can either scream and holler the whole way down or surrender to the experience and ride it with ecstasy. Noticing this is a reminder that the querent has a choice.

Lightning and Fire. The destructive elemental forces are representative of the actual destructive force behind the fall. Make note of how intensely you respond to seeing them, for it is reflective of how intense the situation will be for the querent.

The Falling Crown. The Tower is often topped in some way with a crown that has been knocked off and is falling. This shows that the structure that holds the situation together has fallen.

The Stormy Background. The background of cards is more important than most people understand. Paying attention, the background can give you information. In this case having it draw your attention shows that the situation will affect more than the querent alone.

<><><><><><><><><>

MEDITATION
THE TOWER

Take a few moments before closing your eyes to look at the card in front of you, allowing yourself to take in as many details as you can. Close your eyes and bring your attention to your breathing. Focus on your inhalation

224 ✦ The Tarot

and exhalation as they become balanced and rhythmic, inhaling and exhaling evenly through the nose.

Continuing to breathe deeply, imagine you are standing in a tower. The sky is black, except for flashes of lightning that light up the night. Rain is pouring down, and there is a sense of urgency in the air, and a feeling of anticipation as if something unforeseen is about to happen.

Lightning strikes, hitting the tower and setting the interior on fire. Again, lightning strikes, this time dislodging you from the tower! You are falling. Knowing that the lightning strike and fall from the Tower were what you had been anticipating, how do you fall? Are you screaming and crying? Do you give over to your fate like the Fool stepping off the cliff?

As you fall time slows down. You are in the betwixt and between again, able to see the situation clearly. You see that the top of the tower has been blown fully off, and that it looks like a crown. In that moment your crown chakra seems to expand, as if it has been blown open. Materialistic thoughts and worries that are petty and mundane feel unimportant in this moment. Your focus is on the now—and the bigger matters of existence.

Falling seems to continue on for a very long time; sometimes you are falling with ease and can see a crown upon your head, showing that you are facing the situation with a higher consciousness. Other times the fear comes up and you are screaming—and feeling out of control—as you have no authority in the moment.

Spend a few moments here. Ask yourself how you want to move through hardship: Will you do so with fear, or will you open yourself to trust?

Continuing to focus on your breath, focus your mind on your physical body, wiggling your toes and fingers, moving your consciousness back into your physical form with every movement. Open your eyes and take a few moments to record your experience.

✦ The Star ✦

XVII. The Star is a card of hope, filled with the endless possibilities of bounty. It radiates into the darkness that good times do exist and fills us with dreams and aspirations. It is bountiful and beautiful, heralding opportunity! It's the light at the end of the tunnel, the hallmark that better times are upon us. The Star speaks of joy, love, and celebration, and how deserving we are of such! We do not stumble upon the gifts of the Star sheerly by luck, for they are blessings we deserve.

The Star is dynamic! The happiness it speaks of is not the simple joy of a good cup of coffee or time spent with close friends. It is the kind of happiness that radiates from us like an aura of joy, affecting all we contact. The light of the Star inspires all it touches, illuminating the dreams we focus on with the love we have for them. When the Star comes into our life, we feel infused with purpose, as if the universe is shining a spotlight on the dreams we aspire to.

The Star speaks of bringing celestial sunlight into our being. In most decks the card depicts a woman touching water and land, which symbolizes the ability to be a grounded channel: capable of making wise, thoughtful decisions while simultaneously allowing the wisdom of the heavens to flow through her consciousness. It is the depiction of the awakened human whose energetic body is aware and online, meaning the querent is utilizing both their practical mind and their higher consciousness. It also refers to having an awakened kundalini, in which the person's chakra system is activated, something that requires us to have done the work and cleaned up our old wounds and scars that hold us back from our true potential. This does not mean all who receive the card will be fully healed and ready to take on the world. It simply shows that when the Star arrives in our life, we have made progress in cleaning out the wounding that holds us back, and that our healing has led us to a place in which we can access our potential!

When the Star shows up for us in a reading it reflects who the querent is in the moment: they are the Star! It signifies a time to shine and that the light the querent is radiating through their aura shines outward for all to see. This is a hard card to feel humble around, as it shows the querent how fabulous they really are—and how their happiness and beauty affect those around them. The Star is not selfish; it shines its light for all to see, and it pours abundance on the land and water, offering both stability and expansiveness. It is a time to grow and shine, and it is a time in which one's actions will influence the world around them.

The Star is a deeply personal card that ushers in opportunity and bounty, but it is also a card of responsibility and influence, for when we shine so brightly, we cannot help but influence those around us. Such change in self often comes about after deep soul work and healing of our personal story, with the Star being the reward for such dedication to healing. Metaphysically speaking, when we heal ourselves, we do radiate more: our energetic body (the aura/biofield) gives off more light.

The Major Arcana + 227

What did you notice?

Pouring Water. The Star pouring water onto the land and into the water is symbolic of sharing wisdom and love. It shows that all the energy, love, and joy that moves through them, they graciously share with the world around them.

The Naked Lady. Kneeling naked, the Star is exposed, vulnerable, and empowered at the same time. Noticing this shows that the querent holds their naked body with no shame, accepting themselves for who they are.

Fertile Land. Noticing the fertility of the land symbolizes abundance and good fortune, both physical and emotional.

The Stars in the Background. Noticing the stars in the background shows that the querent is not putting themselves above others, but taking their rightful place of empowerment.

<><><><><><><><><><>

MEDITATION
THE STAR

Take a few moments before closing your eyes to look at the card in front of you, allowing yourself to take in as many details as you can. Close your eyes and bring your attention to your breathing. Focus on your inhalation and exhalation as they become balanced and rhythmic, inhaling and exhaling evenly through the nose.

Continuing to breathe deeply, imagine you are back at the water's edge that you visited in your journey with Temperance. Having survived your fall from the Tower, you are now standing on the rich green Earth, with one foot resting in the water, showing that your mind is balanced intuitively and analytically. You feel renewed, calm, and serene. Your outlook is optimistic as you connect with the sacred waters.

As the Star you are multiple—both the internal, eternal you and the external self that lives your everyday life. Existing inside of you the stars are multiple, as represented by the stars that shine above you, as you kneel by the water. In your mind's eye, the stars above your head are so bright it appears to be daylight. One giant star rests above your head, surrounded by seven other stars. These stars represent the seven chakras that run up your spine, and the large star is your higher self. You are the Star; you are luminous! Take a few moments to experience the light you are radiating out into the universe. (Pause here for a few breaths.)

Take a moment to focus your light, imagining it as a laser pointer. Now focus your intent on the area of your life that needs light shone on it, such as wanting to be recognized in your field, or to attract the right romantic partner. Like a spotlight illuminating the star of the show, you can use the heavenly light you are radiating to attract the attention you need and deserve. Take a few moments here to feel the positive energy flowing through you as you embrace your role as the Star.

Continuing to focus on your breath, focus your mind on your physical body, wiggling your toes and fingers, moving your consciousness back into your physical form with every movement. Open your eyes and take a few moments to record your experience.

✦ The Moon ✦

XVIII. The Moon illuminates the path we must follow, showing us that we are going to face a situation that will change the way we think, by guiding us through the illusions and background bullshit that we fill our minds with. Leaving the waters of the subconscious, we see an illuminated path and a marker that defines the point of no return—in which our view of reality has shifted and our fears are revealed to be illusions!

The imagery of the card displays the illusion and fear that often shows up when we are overthinking, worrying, and sitting in self-defeating thoughts. Framed by two towers, the moon illuminates a path leading from a shallow pool into the distance. The pool of water, like most water in the tarot, is symbolic of the subconscious, intuitive mind. In decks based on the symbolism of the Rider-Waite Tarot, we see a crawfish emerging from the water, symbolizing the shifting of our consciousness from a primitive state into one of greater awareness. On one side of the path we see a domesticated dog, and on the other there is a feral dog or wolf, inviting us to see that there are diverse ways of approaching the situation at hand.

The Moon asks the querent to take the position of the crawfish emerging from the primordial waters, as the card represents a situation that will expand our consciousness by forcing us to face the fears and illusions that bind us. This card speaks directly of the journey to becoming, in which the querent must gaze upon the illusions that bind them before they can proceed. On either end of the path are animals representing opposing ways of being in the world: one domesticated, the other feral. These symbolic creatures live within our consciousness representing the

230 ✦ The Tarot

wild and tame attributes of self and with them the fear, worry, and self-loathing that keep people trapped in painful disillusionment!

When the Moon card shows up in a reading, we must acknowledge both a domesticated dog and a feral dog living within. The domesticated dog speaks to us of obedience and pleasing others, while the feral dog speaks of freedom, doing what we please, and self-preservation. Neither is completely bad; in fact, what we need is a balance between the two. When the domesticated dog speaks to us of our fears, it whispers of the need to do as others would have us do, how we must please others at all costs—and without approval, we will be lost. Meanwhile, the feral dog tells us "Fuck them all! I do what I please!" and bellows narcissistic devotion of how everyone is just trying to control us. Both carry an ounce of truth, and we need both a healthy value of self and others to become balanced.

What did you notice?

The Two Dogs. The two dogs (one feral, one domestic) represent the two aspects of self. If this imagery draws your attention, it is important for the querent to bring themselves into balance, noticing which of the dogs they feed more!

The Crawfish. The crawfish emerging from the water onto the land symbolizes a shift in consciousness. It is important to note how you feel when seeing the crawfish. Does it cause you fear, or do you feel comfortable with the imagery? Make note that this reaction often reflects the querent's emotional state.

The Pool of Water. Water represents the subconscious mind. Noticing it in this card is a reminder to examine how we handle stressful situations, noting that in most cases the actions taken are automatic, directed by our subconscious, and may no longer serve us.

The Two Towers and Path. The path through the two towers shows us that the best way is often the one that runs right through the middle, and that finding harmony will require the querent to balance doing for others and honoring themselves.

The Major Arcana + 231

◇◇◇◇◇◇◇◇◇◇◇◇◇◇

MEDITATION

THE MOON

Take a few moments before closing your eyes to look at the card in front of you, allowing yourself to take in as many details as you can. Close your eyes and bring your attention to your breathing. Focus on your inhalation and exhalation as they become balanced and rhythmic, inhaling and exhaling evenly through the nose.

Continuing to breathe deeply, imagine you are standing at the sacred water, a place you are now familiar with; it is the well that connects us deeply to our intuition, visited by Temperance and the Star. As you look across the water, you see a path leading through the two towers that were presented in the Death card. They are much closer now! Looking at the towers you remember that they are a gateway separating the world of living from that of the dead: a gateway to Heaven.

The Moon is high above you and luminous in its fullness, illuminating the path. On either side of the path there is a dog. On one side there is a domestic dog, always seeking to please others, and on the other the dog is feral, seeking to please its own desires. To move forward on the path toward enlightenment we must seek the aid of both dogs, recognizing that balance is important, and we must be equally feral and domesticated in our pursuits, seeking to help both ourselves and others.

As we begin to set out on our journey, we come across a lobster just coming out of the water. We are reminded that our truth lies in the subconscious mind, at the bottom of the sea that is our soul.

This journey is deeply emotional and intuitive. We can feel a building pressure as our journey moves closer to its end. Walking through the towering portal in the distance will bring us closer to soul consciousness and our ability to exist between worlds.

Continuing to focus on your breath, focus your mind on your physical body, wiggling your toes and fingers, moving your consciousness back into your physical form with every movement. Open your eyes and take a few moments to record your experience.

✦ The Sun ✦

XIX. The Sun is a card of glory, harmony, joy, and good fortune. It is the joyous rebirth awaited after the long dark, in which we celebrate life itself! The card often features a young child naked and illuminated by the sun, representing the newness of life and the purity it offers. The Sun shines its glory on us, rewarding us for enduring the long and arduous road the Major Arcana has taken us on. Its arrival grants us a reprieve from the shadowy corners of our minds, giving us an opportunity to celebrate all that is good and true in life.

The Sun is a card of rebirth, showing that the querent did not arrive where they are by luck, but by traversing the lessons life presented them and overcoming their personal demons; the return of the Sun is

The Major Arcana + 233

the reward for their trials. Within this newfound illumination, the querent is prepared to move forward knowing that God/Goddess/Universe is conspiring with them to bring about something greater.

When the Sun card appears in a reading, the querent should expect an experience of joy and good fortune that is in harmony with their life path. *This is important, for moments in which things are going right can appear suspect to those who have gotten used to the heavy drudgery of burden.* The Sun is a powerful card of rebirth offering us the opportunity to grow in a joyful, loving way, for it is a card of destiny that confirms we are walking our path with the support of the God/Goddess/Universe, and as the road getting there most likely has involved dark pits and tear-filled nights, this rebirth is earned! The querent should embrace the light of the Sun for its path is one of harmony, joy, and personal greatness.

What did you notice?

The Sun. The image of the sun in the Sun card is warm and welcoming, carrying the energy of victory and satisfaction. It is the perfect sun on the perfect day! Noticing the sun shows that the querent has overcome a great struggle to get where they are.

The Child. The child is the image of rebirth; they are young, fresh, naked, and full of joy. Symbolically this shows that the querent will feel a great burden lifted from their shoulders, and a rewilding of their soul, becoming more playful and childlike.

The Sunflowers. The sunflowers are a sign of growth, strength, and bounty. This is a sign that the new path that follows the rebirth will be bountiful.

The Horse. Noticing the mount in the card is symbolic of rapid movement. If you find this image stood out to you, the querent can expect change following rebirth to be quick.

234 ✦ The Tarot

◇◇◇◇◇◇◇◇◇◇◇◇◇

MEDITATION
The Sun

Take a few moments before closing your eyes to look at the card in front of you, allowing yourself to take in as many details as you can. Close your eyes and bring your attention to your breathing. Focus on your inhalation and exhalation as they become balanced and rhythmic, inhaling and exhaling evenly through the nose.

Continuing to breathe deeply, imagine that it is a glorious sunny day, with a bright blue sky and a warm breeze. Sunflowers grow in your garden, and the sun is full and fat in the sky. You have made it through the gateway, after traversing the path by the light of the Moon in your previous journey. Take a moment to soak in the light of the Sun.

In front of you is a golden-haired child riding a white horse, a crown of yellow flowers upon their head. A large red banner flutters behind them— a sign of celebration, victory, and glory! Looking upon the child you feel buoyant and happy, renewed and vibrant. This is a moment of goodness along the path, a time of respite and rejoicing. Take a moment here to think on what brings you such joy, and how you experience it in the physical world. (Pause here for a few breaths.)

Sunflowers wave in the breeze catching your eye; standing straight beside each other in rows, they remind you of loyalty, adoration, and happiness. Their presence reminds you that you are supported, that others value you and celebrate your wins along with you. Take a moment to think on how you are supported in your physical life. Who are the people who celebrate your accomplishments with you? Who are your loyal companions?

Sitting in our garden celebrating our victories, in the Sun we feel reborn. Having survived the trials of the Hanged Man, walked the lonely path of self-discovery as the Hermit, spun the Wheel of Fortune, been weighed and measured by Justice, explored Death and the darkness of our soul with the Devil, and survived the crashing of the Tower and all the lessons in between, you have been reborn, shining as the Sun! Your journey so far has been epic! Take a few more minutes to sit in the glory of what you have overcome. (Pause here for a few breaths.)

Continuing to focus on your breath, focus your mind on your physical body, wiggling your toes and fingers, moving your consciousness back into your physical form with every movement. Open your eyes and take a few moments to record your experience.

✦ Judgement ✦

XX. Judgement illustrates one's righteousness being assessed at the end of times. Having traveled the path crafted by the Major Arcana we witnessed the progression of the soul—from stepping off the edge of the cliff as the Fool, gathering our tools as the Magician, facing our fears

and shadow with the Devil, and expanding our consciousness through many a trial and tribulation along the way—we now stand in a place of evaluation in which we are judged. But where old-school, biblical fear may have us quivering in fear at such a thought, the images on the card speak otherwise, often showing calm and joyful faces looking to the heavens.

While the Judgement card can be a joyous card of earned recognition and aspired growth, it is also a card that holds the power of true sight. It is often depicted with an angel overlooking a man and a woman revealing the truth of their souls and passing judgment. When it shows up in a reading it is important to feel into it, and really look at the other cards that surround it; Judgement has no bias!

When our psychic mind focuses on the symbolic imagery of angelic rapture, we may interpret it as a sign of rebirth and forgiveness. By seeing the card in such a manner our view becomes one more focused on the growth of the soul and less on punishment. This is important when using the Major Arcana as a map for soul development. Judgement is a rite of passage in which we move forward into a new, wiser incarnation of self.

This card may reflect judgment passed on the querent or a need for the querent to examine their own judgment. Are their judgments biased? Are they judged falsely? Judgement requires a clear evaluation of situations from a point of balance and truth. *If you are experiencing this in a personal reading, taking time to center yourself before doing a reading will help you get a better assessment of the situation.* When Judgement comes in about others, it is generally meant as a heads-up that the truth will be revealed and the person/situation in question will receive what they deserve. This is a quiet reminder that we do not need to obsess over it, that it is not our place to dole out punishment or right the wrongs, but that a higher power is at play in the situation. Regardless of whether Judgement shows up for the querent personally or for another, it is a powerful card that shows that the situation is being minded by the Universe and things will be set right and true!

The Major Arcana + 237

What did you notice?

The Angel. Featured above the people in a place of judgment, the angel represents the dual role of gatekeeper and illuminator of souls. The angel shows that the querent should be cautious, but ultimately approach the situation with a desire for truth, reserving judgment until all facts are presented.

The Risen Dead. Standing in their graves the souls of the dead are symbolic of rebirth, showing the querent's evolution on a soul level, elevated and transformed by a death of some part of their life.

The Trumpet. The trumpet can represent a need for the querent to wake up and look clearly at the situation. It can also represent the triumph of success; let your intuition as a psychic storyteller determine which.

The Background. The bright blue sky and vantage point above the clouds symbolically shows that the querent has ascended, as such images are often associated with the Christian heaven. As a background it adds support to the querent showing that there is an elevated level of moral decency in the situation.

◇◇◇◇◇◇◇◇◇◇◇◇◇

MEDITATION
JUDGEMENT

Take a few moments before closing your eyes to look at the card in front of you, allowing yourself to take in as many details as you can. Close your eyes and bring your attention to your breathing. Focus on your inhalation and exhalation as they become balanced and rhythmic, inhaling and exhaling evenly through the nose.

Continuing to breathe deeply, imagine you hear the sound of trumpets calling you to wake. The sound is triumphant and welcoming. There is a feeling of awakening, as if your consciousness is being elevated. The sky around you is illuminated, and you feel the presence of a supernatural being. For some this may appear as an angel, for others a guide or a venerated

238 ✦ The Tarot

ancestor. Take a moment to sit with the call and your response to it. Do you feel threatened or welcomed by the call? (Pause here for a few breaths.)

You rise up from your slumber and stretch your body toward the sky; you are once again naked, something you have come to see as a sign of vulnerability and having nothing to hide. Take a moment to see how that feels. Are you comfortable being vulnerable? Do you struggle to trust? Are you afraid of being judged? Take a few breaths here, allowing yourself to work through the emotions that come up. (Pause here for a few breaths.)

While many may fear Judgement, you have been tempered by your travels through the Major Arcana and have proven yourself time and time again. You have faced your fears and your darkness, and you have embraced your light. Do not be afraid of Judgement!

You see the illuminated being above you—be they angel, ancestor, or deity. Seeing them you recognize that it is your soul that is being judged. Judged to see whether you are living your life in accordance with what is best for you. You lock eyes with them and ask, "What is your Judgement?" Take a few moments here to receive your judgment, knowing that ultimately this knowledge is coming from your guides and higher self. (Pause here for a few breaths.)

Having experienced your own judgment you are now able to see that there are people all around you being judged. Some are doing so fearfully—pleading with the higher power for mercy—while the majority are doing so with their arms raised high toward the heavens. You see that Judgement is fair, and meant to bring about a period of awakening in people. It is helping us to find our true purpose.

Take a few moments here to think of how you pass false judgment on yourself, and how releasing that constant fear of not being good enough can help you.

Continuing to focus on your breath, focus your mind on your physical body, wiggling your toes and fingers, moving your consciousness back into your physical form with every movement. Open your eyes and take a few moments to record your experience.

✦ The World ✦

XXI. The World speaks of greater perspective and the need to look at how the situation affects the big picture, requiring us to take into consideration the importance of how our actions will affect others. In many decks a woman is suspended in the sky surrounded by animals and birds or alchemical symbols for the elements of Earth, Air, Fire, and Water—either way representing the building blocks of our world. The World is a card pertinent to the times we live in, as we must start thinking outside of our small personal box of comfort about the greater issues facing our planet.

The World asks us to broaden our perspective to include the world around us, but it is not a heavy card of weighted despair. It is a card of

240　✦　The Tarot

possibilities and cycles, which reminds us that as we are all born, we all must die, and that the world goes on regardless of the hardships and joys that we face. It is an invitation to live life fully, travel, and taste the sweetness of the world, to open our eyes to the beauty and wonder that now is fragile. When the World shows up in a reading it asks us to look at the situation from outside our personal bubble, to take into consideration the greater ripple effect caused by our actions.

The World speaks of change, the kind of change that affects more than just us, for it is all-encompassing in its reach. The World represents the complexity of situations and the connection between all things. If the World is showing up a reading, it is advising us to look at the big picture, see how the pieces go together, and realize how moving one, moves another. This viewpoint will often allow us to maneuver with more ease and flow as we will not be hitting unexpected obstacles; instead, we will see the obstacles beforehand and include them in our navigation.

What did you notice?

Beings in the Corners. In each corner of the card there is a face in the cloud: man, ox, lion, and eagle. These creatures have fixed astrological correspondences and elemental connections: man/Aquarius/Air, ox/Taurus/Earth, lion/Leo/Fire, and eagle/Scorpio/Water. (These images are also in the Wheel of Fortune as winged beings.) Make sure to take note of which of the beings stand out to you, and ask yourself how that element and its astrological traits are influencing the situation.

The Laurel Wreath. Laurel is often a sign of victory. Noticing this imagery in the card shows that the working of the querent will be successful and important.

The Woman. The woman in the center of the wreath is symbolic of the querent; we see she is confident, strong, and open. Noticing this shows the querent has something to offer to the greater world.

The Batons. The batons held in each of the woman's hands are a sign of

The Major Arcana ✦ 241

balance; noticing them is a reminder to the querent that they must keep their needs and the needs of the greater world in perspective.

◇◇◇◇◇◇◇◇◇◇◇◇

MEDITATION
THE WORLD

Take a few moments before closing your eyes to look at the card in front of you, allowing yourself to take in as many details as you can. Close your eyes and bring your attention to your breathing. Focus on your inhalation and exhalation as they become balanced and rhythmic, inhaling and exhaling evenly through the nose.

Continuing to breathe deeply, imagine you are floating in the sky, suspended by supernatural powers, with a laurel wreath surrounding you as a sign of your success.

Having passed through Judgement, you are now experiencing a life review as you end a cycle of life and prepare to start the next cycle of your life as the Fool again.

Recognizing you are at the end of a cycle, you look around you for clues to who you have been. As you float above the Earth, you see familiar images in the clouds surrounding you: the man, eagle, ox, and lion you saw while spinning the Wheel of Fortune. You know they are watching you as you move through this incarnation into another, representing the physical world.

Take a few moments to review your last life cycle, recognizing that we all go through many beginnings and endings in our lifetime. Spend a few minutes here breathing and remembering.

Continuing to focus on your breath, focus your mind on your physical body, wiggling your toes and fingers, moving your consciousness back into your physical form with every movement. Open your eyes and take a few moments to record your experience.

The Suits— The Minor Arcana

Having completed our exploration of the Major Arcana, we are now ready to step onto the supportive path of the Minor Arcana, beginning with our exploration of the tarot suits. Like the Major Arcana, each Minor Arcana card has its own meaning; however, where the Major Arcana holds deep energetic resonance, usually showing outside influence and situations that are harder to avoid, the Minor Arcana represents things that are easier to change.

Much like traditional playing cards, the Minor Arcana of the tarot is broken into four suits. However, where traditional cards have Hearts, Clubs, Spades, and Diamonds, the tarot has Cups, Wands, Swords, and Pentacles. Each suit has its own Court (King, Queen, Knight, Page) and ten numbered cards.

The suits are like kingdoms, each with different rules, values, and personalities. Understanding the nature of the suits allows the reader to get a feel for the reading before settling into the details. The more we build a relationship with the cards the easier it is for our intuitive mind to understand what they are telling us.

When developing our ability to read the tarot's story, it is important to look for patterns, such as the dominance of a suit in a spread, showing the reading will be in the suit's nature. This information contributes to the framework of the reading, similarly to how background scenery creates the environment of a play.

✦ Wands, Staves, and Clubs ✦

The suit of Wands (also called Clubs or Staves) represents thoughts, dreams, and the workings of the mind. Wands carry information about our thought process: inspiration, inner strength, intuition, creativity, and psychic knowing. When they appear in a reading, they represent things that take up space in our mental process, such as decisions that need to be made or projects we are dreaming into being. The shadow work of our consciousness is often played out through its numbered cards and Court cards.

The tarot suits are associated with the four elements: Earth, Air, Fire, and Water. The associations of Cups with Water and Pentacles with Earth are clear; however, there are differing opinions on which elements represent Wands and Swords. Wands are associated with communication, inspiration, and the workings of our mind, which connects most closely to the element of Air. Others argue that wands are flammable and represent passion, connecting them with the element of Fire. Ultimately this is a choice for you to feel out.

Many Wands in a reading show the querent has a busy mind spinning with ideas. The energy surrounding Wands is often fast-paced, showing a forward momentum with our thoughts moving into action. Wands ask us to think, to make choices, and to explore the direction we are going in in our mind first before putting it into action. Even the more challenging cards connected to the suit take on a "King of the Mountain" kind of mentality, in which the problems they present are often less than we are making them. We may experience a battered and bruised feeling when dealing with the issues they present, but—unlike Swords—they are not absolute, and they are unlikely to cause us lasting harm. If Wands are making themselves noticeable in your readings, note that you most likely have a problem you are overthinking and that

244 ✦ The Tarot

spending some time in mediation looking at the issue from a different perspective would most likely be helpful.

What did you notice?

Movement. Many of the Wand cards are action cards. When reading the symbolism of movement, pay close attention to how you feel and whether the card depicts fast or slow motion. Noting the movement is coming is one thing, being able to see how (timing, intensity, and whether it's avoidable) comes from examining all the cards and sitting with our intuition.

Thoughtfulness. As Wands are connected to the mind, noticing the expression of the people on the cards can tell a lot about the mental state surrounding the situation. Contemplation is common in Wands; when cards representing this aspect of Wands catch your attention, the querent likely has a big issue to figure out.

Struggle and Victory. The struggle depicted in the suit of Wands comes in various forms. When drawn to the struggle take note of the fact that there is more often bruising than loss of limb, as there is more of a local town victory parade feel than great warlord! In this symbolism, Wands often depict issues that can be resolved with words and thoughtful actions.

Background. The background of most Wand cards is sunburnt or not yet ripe, showing a somewhat barren environment. Symbolically this shows us that the ideas have been planted like seeds, but the time of harvest is not yet here. Wands hold potent ideas!

✦ Pentacles, Coins, Discs, and Shields ✦

Pentacles are the most solid, structured suit of the tarot. Connected solidly to the physical world, they ask us to look at our earthly affairs. Also known as Coins, Discs, and Shields, Pentacles speak to us about finances, home, work, and education. In many ways they are the basest

The Suits—The Minor Arcana + 245

of our needs, those needs that are part of all people's lives. Skill, as seen in the arts and in our work, is represented in the suit of Pentacles—so, too, is the fertility of our land, womb, and bank account.

Often associated with the element of Earth, Pentacles speak to us of the solid three-dimensional aspect of life. I have interpreted Pentacles reversed (upside down) as being associated with the spirit world. This interpretation came out of necessity. As a spirit speaker (psychic medium) I spend a lot of time in the spirit world—and helping others who are having awakenings to the world of spirit. Using Pentacles this way is like having a fifth suit: one dedicated to the working of the spirit world.

If you are looking to understand the suit of Pentacles, take a walk in the forest or a city street, practice your favorite craft, work in a garden, or spend time with your family and community. These are the things ruled by the suit of Pentacles! Remember, Pentacles' equivalent in playing cards is the suit of Diamonds.

What did you notice?

Background. Noticing the background of Pentacle cards you will see that they are either very harsh, dark, and weathered, or they are lush and appealing. This symbolically gives the reader an understanding of whether the situation is favorable or a struggle.

Craft. Pentacles are cards of skill, education, and talent. When the card is presenting a skill, it is likely the querent has something going on in this part of their life, such as going back to school, getting a new job, or recognition for their skill. Make note of the surrounding cards and feel into it with your intuition.

Gardens. Gardens are symbolic of abundance and the ability to provide. Pentacles that take place in gardens symbolically represent family life, community, and financial abundance.

Pentacles Reversed. Pentacles reversed are connected to the spirit world, particularly ancestral spirits. If you feel drawn to Pentacles reversed in this manner, often the querent is experiencing some kind of spiritual contact.

246   ✦   The Tarot

✦ Cups, Chalices, and Goblets ✦

The suit of Cups, sometimes referred to as Chalices or Goblets, is an emotional suit. Where Pentacles dealt with the physical world and Wands spoke to us about our ideas and inspirations, Cups with their connection to the element of Water are all about the way we feel, how things affect us emotionally, and the ability to perceive the world empathically. Romance, family, friendship, and all the good and bad that come with it are mixed into the Cups we are served by; learning their language is to understand the depth of importance that comes through our emotions and how we can best manage them, including how we heal.

When it comes to the healing aspect of Cups things can get deep, as they speak of the wounds that are bound in layers of emotional silt, covered in debris, and often hiding in plain sight. Cups ask us to explore the inner workings of our emotional self. They invite us to dive deep, and simmer in our feelings. They celebrate the good in life and lament the losses, showing us a complete range of human emotions: personal soul searching, journeying on our life path, intimate love affairs, marriage, and birth can all be found when gazing into the depths Cups have to offer. The story of Cups often leads through mire and bramble, and over treacherous terrain, so that we may find our truth.

If Cups are dominant in a reading the querent can expect a time of emotional immersion, in which their feelings will play a key role in their life. New love, marriage, childbirth, chasing one's dreams, betrayal, and grief are all found within the suit of Cups. Additionally, the suit of Cups can represent healing, showing up when the querent needs to process emotional trauma, or when they are being called to the role of healer.

What did you notice?

Missing Cups. If a reading includes a lot of cups that are spilled, missing, or come with a feeling of searching, the reading will most likely involve the querent feeling like they are missing something

The Suits—The Minor Arcana ✦ 247

in their life. Make note of the surrounding cards and what you feel intuitively.

Celebration. Cups raised in celebration present a background of good times to come. If these cards are noticeably present in a reading, the querent is likely moving in a positive direction in regard to their heart.

Family. Cups often have children in them and come with a feeling of family and community-building. Noting these cards in a reading will show the importance of family to the querent, and often the reading will be focused on the building and maintenance of such.

Romance. Cups are also about intimate relationships. Cup cards that depict such are symbolic of romantic relationships. Pay attention to surrounding cards, the positioning, whether reversed, and what you feel intuitively.

✦ Swords, Spades, and Blades ✦

Swords are the most aggressive of the tarot suits; they are the "shit's going to happen" cards of the deck that speak of action and change, often with a ripping-the-bandage-off approach to doing so! With the representation of Sword, Blade, or Spade, you get the point . . . it's a weapon, and chances are it's going to be a bit uncomfortable to deal with!

I like to see Swords as agents of change! They are the badass, boots-on-the-ground cards of the tarot that come into our lives to show us things are going to get real, and that action is needed to move forward. With this message, it is not surprising to find heartache, betrayal, and strife, but just as often they can represent victory, survival, and clarity. Clarity is, in fact, one of the suit of Swords' best attributes, as they often shine a light on the things we didn't want to see, making it crystal clear so we cannot deny the truth.

Often the clarity gained by Swords comes through heavy thought,

248 + The Tarot

intuitive contemplation, and puzzle-solving. We don't suddenly get all the answers because a bunch of Swords show up in our reading. Instead, the cards show us what's going on—and what needs to change! They depict the hours of anxiety the situation is causing us, shining a light on it so we can no longer keep it tucked away in the closet for no one to see. They show us our burden for what it is, often confirming what we already know.

Swords come with repercussions! While they do not always represent high-speed, action adventures, they do all lead to a conclusion. When a reading is filled with Swords you can expect to make difficult decisions, ones that are likely, at some point, to keep you up at night or cause your mind to be filled with anxiety. If such is the case do not hate the messenger, for often they are simply showing us what we already know and have been avoiding. They have come in to let us know for sure that we need to make some changes. Swords are also about clarity and victory! This means all the hard work and discomfort of moving through the travesty of false illusions we have kept ourselves in—pretending things are OK and will work out somehow—is worth it!

What did you notice?

Hardship. Many cards in the suit of Swords depict hardship. If you see this heavily being played out in a reading, center yourself and look for the ways the querent can find support as they go through the difficult times ahead of them.

Bound. There are cards in the suit of Swords that show a person bound and blindfolded with swords. If you look closely, there is a way in front of the person that is open. This shows that they must rely on intuition to help them navigate the situations they are facing.

Death. There are a couple of cards in the suit of Swords that depict death. It is important when seeing these cards to keep yourself centered and not immediately jump to death as the answer. Like the

The Suits—The Minor Arcana + 249

Death card, these cards can also be depicting betrayal and a painful ending.

Background. The background in the suit of Swords is often chiseled from stone and appears cold. Being drawn to the background, the reading can feel emotionally void, or even painful, and cold. Gentleness is often needed for the querent.

The Court Cards

In the tarot, each suit has a Court consisting of a Page, a Knight, a Queen, and a King. As mentioned before, the Court cards are the Minor Arcana cards that will most often depict people in readings. As we will see, these personalities also have characteristics that are intertwined with their suits. One of the things that I think is important to mention—particularly when speaking of the Court cards—is that the cards are gender-fluid! This is important to know as Court cards show up in the representation of people in our life more often than other cards do, which means we may pull a Queen in the representation of ourselves or another regardless of our sexual identity, as the card is showing more in connection to how we think, act, and respond than to our body parts and outward presentation.

✦ The Pages ✦

Pages are the messengers of the court. They carry important documents, share ideas, and introduce concepts to the querent. Each Page has a different flavor depending on the suit it is attached to.

The Page of Wands comes with messages of growth, particularly that of soul growth. Their arrival heralds opportunity, inspiration, and new ideas. The Page of Wands is the adventurous traveler who points the way to the path we should take. Remember that Wands

are all about the expansion of our thoughts and the contemplation of ideas. The Page of Wands' appearance in our reading tells us things are going to change; we are going to see the world differently whether we want to or not. Ushering in new adventures, travel, and concepts that will ultimately bring about spiritual growth, the Page of Wands often opens new channels of communication for us—both with ourselves and others. The bold step onto the path they represent, which invites us to become more! *Physically the Page of Wands has an outdoorsy, sun-kissed look about them, with a practical fashion sense.*

The Shadow Page of Wands (reversed) carries messages from our higher self.

The Page of Pentacles is the ambitious doer of the Pages, the manifester, who shows up to remind us that it's time to take our dreams into the physical world. Remembering that Pentacles are the suit that tells of the earthly realm of home, job, building, and creating, we can see the Page of Pentacles as a sign it's time to make things happen, to step up to the crafting bench and start getting things done. The Page of Pentacles, being focused on our earthly world, carries messages of creation. This can be a powerful card that invites us to become co-creators of our reality! *Physically the Page of Pentacles has contrasting or striking features and tends to be a bit more groomed and glamorous.*

The Shadow Page of Pentacles (reversed) carries messages from the spirit world.

The Page of Cups is the most emotional of the Pages, often considered the messenger of love. When the Page of Cups comes into our life, they are there to make us aware of an emotional situation that needs our attention. It is easy to assume that as a messenger of love they would be all about romance, but love comes in many different forms, so it's important to check in with your intuition and the cards surrounding the Page to get a clear look at the message they carry. Generally, the Page of Cups is seen as a messenger of good news, carrying whispers of romantic love, budding friendships, and opportunities that carry an emotional component. One of my favorite ways to view the Page of Cups is as the messenger of healing, who shows up to point the way toward the path of wholeness. *The*

PAGE of CUPS.

Page of Cups has a softness to their appearance. This may be in their physical appearance in the form of rounded face and youthfulness. They tend toward a softer, more romantic style.

The Shadow Page of Cups (reversed) carries messages of our personal emotions.

The Page of Swords carries messages of action! Stepping forward they announce that shit is going to happen. While they do not carry the immediate activation of a Knight, they are the boldest of the Pages. Their messages are often direct, and their tongue can be sharp. Little energy is wasted on emotions when the Page of Swords shows up; they are quick of mind and hold the direction of leadership,

PAGE of SWORDS.

The Court Cards   +   255

telling us we need to get moving *now* . . . much like an alarm clock going off, they are not to be ignored. They are eager to get on with the business at hand and often their appearance in our life feels like being prodded with a pointy blade. We can't sit around comfortably procrastinating, as they will poke us with the sharp end until we are uncomfortable enough to move. The Page of Swords is not meant to punish us; they are simply a no-nonsense kind of messenger. They see change needs to be made, and they are going to speak up until we do! *Physically the Page of Swords is more angular in appearance and leans toward uniform or clean fashion.*

The Shadow Page of Swords (reversed) carries messages of our internal strife.

What did you notice?

Physical Appearance. If you find yourself drawn toward the physical appearance of the Page, the card is most likely showing you a person who is either in or entering the querent's life. Looking into your third eye, see if you can pull out any other details.

Their Tool. Each of the Pages carries an implement of their office. Being drawn to the tool indicates that the message they carry will be connected to the workings of their suit.

Their Bearing. The Page's stance helps determine how the message will be delivered.

The Background. Backgrounds frame the reading, showing the energy and warmth of the message the Page is carrying. The background of Court cards can also be used to determine seasons. Notice how the land feels, and ask your intuitive mind what season you believe this message will come in.

+ The Knights +

Where the Page politely delivers a message like an errand boy, the Knight barges onto the scene insisting that something needs to be done about the situation. Knights are bold—and mounted! Like cavalry units of the military, they are mobile and fleet, often taking us by surprise. Regardless of their suit they are action cards, and the appearance of a Knight in a reading means things need attending to. More than one Knight in the reading, you should prepare for shit to get moving—and most likely for there to be a momentum involved that leaves us little choice but to do so. Unlike the Page, whose message we can conveniently tuck away in the recesses of our mind, the appearance of Knights will not be ignored!

The Knight of Wands announces bold changes in the way we think, filling our minds with opportunities to grow. They are enthusiastic, capable of getting others interested in the news they carry. They

carry a youthful, sometimes hyper energy that expands their ideas in grand ways with plans often many steps ahead of the beginning. They are playful and often athletic, with a grace to their movement. They share the same sun-kissed features as their entire Court family.

The Shadow Knight of Wands (reversed) can represent the spirit of inspiration, rushing forward and filling the querant with creativity and drive.

The Knight of Pentacles comes bearing gifts, documents, and opportunity for growth in the physical world of the querent. The Knight of Pentacles is bold in nature with a gregarious, showy personality. While this is often just confidence, in some cases the Knight

of Pentacles can be seen as arrogant—or as carrying expectations that they expect filled due to their station. The Knight of Pentacles often enters our lives in the form of business opportunities. In life, those represented by the Knight of Pentacles are drawn to the nicer things in life, often having expensive taste or being flamboyant in style.

The Shadow Knight of Pentacles (when reversed) can represent a visitation from spirit, happening in such a way that it cannot be ignored.

The Knight of Cups comes forward announcing love, like the fabled knights of old who joust in the name of their fair lady. They are the most romantic of the Knights, and in truth of all the Court!

They are deeply connected to their emotions, which can be good or bad. In most cases the Knight of Cups is showy in love; however, in the negative aspect they can be clingy and possessive. Make sure to check in with your intuition when encountering the Knight of Cups to help you see the nature of their emotions. In appearance the Knight of Cups can be seen as a player, in the sense that they often dress and groom themselves to attract a mate. Love and lovemaking are some of their favorite things!

The Shadow Knight of Cups (reversed) can represent personal healing, and self love.

The Knight of Swords cares little for our comfort; instead, they rip off the Band-Aid and make us look at the trouble festering beneath

260 ✦ The Tarot

the surface. They lean toward a military stance and a briskness of speech, often taking a direct route, speaking analytically with a focus on clarity of information. This can make the Knight of Swords come across as lacking in emotion. Physically the Knight of Swords can appear imposing, their stance often coming across as aggressive or ready to spring into action. Their features can be seen as dark and foreboding, or angular like the rest of their court.

The Shadow Knight of Swords (reversed) often represents our personal shadow, the part of our self we battle with.

What did you notice?

Physical Appearance. If you find yourself drawn toward the physical appearance of the Knights, the card is most likely showing you a person who is either in or entering the querent's life. Looking into your third eye, see if you can pull out any other details.

Their Tool. Each of the Knights carries an implement from their office. If you find you are drawn to the tool the Knight carries, the suit they serve plays a big part in the message they carry.

Their Bearing. Noticing the stance of the Knight helps determine how the message will be delivered.

The Background. Backgrounds frame the reading, showing the energy and warmth of the message the Knight is carrying. With practice you will develop an understanding of time and season when looking at the background of cards. Make sure to keep track of your progress in your Book of Shadows.

✦ The Queens ✦

Oh, the Queens! I personally love the Queens of the tarot. They are receptive and deep, and they often carry an air of mystery that makes them somehow both royalty and priestess at the same time. Carrying the feel of magic that is almost palatable, these powerful ladies of the Court hold the very essence of feminine power. Queens are contemplative and thoughtful, and they must be pursued! This means if you want something from the Queen you will need to ask, offer, or present your idea. She expects you to come to her! It's easy to understand if we take a moment to think of how a Queen functions in any court. For the most part, she stays in the castle, doing business on the home front while the King is off warring, negotiating, and outwardly achieving. A Queen in many ways is like the mother of a country; she rules with a softer touch than her husband and is seen as a bit more rational and willing to compromise.

The Queen of Wands is the creative, hands-on Queen who leads through enthusiasm, following Awen (the spirit of creativity) as if her life was a quest of becoming. In many decks, she is pictured with sunflowers, a sign of regenerative growth, as they are known

for their ability to clean soil and replenish damaged land. The Queen of Wands has an adventurous spirit and a quick mind. She is open to new ideas and desires to make the world she serves a better place. *Physically she is likely to be strong, agile, and often athletic. Like the rest of her court, she is sun-kissed and has a strong love of the outdoors. Her style is often practical and suited for adventure.*

The Shadow Queen of Wands (reversed) represents creative thinkers, and artists prone to loosing themselves in fantasy.

The Queen of Pentacles is the earthliest of the Queens; she is deeply connected to the material world. She represents prosperity and abundance, and she is often seen as the most generous of Queens. Rich gardens and ornate events surround this Queen, for she is fully

settled into her position. *This Queen is often dramatic in her dress with a love of rich fabrics, accessories, and quality. Her features, like the rest of her court, are striking, often with much contrast.*

The Shadow Queen of Pentacles (reversed) represents mediums and all who communicate between the veil of the living and the dead.

The Queen of Cups is the most compassionate of the Queens, as she is emotional, empathic, and deeply connected to her intuition. Regardless of the deck, she tends to seem a bit ethereal, as if she has one foot in this world and one in another. When representing a person this may mean she is highly sensitive and dreamy. She is the nurturing mother and the empathic feeler who rules through her heart.

Physically she has softer features and a gentleness to her demeanor. Her fashion is often romantic and dreamy like her personality.

The Shadow Queen of Cups (reversed) represents empaths and those who are natural healers.

The Queen of Swords often reminds me of an M&M. She has a hard (candy) shell but is super soft on the inside. In most cards her sword is held in front of her in some sort of protective stance, showing that she expects you to approach her with respect and to keep your distance a bit, for she does not open her arms to strangers. Like all the Queens she is seen as receptive and wise, but her wisdom is much more analytical than some of the others. She weighs things

QUEEN of SWORDS.

The Court Cards ✦ 265

out at arm's length before she makes a move. However, she is far softer than she lets on, and once wounded it is unlikely she will ever forget the affront. While she may publicly act as if she has not been bothered by your actions, she will remember it always. Words matter with this Queen, so be careful how you approach and how you speak your mind, for she is likely to take you literally. *Physically the Queen of Swords is tight in posture, often holding her body in a defensive stance. She prefers simple, clean lines as she prefers to be recognized for her mind, not her appearance!*

The Shadow Queen of Swords (reversed) represents those who are drawn to relationships with people who mistreat them.

What did you notice?

Physical Appearance. If you find yourself drawn toward the physical appearance of one of the Queens, the card is most likely showing you a person who is either in or entering the querent's life. Looking into your third eye, see if you can pull out any other details.

Their Tool. Each of the Queens carries an implement of her office. If you find you are drawn to the tool the Queen holds, the suit plays a big part in the message she carries.

Their Bearing. Noticing the body posture of the Queen helps determine how the message will be delivered or received.

The Background. The throne and background of the Queen say a lot about the situation surrounding the person or question associated with the card.

✦ The Kings ✦

The Kings of the tarot are the most commanding of the Court cards. Having the perspective of those who have traveled through life overcoming obstacles, gaining wisdom and power, they now reign through thought and deed. When a King appears in our reading there is little room for maybes and think-so's, as we are being commanded to look at the information they bring to light! Their presence alone is a sure sign that we will need to do something about the situation, and most likely that something will involve action. As the highest of the Court cards the Kings trump all other tarot royalty. While they are persistent, they will quickly become annoyed at having to remind us more than once, making our lives uncomfortable until we do as we are advised.

The King of Wands is an inspired leader, his mind often alight with ideas and purpose. He is keenly aware of his physical prowess and is often seen poised upon his throne as if he could spring to action at any time. When representing a person, he has a tendency to be connected to those who are movers and shakers, with creativity and growth springing up around them. When the King of Wands shows up in a reading, the querent should pay attention to dreams that are

percolating around them and have faith that it is time to act upon those that speak loudest. *Physically the King of Wands is outdoorsy, sun-kissed, and practical. His style is often adventurous, and he may have a leaning toward physically demanding careers or hobbies.*

The Shadow King of Wands (reversed) represents a person who overthinks everything.

The King of Pentacles represents success on the physical plane. He is abundant, rich, and successful, and he has earned his throne! Often representing those who are self-made, achieving their position through hard work and dedication, the King of Pentacles is proud—and may even lean toward arrogance. This is a card that

KING of PENTACLES.

often comes up for those who are self-made entrepreneurs, who blaze the path of their own destiny. The King of Pentacles likes being King and does not expect his generosity to go unnoticed. When he shows up in a reading, he often refers to success through hard work and dedication. *Physically the King of Pentacles is well groomed, with a desire to show his success through expensive items. He has striking or contrasting features much like the rest of his Court.*

The Shadow King of Pentacles (reversed) often shows us that a powerful spirit is trying to make contact with us, often a personal spirit guide.

The King of Cups is highly intuitive and connected to his emotions. In the best-case scenario, he is ruler of his emotions; in the worst, he

KING of CUPS.

The Court Cards ✦ 269

is ruled by them! Knowing which qualities he possesses comes from developing our intuitive ability to read the story the card is telling us. He is diplomatic, preferring conversation and communication over swords and shields. When the King of Cups is reversed, he may find his emotions overwhelming, and/or be prone to addiction and overindulgence. If the King of Cups shows up in a reading, he may be showing you something of yourself you need to see, particularly if you are easily ruled by your emotions. Learning how to navigate our emotions is paramount to our growth as awakened humans, for the clarity of our intuition can be dulled when we let our emotions run rampant around us. *Physically the King of Cups is the gentlest of the Kings, often carrying a youthful face long in life. They prefer comfortable clothing and have a tendency toward enjoying the comforts of life (food, drink, smoke).*

The Shadow King of Cups (reversed) represents a person whose emotions have become overwhelming.

The King of Swords is the warlord King. He has won his seat through battle, and he intends to keep it! The King of Swords is not content to wait for trouble to come to him; he is ever vigilant in the search for his next obstacle. As a master strategist, he relies on his wit as often as his might. He can often come across as cold or lacking in emotions, and, in truth, this is the most difficult of Kings to have an intimate relationship with, as they struggle to express their emotions, often coming out cockeyed or backward. When the King of Swords shows up in a reading the querent may be expected to use force to achieve their goal. (Please note that *force* and *violence* are not necessarily the same thing!) *Physically the King of Swords is often militant or utilitarian in his appearance, often preferring a uniform. They often have careers in areas that rely heavily on strategy.*

The Shadow King of Swords (reversed) represents a person who struggles with rage or anger, affecting their ability to self-regulate.

What did you notice?

Physical Appearance. If you find yourself drawn toward the physical appearance of one of the Kings, the card is most likely showing you a person who is either in or entering the querent's life. Looking into your third eye, see if you can pull out any other details.

Their Tool. Each of the Kings carries an implement of his office. If you find you are drawn to the tool the King holds, the suit plays a big part in the message he carries.

Their Bearing. Noticing the body posture of the King helps determine how the message will be delivered. This is particularly noteworthy with Kings!

The Background. The throne and background of the King say a lot about the situation surrounding the person or question associated with the card. For the King his throne is a place of leadership; if this is shown in a reading as significant, it often represents the project's physical surroundings and support.

| THE CHARIOT. | DEATH. | THE EMPEROR. | THE EMPRESS. | THE FOOL. | THE HERMIT. | THE HIEROPHANT. | JUDGEMENT. |

Numerology and the Tarot

Numerology is the art of divination through numbers, recognizing that situations such as births, marriages, and important dates—as well as phone numbers, addresses, and even names—carry an energetic vibration based on their numerological value. In numerology, numbers are broken down to their base value by adding their digits together until you reach a single digit. For example, the number 12 would become 1 + 2, which equals 3, so it would carry the numerological quality of the number 3. (Note that the master numbers 11, 22, 33, 44, etc. are the exception to this rule; they are not broken down to single digits because they carry their own energetic signatures.) In our study of numerology within the tarot, we will focus on the numbered cards that are present in each of the suits: Aces (Ones) through Tens.

It is important to remember that the numerological value can sway in meaning a bit depending on what suit it is present in, just as the position where the card appears in the spread also influences the meaning. Think of the position in the spread as the question being asked, and then use the numerological meaning and your understanding of the suit to help arrive at your answer. The more cards in a reading of the same number, the stronger the numerological influence. So, if you have all

Numerology and the Tarot ✦ 273

four Threes show up, or there are multiple of them back-to-back, you know the number influence is potent!

✦ Ace ✦

Ace (One) in readings represents the activation point of things we have chosen to learn in this lifetime; it shows us what is inevitable! While we cannot change the fact that these events will be, we can determine how we will navigate them.

The Aces have taken on a special meaning in my working with the tarot as a storyteller, as they represent both the number one and something more. In numerology, the number one represents new beginnings, independence, leadership, and pioneering spirit; the number one also has a special meaning to me, that of karmic connection. Aces in playing cards can represent the number one, but they more often are seen as one of the highest-ranking cards in the deck, and the same is true for the tarot. In this way Aces represent the big "1"—carrying the master number energy of 11, the karmic vibration of something extraordinary. In most decks, Aces are depicted as a single item (pentacle, cup, wand, or sword) being presented by the hand of divine, showing that what is being presented is special!

Aces, like the master number 11, carry the vibration of teacher, surfacing in readings as reminders of lessons the querent has chosen to learn! They are not to be feared; instead, it is important to remind the querent that they were the one who created the plan in the first place. In my experience, when we engage with the lessons presented by the Aces, we will find things move smoothly, and when we resist the teachings of the Aces, we tend to get kicked around a bit. *I will revisit number one at the end of this chapter, when we discuss the numerological transformation of ten back into one.*

The Ace of Wands is filled with inspiration, dreams, and ideas. Remembering that Aces are connected to our destiny, that which must happen, the Ace of Wands often speaks to us of that which we

ACE of WANDS.

ACE of PENTACLES.

ACE of CUPS.

ACE of SWORDS.

Numerology and the Tarot ✦ 275

hold deep inside ourselves that wants to be birthed. It is the dream that speaks to us over and repeatedly, until we cannot help but take action.

The Ace of Pentacles affects our physical world; it is the personification of manifestation. When present in a reading it is speaking of things that *will happen*! Often it is associated with things we build, create, and birth: businesses, children, art, and so on. When the Ace of Pentacles is upside down (reversed), showing its shadow aspect, it often refers to things that are happening in the world of spirit. This is more likely to happen in a reading if the querent is a spiritual seeker.

The Ace of Cups is all about love and healing. When the Ace of Cups shows up the reader is well advised to pay close attention to the other cards and the position the Ace of Cups holds in the spread, as there are different ways of seeing this card. In its first incarnation the Ace of Cups represents love in all forms. It can be speaking of a child, lover, or platonic relationship. It can also be telling a tale of health, as it is connected to healing. Really feel this one out, don't rush, and let your intuition tell you the tale.

The Ace of Swords is a card of action. It is sharp and direct, cutting through all the bullshit we tell ourselves. When the Ace of Swords shows up things are going to get intense quickly. "Victory through action!" is one of my favorite sayings I use to describe this card. It is quick and to the point, and it generally is cold and unemotional in doing so. This does not mean you will not feel emotions; instead, it comes with little regard for our comfort, being focused on getting the job done. This is not necessarily a bad thing, as many people prefer to get the situation over with before healing. It is a card of endings . . . and beginnings.

What did you notice?

The Hand. The hand presenting the Ace speaks of a higher power. Noticing this emphasizes the importance of the situation.

276　✦　The Tarot

The Suit. This shows us what area of the querent's life will be affected by the Ace.

More Than One Ace. Having more than one Ace in a reading is a sign that the querent will be dealing with a major life-changing event that, while part of their life plan, will likely demand a lot of their attention.

The Background. Just as in all cards, the background creates the scene for the story of the card.

✦ Two ✦

Two is the number of partnerships, connections, and duality. Representing the pair or duo, in numerology it speaks of receptivity, gentleness, understanding, and adaptability. While Twos in the tarot often speak of personal relationships, these relationships are not always with other humans, but instead speak simply of a relationship between two beings, which expands the possibilities to include our relationship with spirit guides, deities, and otherworldly beings. Another important piece to remember when thinking about the Twos is that they are not always of a romantic nature, and in fact they may have nothing to do with our personal life at all.

Two also represents choice and opposition. It shows us that there is more than one way to approach a situation, and the options are often of equal value; this makes it necessary for us to bring our intuition into the mix, as the intellect of weighing the pros and cons of the situation comes out too close for a clear decision to be made. It is important to remember in such cases that in numerology two is a receptive number of give-and-take; it is soft and malleable. Where one is direct and self-absorbed, two is considerate of more than themselves, often coming with a feeling of responsibility to others. Slow and pragmatic, Twos in the tarot often present a need to contemplate our actions before taking them, whether speaking of an intimate relationship or a trying decision.

The Two of Wands is a card of choices and contemplation. There is no pressing agenda when the Two of Wands appears; instead, it is an

Numerology and the Tarot ✦ 277

278 ✦ The Tarot

invitation to think on something that perplexes you. It invites you to weigh out the choices and engage your intuition.

The Two of Pentacles is a card of balance. It speaks of the querent's need to balance a situation in their life. It can also be connected to physical balance and, as a card of earthly things, the balancing of our finances.

The Two of Cups is a card of lovers and partnership. While it can show up in platonic situations such as business partners, it most often is speaking of an amorous relationship.

The Two of Swords is a card of decisions. Blindfolded and holding two blades, the querent must make their decision based on their intuition; what they feel is best!

What did you notice?

Opposing Forces. Here we see Two as involving choice. The querent must still their mind and make their decision from a point of intuition, trusting that they know what is best.

Body Language. The body language of the Twos is very important. If you are being drawn to this imagery feel out the emotions of the situation.

Entwinement. If Two presents itself to you in this form (for example, the lemniscate in Two of Pentacles or the entwined snakes on Two of Cups), it is speaking of relationship.

Background. Noticing the background shows the support systems or opposition that surrounds the issue.

✦ Three ✦

Three resonates with the vibration of creation, carrying the energy of manifestation and the resonance of time. Time as we know it is divided into three parts: past, present, and future. Aging, too, comes in the three forms of youth, maturity, and old age. It is my belief that the separation of time is partially responsible for the creative force that emanates from situations associated with the number three, for the pressure of time

Numerology and the Tarot ♦ 279

280 + The Tarot

and the understanding of our own aging is what motivates most of us to get things done!

Through this power of creation the number three gains its association with the divine, something quite noticeable in the Christian portrayal of God as Father, Son, and Holy Spirit and in Goddess-worshipping religions in the form of the Maiden, Mother, and Crone. While the influence of divinity is notable in the Three cards, it is through the aspect of co-creation, as the querent is an active participant in any workings associated with it. When a Three shows up, regardless of the suit, we are being asked to explore the nature of who we are and what we are here to do.

The Three of Wands is about incoming opportunity. It is connected to entrepreneurship and the creative force that flows through us. When it shows up in a reading it signifies an opportunity or issue that is on the horizon; having moved from the comfort of our mind, it is now within our sight—but not yet upon us.

The Three of Pentacles represents the creative/craftmanship aspect of the number three. It is the creative force in motion and the appreciation that comes with a job well done. This is a skill that others recognize, admire, and respect.

The Three of Cups is a card of friendship and celebration, showing good times.

The Three of Swords represents the painful aspect of separation and crossing of points, in which the querent most often goes forward alone.

What did you notice?

The Symbols of Suit. Noticing the items of the suit shows that the nature of the suit greatly influences the card.

Body Language. The body language of the Threes (such as standing still or dancing) are very important. If you are being drawn to this imagery feel out the emotions of the situation.

Numerology and the Tarot ✦ 281

Entwinement. If Three presents itself to you in this form it is speaking of relationship and how the querent is viewed.

Background. Noticing the background shows the support systems or opposition that surrounds the issue.

✦ Four ✦

Four is the number of stability! As children, we soon learn to connect the number four with rectangles and squares: those solid, sturdy shapes that make up the building blocks of our reality. Tables, chairs, buildings, and monuments are generally created with four sides, or four points creating the base of the structure. Numerology is practical, designed to make sense, so when we think of the numerological value of something we should always take some time to see how it plays out in our regular day-to-day reality. Doing so helps us create mental pathways that allow us to turn abstract things, such as signs and symbols, into something solid and predictable. Moments and events that resonate with the number four will naturally be more solid, stable, and practical. Fours are never frivolous! They are balanced, thoughtful, and often represent a time of planning and building in our lives. They are cautious and love plans.

If you have a bunch of Fours showing up in a reading, remember this is a time to think deeply on your next moves, to evaluate your relationship with structure, and to make plans! Fours require us to use strategy and analytical thinking.

The Four of Wands is a card of celebration; it's generally depicted as four poles decorated with festive greenery, being placed for a wedding or celebration.

The Four of Pentacles represents a need to be thoughtful with our finances.

The Four of Cups is a reflective card that often shows the imbalance of focusing all of our mind on what we want or feel is missing while ignoring the other parts that lay at our disposal.

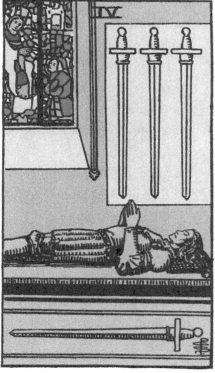

The **Four of Swords** speaks of a need to find stillness, to return to one's personal balance! It also can speak of eternal rest (death). *Intuitively, if it is the latter you would likely get a strong energetic hit.*

What did you notice?

The Symbols of Suit. Noticing the items of the suit gives you an understanding of where things will play out in the querent's life.

Body Language. The body language of the Fours varies; noticing this shows a lot about the energy surrounding the issue. As the number four is associated with strategy, make sure to engage your analytical thinking as well as your intuition. Four asks us to think like a detective!

Thought. Four is an analytical number, connecting these cards to problem-solving and critical thinking.

Background. As four is a number associated with structure, the background of the card will likely inform the reader of the physical location or environment where the situation will take place.

✦ Five ✦

Five in numerology is symbolic of free will, exploration, and overcoming obstacles. In tarot, the vibe seems to be most prevalent in the latter. In numerology the number five represents being at a point in which you have all the ingredients needed to succeed; however, you now must figure out how to use them. It's the halfway point, as numerology works with single-digit numbers (except for master numbers 11, 22, 33, etc.). Being the middle marker, five is where the real work begins; the prior work was simply the foundational support. Five in the tarot calls upon our ability to be resourceful, which includes knowing when to seek out help!

Often when the Fives are dominant in a reading (when you have three or four of them, or when you have them doubled up next to each other), the querent can expect hard work and a bit of upheaval in achieving their goal. It is also a sign that the things we need to succeed are within our grasp if we are willing to put a bit of work into them.

Numerology and the Tarot ✦ 285

The Five of Wands reminds me of King of the Mountain: a game of strength, as opposed to a real fight! Most likely the querent will struggle to reach their goal but with no serious wounding.

The Five of Pentacles is a card of struggle and refuge, telling the story of support and how the querent or situation may need help from others.

The Five of Cups is the "licking our wounds" card of the deck! It shows us the querent is spending too much time lamenting over what they do not have—and not enough time appreciating what they do!

The Five of Swords depicts winning a battle, but not without losses.

What did you notice?

Struggle. Struggle is a common feature with the Fives; notice what side of hardship you intuitively see the querent on.

Body Language. The body language of the Fives often comes across as being weary, tired, and wrung out. If you note this imagery in the card the querent is most likely feeling at the end of their ability to cope, alone, and should be advised to seek help.

Clothing. The people in the Five cards are often wearing torn and tattered clothing. If you are drawn to this aspect of the card, there is likely to be true hardships.

The Weather. The Five cards often feature weather in the background. If you find yourself drawn to this imagery in the card, make note of how weather is symbolic of our emotions.

✦ Six ✦

Six represents responsibilities, family, and community; it asks us to think about people and situations outside of ourselves. Six is thoughtful and conscientious, seeks true harmony, and understands that it cannot exist while others are suffering. Sixes in the tarot focus on the refuge and peace that comes through community.

The Six of Wands is a card of victory! While it can show up in a reading as a sign of personal victory, it is more a card of winning the

battle for the team or community. The victory is shared, and often the querent is celebrated for their part in it.

The Six of Pentacles shows us the true aspect of the Sixes' generosity. As Pentacles are the suit that represents our earthly needs, this card carries the physical component of generosity.

The Six of Cups is a gentle card, one often associated with childhood love, or the simple act of giving. It is kind and holds a sense of innocence, as the gifts are given with a feeling of purity, holding no expectation or need of gifts returned.

The Six of Swords is a card of refuge, often showing someone being rowed to safety, representing the overcoming of difficulty and the ability to recuperate.

What did you notice?

The Support. Support is a common feature with the Sixes. Noticing the helpers and supporters on the card is a sign that the querent will have the help that they need.

Body Language. The Body language of the Sixes is an important feature, as is identifying which person in the card is the querent.

Symbols of the Suits. If you are drawn to the symbol of the suit, remember it shows that the qualities of the suit are of particular interest.

The Background. The background of sixes is often less important than the foreground, depicting that the situation is represented by sixes is usually of a personal, up close nature.

✦ Seven ✦

Seven is a number associated with big thoughts and serious contemplation. In tarot, the Sevens collectively represent the need to see behind the veil, understanding that big decisions are often more complex than we initially believe them to be. In numerology the number seven is connected to our mind, and when it is depicted in the tarot it is generally showing us things that are taking place internally, preparing us for what we should/could/must do next! When the Sevens

Numerology and the Tarot ✦ 289

are dominant in a reading (showing up in a pair close together, or having three or four of them), it is a good idea to take a moment to think about the situation at hand. Deeply connected to spiritual awareness, when we sit with the lessons of the Sevens, we often see the problems associated with them resolve themselves with little physical effort. Seven is deeply connected with the divine, be it God/Goddess/Universe or collective consciousness. When the number seven is dominant in your life, know that you are being asked to examine the fundamental workings of your life, the way you engage with the world, and the world you want to create!

The Seven of Wands is a defensive card that shows we have taken the high ground and now simply need to defend it. The obstacle in front of the querent should be faced with a flexible mind and the understanding that it will not overwhelm them, for they have the vantage point!

The Seven of Pentacles is a card of planting, harvestings, and saving for a later date. It is a card that speaks of investment in things and following them into fruition.

The Seven of Cups is a card of dreams, often depicted with a person looking at cups filled with different kinds of treasure floating in the clouds. The card shows dreams, potential realities, and the illusions we must face. Remember, Cups are connected to our emotions.

The Seven of Swords card can both be interpreted as having to leave something behind to move on, as well as pointing to betrayal, trickery, and theft. Knowing which way to interpret the card lies in examining the cards surrounding it and the story that appears to be playing out of the querent.

What did you notice?

All Consuming Vision. A common theme for the Sevens is hyperfocus. Regardless of the reason, the people in the Seven cards are hyperfocused on what's in front of them. If you notice this aspect of the

290 ✦ The Tarot

card, then the situation facing the querent will be of great importance to them.

Body Language. The body language of the Sevens shows much about the thoughts and emotions that they have when facing the situation in front of them. Noting how they feel is relevant to the querent.

Secret. There is an aspect of secret or hidden for each of the Seven cards, whether defending the unknown, dreaming of the unknown, or performing actions in secret. If you are drawn to these images then there is a need to be secretive associated with the issue, or someone is keeping a secret. Use your intuition to figure out which feels right.

The Background. The background creates the framework for the card; noticing it shows you how the situation is supported or hindered.

✦ Eight ✦

Eight is a number associated with prosperity and success, and the road traveled to achieve such. In numerology it relates to the success achieved through dedication and persistence, and it often shows a person or situation that is self-made! Beneath the shiny veneer of success that comes with the vibration of the number eight, there are often many hours, days, weeks, and years of dedication to one cause. Favored by athletes and artisans, eight carries the energy of striving toward one's personal greatness. In business, the number eight often represents a turning point in one's journey, in which their skill becomes noteworthy. Goals achieved, the journey that follows is often about choosing the next leg of our journey and making decisions on where we want to expend our energy.

The Eight of Wands represents the beginning of the journey; the Eight of Wands shows ignition! It is a card of movement, in which projectiles are being launched in the direction of our dreams. When the Eight of Wands comes in, we can expect things to start moving at a bit of a clip.

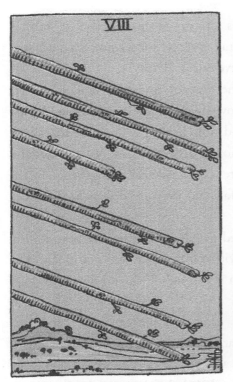

292 ✦ The Tarot

The Eight of Pentacles represents mastery of one's skill. The journey from novice to master having taken place, we are now seen as holding the skill necessary to achieve our goals.

The Eight of Cups represents the journey toward personal growth, completion, and success. It shows that the querent has found their way through the obstacles and now has eight cups behind them. The querent has achieved enough to no longer be considered a beginner on their path; they are weathered and strengthened by the road they have traveled thus far, and they are determined to seek out that which they desire.

The Eight of Swords shows a need to rely on our intuition and faith. The querent is surrounded with obstacles and blindfolded. The only way through the situation is through faith and intuition.

What did you notice?

Confidence. Regardless of the situation, the people featured in the Eight cards all have confidence and an aura of calm around them, even when they are facing challenges. It is helpful to point this out in a reading, as it can change how the querent approaches the situation.

The Process. Eights are action cards. While the processes may be different, on each card the person is deeply in the middle of doing something. This shows that the querent must do the work, that no one else can do it for them.

Alone. There is only one person in each of the Eight cards; noticing that they are alone shows that there will be a level of loneliness to the querent's journey.

The Background. The background creates the framework for the card; noticing it shows you how the situation is supported or hindered.

<h1 align="center">✦ Nine ✦</h1>

Nine carries a transient or temporary feel as if the things we have achieved are not firmly anchored. Numerology focuses on the energetic value of single-digit numbers (except for master numbers). Within this

Numerology and the Tarot ✦ 293

294 ✦ The Tarot

format, the number nine represents the ending point: the crossroad tipping point of contemplation before stepping into something new. It is neither the ending nor the beginning, but the space just before such things percolate!

The Nine of Wands is a card that reminds us to be attentive to that which we have acquired as it is not yet fully secure. We have captured the flag, and now must secure the castle!

The Nine of Pentacles is deeply connected to intellectual knowledge and our physical world. It tells the story of prosperity and achievements, recognizing that we have gained a level of success through our hard work and perseverance.

The Nine of Cups steps away from the fear that causes us to grip our dreams with clenched hands and tight breath . . . to a space of love and joy in which we can ponder the wonder of our life and the joy of arrival. It is a place of recognizing the fruits of our harvest, the hard work we have put in paying off, and the celebration of life!

The Nine of Swords brings our thinking into the darker realm of shadow and fear, representing nightmares and worries. When it shows up in a reading the querent is experiencing heavy thoughts that weigh them down. When the Nine of Swords shows up in a reading it is important to remember that our thoughts are being amplified by our fears and that often the thoughts we are stuck on are distorted because of such.

What did you notice?

The Emotions. The Nines are very emotion driven; making note of how you feel when looking at the card gives a good idea of how the querent will experience this space before transition.

The Contrast. The Nines are filled with contrasts often showing in their coloring. Noticing the contrast is significant to how different the querent's transition will be when it takes place.

Protective Space. In each of the Nine cards the person is in a secure location: garden, bed, behind a perimeter. This shows security and protection for the querent or situation.

The Light. The Nine cards all have light shining on the querent, showing that the transition to come will be uplifting. If you are drawn to the light, note this in the reading.

✦ Ten ✦

Ten in numerology is the first number to be transformed, moving from a double-digit number to a single digit (10 becomes 1 + 0, which equals 1). Being the first number to be broken down adds a special something to ten, as it can be seen as both an ending and a beginning!

The Ten of Wands is a card of completion, showing a person carrying a full and abundant load. The card often shows a fruitful, picturesque setting, giving the card a feeling of accomplishment and bounty. When it shows up in a reading it is generally there to show that the querent will soon be able to put down their burden, finish up their endeavor, and harvest their hard work. Recognize that doing so is simply a part of the circle of life and that new projects and obligations will eventually return, but for right now they are experiencing a point of completion!

The Ten of Pentacles is a card of legacy! It speaks of the foundation we have built—not only for ourselves, but for our family, business, or organization. It is the result of hard work and ambition; it is fruitful, generational, and abundant. The Ten of Pentacles represents reaching a completion point in the pursuit of our dreams. Being connected to the physical world, it is also seen as a card of material gain. When the Ten of Pentacles shows up it is time to stop and appreciate all we have worked so hard to create, recognizing that—like all things—it is transient, and we will again have something to strive toward one day.

The Ten of Cups is the sweetest of endings and beginnings, representing the transitional point in a relationship upon which dreams

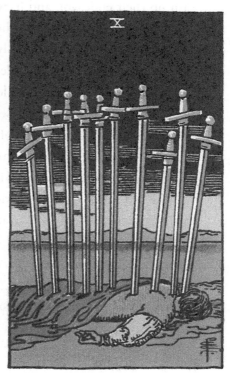

Numerology and the Tarot ✦ 297

are built. The card generally depicts a couple contemplating their dreams, with an arbor or rainbow of cups above them. It speaks of dreams shared, and the growth from lovers and friends to partners, building a life together. It is built upon hard work and investment and carries the promise of a possibility! Unlike the Lovers and the Two of Cups that speak of passion, connection, and spark, the Ten of Cups speaks of commitment, mature love, and true intimacy. It is what we all strive for, the relationship that has lasting potential, strength, and endurance; and—like all Tens—in truth, it is merely a transition point to grow upon.

The Ten of Swords is one of the most painful cards in the deck, and—like all Tens—it is a temporary state, a turning point in which things can be transformed. The card depicts a person lying prone on the ground with ten swords sticking out of their back. Often seen as a sign of betrayal, hence the swords in the back, it is generally seen as a painful ending. While this ending can be painful and overwhelming, it is important to recognize the light blue of dawn on the horizon! This symbolizes the transient nature of the card, the fact that these pains will pass. Yes, it is true that it can represent death, but it is unlikely to depict such. Instead, it generally depicts painful transitions such as breakups and circumstantial endings.

What did you notice?

The Feeling of Completion. Representing the end of a cycle and the beginning of a new, the Tens often feel complete and final. If you are drawn to this energy in the card, note that to the querent.

Fullness. The Ten cards are often filled with imagery, giving them a feeling of fullness. If this draws your attention in a reading, note that the querent will have little time for anything else when the situation will have full hold of their attention.

Protective Space. Like the Nines, there is a feeling of security that comes from the protective space surrounding the people in the Tens (except for the Ten of Swords, which carries the feeling that nothing worse can happen). This shows that the place the querent is in is safe from outside disturbances.

The Light. Light is very important in the Tens as it represents hope!

A Final Wish
for the Seeker

Psychic development is like a rabbit hole. Once you go down it you will likely find it goes on forever, with different paths leading you into greater understanding of the universe. I have been studying the psychic arts my entire life, and I fully expect to continue doing so for the rest of it. For those of you who have a deep passion for understanding and utilizing this knowledge, I wish you well and hope that the universe provides you with interesting tidbits to keep you going!

Trust yourself, take lots of notes in your Book of Shadows, and think outside the box . . .

SPREADING LOVE,
SALICROW

Index

Ace (One), 273–76
activated prayer
  about, 122
  cartomancy in, 122–25
  with oracle cards, 123–24
  in a pinch, 125
altars, 17–18, 140–45
angel deck, 122
apps, tarot and oracle, 125
April (Pink Moon), 19
astral realm, 38
August (Sturgeon Moon), 20
autumn equinox (September 21–23)
  about, 24
  in Wheel of the Year, 80
  Year in Review spread, 93

balancing personal energy (spring
    equinox) spread, 83–84
Beltane (May 1), 23, 80
black moon (soul healing) spread, 98
blessings
  fertility, 130–31
  house, 131–33

marriage, 130–31
  prosperity, 133–34
blessings and bounty (summer
    solstice) spread, 90
blue moon (self-viewing) spread,
    96–97
body dowsing
  about, 32
  advanced, 34–35
  blocks and, 33
  expanding, 34
  practicing, 32–33
Book of Shadows, 39, 51–52

cards
  blessing and programming,
    54–56
  choosing a deck, 53–54
  difficult situations and, 66–67
  in divination, 9–10
  handling, 58, 61
  karma in, 65–66
  selection at session beginning,
    58

300

Index + 301

spells and, 127
storing, 56–57
types of, 10–11
unconventional use, 119–20
understanding symbols and,
36–37
card spreads. *See* spreads
Career/Life Path (Lughnasa) spread,
91–92
cartomancy
about, 8
in activated prayer, 122–25
cards, 9–11
practice of, 9
as psychic skill, 8–9
symbolism and, 36, 57–58
Celtic Cross, 76, 77
chakras, 33, 41–42, 228
Chariot, the
about, 184–85
in challenging times, 186
details, 186–87
guided meditation, 187–88
in readings, 184, 186
representation, 185–86
charms
card, 127–28
House Blessing, 131–33
Marriage Blessing, 130–31
Prosperity, 133–34
Soul Mate, 128–29
clairaudience (psychic hearing), 7
claircognizance (psychic knowing), 7
clairsalience (psychic smelling),
7–8
clairsentience (psychic feeling), 7
clairvoyance (psychic seeing), 6–7

communication, 13–14, 38, 69, 82,
105, 243
connection questions, 71
Court cards
about, 250
Kings, 265–71
Knights, 255–60
Pages, 250–55
players and, 59
Queens, 260–65
Cups
about, 246
Ace of, 274, 275
details, 246–47
Eight of, 291, 292
Five of, 284, 285
Four of, 281, 282
King of, 268–69
Knight of, 258–59
Nine of, 293, 294
Page of, 253–54
Queen of, 263–64
in readings, 246
Seven of, 288, 289
Six of, 286, 287
Ten of, 295–97
Three of, 279, 280
Two of, 277, 278

Daudra Dura (Forndom), 147
Death
about, 209–10
details, 211–12
guided meditation, 212–13
meditation on, 211
in readings, 211
representation, 210–11

302 ✦ Index

December (Cold Moon), 21
Devil, the
about, 217
guided meditation, 220–21
in readings, 218–19
divination
about, 5–6
accuracy, 14
altars, creating, 17–18
intuition in, 63–64
journey work, 146
as mainstream, 12–13
practice of, 6, 8
as psychic storytelling, 6, 57
timing and, 72–73
use of, 9
web of fate and, 61–62
divine timing, 18–24
documentation, not keeping, 48–49
doubt words, 26
dreaming, 38, 146, 243

ecstatic dance, 27
Eight, 290–92
empathy, 13–14, 102, 202
Emperor, the
about, 171–72
details, 173–74
guided meditation, 174–75
in readings, 173
Empress, the
about, 167–68
details, 169–70
forms of, 168, 169
guided meditation, 170–71
in readings, 168–69
ethics and morals, 47–49

fate
about, 61–62
connection to, 63
karma and, 66
web of, 61–65
February (Snow Moon), 19
Five, 283–85
Fool's Dog, The (tarot app),
125
Fool, the
about, 156–57
details, 157
guided meditation, 158–59
in readings, 157
Four, 281–83

guided meditations, 38–43, 146.
See also specific meditations
guides, lessons from, 94–95

Halloween (Samhain), October 31
about, 21–22
lessons from guides spread,
94–95
in Wheel of the Year, 80
handling cards, 58, 61
hands
balancing personal energy spread,
83–84
healing for, 98
what it needs, 95
Hanged Man, the
about, 205–6
details, 207–8
guided meditation, 208–9
in readings, 207
representation, 206–7

Index + 303

head
  balancing personal energy spread,
    83
  healing for, 98
  what it needs, 94
healing
  for head, hands, heart, 98
  intuition and, 134
  personal, 43–45
  prayers of, 122
  soul, 98
healing boards
  about, 134–35
  Long-Term Healing Mental Health,
    138–39
  Long-Term Healing Physical
    Health, 139–40
  Medical Instant Need, 135,
    136–37
  Mental Health Instant Need, 135,
    136
heart
  balancing personal energy spread,
    83–84
  healing for, 98
  what it needs, 94–95
Hearth and Home spread, 81–82
helpers, 68–70, 92, 287
herbal oracle, 122
Hermit, the
  about, 192–93
  details, 195
  guided meditation, 196
  journey, 194–95
  representation, 193, 195
hidden potential (lunar eclipse)
  spread, 99

Hierophant, the
  about, 175–76
  details, 178
  exploring, 177–78
  guided meditation, 179–80
  representation, 177
High Priestess, the
  about, 163–64
  details, 165
  guided meditation, 166–67
  in readings, 164
  representation, 164
House Blessing charm, 131–33
House of Cards
  about, 140
  Activating the House of Cards
    spell, 142–44
  choosing, 141–42
  custom, creating, 144–45
  Guardians, 142, 144–45
  Speaker of the House, 141, 143,
    145

imagination, 8, 58
Imbolc (February 2)
  about, 22
  Hearth and Home spread, 81–82
  in Wheel of the Year, 79
instant need healing boards,
    135–37
intuition
  in divination, 63–64
  guided meditation and, 38–43
  healing and, 134
  symbolism as language of, 35–36
intuitive healing boards. See healing
    boards

304 ✦ Index

January (Wolf Moon), 18–19
journal, sacred. *See* Book of Shadows
journey work
    divination, 146–47
    guided meditation and, 38–39, 146
    music in, 146–47
    one-card journey, 147–48
    preparing to journey and, 39–41
    storyline journey, 150–52
    three-card journey, 149–50
Judgement
    about, 235–36
    details, 237
    guided meditation, 237–38
    in readings, 236
July (Buck Moon), 20
June (Strawberry Moon), 19
Justice
    about, 201–2
    details, 203–4
    guided meditation, 204–5
    in readings, 203
    vibrations, 202

karma, in the cards, 65–66
Kings. *See also* Court cards
    about, 265–66
    details, 270–71
    King of Cups, 268–69
    King of Pentacles, 267–68
    King of Swords, 269–70
    King of Wands, 266–67
Knights. *See also* Court cards
    about, 255–56
    details, 260
    Knight of Cups, 258–59
    Knight of Pentacles, 257–58

Knight of Swords, 259–60
Knight of Wands, 256–57

lessons from guides (Halloween)
    spread, 94–95
light trance, 25–26, 27, 29, 61
long-term draw, 121
long-term healing boards. *See also*
    healing boards
    about, 137
    digital, 137–38
    Long-Term Healing Mental Health
        board, 138–39
    Long-Term Healing Physical
        Health board, 139–40
    physical, 137–38
looking for love (Beltane) spread, 86–87
Lovers, the
    about, 180–81
    details, 182–83
    guided meditation, 183–84
    in readings, 181–82
    in soul evolution, 182
Lughnasa (August 2)
    about, 23–24
    Career/Life Path spread, 91–92
    in Wheel of the Year, 80
lunar cycles, 18–21
lunar eclipse (hidden potential)
    spread, 99

Magician, the
    about, 159
    details, 161
    guided meditation, 162–63
    infinity and, 159–60
    in readings, 161

Index ✦ 305

Major Arcana cards. *See also*
 individual cards
 about, 53–54, 154
 the Chariot, 184–88
 Death, 209–13
 the Devil, 217–21
 the Emperor, 171–75
 the Empress, 167–71
 the Fool, 156–59
 the Hanged Man, 205–9
 the Hermit, 192–96
 the Hierophant, 175–80
 the High Priestess, 163–67
 Judgement, 235–38
 Justice, 201–5
 the Lovers, 180–84
 the Magician, 159–63
 meditating on, 155–56
 the Moon, 228–31
 readings with, 154
 the Star, 224–28
 Strength, 188–92
 the Sun, 232–35
 Temperance, 213–17
 the Tower, 221–24
 using, 154–55
 Wheel of Fortune, 197–201
 the World, 239–41
March (Worm Moon), 19
Marriage Blessing charm, 130–31
May (Flower Moon), 19
Medical Instant Need healing board,
 135
meditation. *See also* guided
 meditations
 ecstatic dance, 27
 finding form of, 27

importance of, 26
journey work as form of, 38–39
rocking, 27, 28–29
third eye opening, 29–31
traditional, 27
types of, 27
vocal toning, 27
Mental Health Instant Need healing
 board, 135, 136
Minor Arcana cards
 about, 53–54, 242–43
 Cups (Chalices, Goblets), 246–47
 Pentacles (Coins, Discs, Shields),
 244–45
 suits, 242–49
 Swords (Spades, Blades), 247–49
 Wands (Clubs, Staves), 243–44
Moon, the
 about, 228–29
 guided meditation, 231
 in readings, 230
 representation, 229–30
music, in journey work, 146–47

Nine, 292–95
November (Beaver Moon), 20
numerology, 272–73. *See also specific*
 numbers

October (Hunter's Moon), 20
one-card journey, 147–48
oracle cards. *See also* cards
 about, 10–11
 activated prayer with, 123–25
 angle deck, 122
 availability of, 119
 choosing, 53

306 + Index

in creating ambiance, 58
herbal oracle, 122
soul-level spreads and, 101
oracular storytelling
about, 57–58
players, 59
setting the stage, 58–59
situations and circumstances, 61

Pages. *See also* Court cards
about, 250
details, 255
Page of Cups, 253–54
Page of Pentacles, 252
Page of Swords, 254–55
Page of Wands, 250–51
parallel lives, 114–15
past life readings
about, 108
decks for, 108
past life, 109
past life relationship, 111–13
past-life triangulation, 114–18
past life relationship spread,
111–13
past life spread, 109–11
past-life triangulation
about, 114
change throughout life, 114–15
spread illustrations, 116–17
steps, 115–18
Pentacles
about, 244–45
Ace of, 274, 275
details, 245
Eight of, 291, 292
Five of, 284, 285

Four of, 281, 282
King of, 267–68
Knight of, 257–58
Nine of, 293, 294
Page of, 252
Queen of, 262–63
Seven of, 288, 289
Six of, 286, 287
Ten of, 295, 296
Three of, 279, 280
Two of, 277, 278
players, 58, 59, 61, 68, 70, 73, 77
playing cards, 10, 53, 127–34.
See also cards; charms
programming and blessing cards,
54–56, 57
programming the empathic pool,
49–51
Prosperity charm, 133–34
psychic abilities
developing, 1, 25
healing and, 43
journaling and, 10
spell work and, 127
trusting, 32
psychic evolution, 11–13
psychic readers
ethics and morals, 47–49
personal healing and, 43–44
reputation, 49
psychometry, 55

Queens. *See also* Court cards
about, 260–61
details, 264–65
Queen of Cups, 263–64
Queen of Pentacles, 262–63

Index ✦ 307

Queen of Swords, 264–65
Queen of Wands, 261–62
questions
    asking, keep, 52, 66–67
    connection, 71
    handling cards and, 58
    information reveal, 47
    for precognitive anxiousness, 34
    right, asking, 1, 66–68

rare moon spreads, 96–99
reading(s). *See also specific cards*
    helpers in, 68–70
    karma in, 65–66
    leaning into, 67–68
    with Major Arcana cards, 154
    past life, 108–18
    questions, 67
    relationship, 70, 85–89
    seeking clarity in, 63
    side investigations in, 67
    timing in, 72–73
    white raven (psychic gifts),
        105–7
rebirth, 210, 211–12, 232–33, 236
relationship readings
    about, 85
    current relationship spread, 87–89
    helpers in, 70
    looking for love spread, 86–87
relationships
    current, 87
    family, 82, 111, 118
    past, 86, 87
    past life, 111–13
    personal, 111, 118, 276
    with self, 82, 86

Rider-Waite deck, 54, 205
rocking, 27, 28–29

sacred circle, creating, 105
sacred space
    about, 14
    creating, technique, 16
    creation of, 14–15
    intention and, 14–15, 18
sacred space spray, 15–16
seasonal spreads, 78–95
Seers, 4–7
self-care, 45–56
self-viewing (blue moon) spread,
    96–97
September (Corn Moon), 20
Seven, 287–90
shadow work, 193, 194, 243
sigils, magical, 56–57
situations and circumstances, 61
Six, 285–87
solar cycles, 21–24
solar eclipses, 24
soul healing (black moon) spread, 98
soul-level spreads
    about, 100–101
    oracle and tarot cards, 101
    past life readings, 108–18
    soul purpose, 102–4
    white raven, 105–7
Soul Mate charm, 128–29
soul purpose spread, 102–4
spells
    about, 126
    Activating the House of Cards,
        142–44
    blessing, 127

card representation, 127
foundation of, 127
House Blessing charm, 131–33
instant need healing, 135–37
long-term healing, 137–40
Long-Term Healing Mental Health board, 138–39
Long-Term Healing Physical Health board, 139–40
Marriage Blessing charm, 130–31
Prosperity charm, 133–34
Soul Mate charm, 128–29
working, 126–27
spirit communication, 12–13
spreads
about, 76
black moon (soul healing), 98
blue moon (self-viewing), 96–97
Career/Life Path (Lughnasa), 91–92
Celtic Cross, 76, 77
current relationship (Beltane), 87–89
exploration through, 76–77
Hearth and Home (Imbolc), 81–82
lessons from guides (Halloween), 94–95
long-term draw, 121
looking for love (Beltane), 86–87
lunar eclipse (hidden potential), 99
outside influence and, 68
past life, 109–11
past life relationship, 111–13
past-life triangulation, 114–18
rare moon, 96–99
seasonal, 78–95
soul-level, 100–118
soul purpose, 102–4

spring equinox, 83–84
summer solstice, 90
Wheel of the Year, 78
white raven, 105–7
winter solstice, 78–80
Year in Review (autumn equinox), 93
spring equinox (March 21–23)
about, 22–23
balancing personal energy spread, 83–84
in Wheel of the Year, 80
Star, the
about, 224–26
details, 227
guided meditation, 227–28
in readings, 226
storyline journey, 150–52
Strength
about, 188–89
characteristics, 190
details, 191
guided meditation, 191–92
in readings, 190
suits
about, 242
Cups (Chalices, Goblets), 246–47
Pentacles (Coins, Discs, Shields), 244–45
Swords (Spades, Blades), 247–49
Wands (Clubs, Staves), 243–44
summer solstice (June 21–23)
about, 23
blessings and bounty spread, 90
in Wheel of the Year, 80
Sun, the
about, 232–33
details, 233

Index ✦ 309

guided meditation, 234–35
in readings, 233
supernatural, 5
Swords. *See also* Minor Arcana cards
about, 247–48
Ace of, 274, 275
details, 248–49
Eight of, 291, 292
Five of, 284, 285
Four of, 282, 283
King of, 269–70
Knight of, 259–60
Nine of, 293, 294
Page of, 254–55
Queen of, 264–65
Seven of, 288, 289
Six of, 286, 287
Ten of, 296, 297
Three of, 279, 280
Two of, 277, 278
symbolic language, 36–38
symbolism
about, 35–36
cartomancy and, 36, 57–58
developing understanding of, 36–38
effects of, 36
handling cards and, 58
sources of, 37

tarot cards. *See also* cards; Major
Arcana cards; Minor Arcana cards
about, 11, 53–54
availability of, 119
choosing, 53–54
soul-level spreads and, 101
techniques
advanced body dowsing, 34–35

card blessing/programming, 55–57
creating divination altars, 17–18
creating sacred space, 16
guided meditation to open the
third eye, 41–43
meeting the court, 59–61
preparing to journey, 39–41
programming the empathic pool,
49–51
rocking, 28–29
third eye opening, 29–31
visualizing the web, 63–65
Temperance
about, 213–14
details, 215–16
guided meditation, 216–17
in readings, 215
as Witch Card, 215
Ten, 295–98
third eye opening, 29–31, 41–43
Three, 278–81
three-card journey, 149–50
timing and timelines, 72–73
Tower, the
about, 221–22
details, 223
guided meditation, 223–24
in readings, 222–23
representation, 222
travel altar, 140–45
Two, 276–78

vocal toning, 27

Wands
about, 243
Ace of, 273–75

310 ✦ Index

details, 244
Eight of, 290, 291
Five of, 284, 285
Four of, 281, 282
King of, 266–67
Knight of, 256–57
Nine of, 293, 294
Page of, 250–51
Queen of, 261–62
in readings, 243–44
Seven of, 288, 289
Six of, 285–86
Ten of, 295, 296
Three of, 279, 280
Two of, 276–78
Web of Fate, 61–65
Wheel of Fortune
about, 197–98

details, 199
guided meditation, 200–201
in readings, 198–99
as sentient being, 198
Wheel of the Year spread, 78–80
white raven (psychic gifts) spread,
105–7
winter solstice (December 21–23), 22,
78–80
World, the
about, 239–40
details, 240–41
guided meditation, 241
representation, 240
wyrd, 5–6, 63, 100

Year in Review (autumn equinox)
spread, 93